First World War
and Army of Occupation
War Diary
France, Belgium and Germany

39 DIVISION
Headquarters, Branches and Services
Adjutant and Quarter-Master General
1 March 1916 - 10 July 1919

WO95/2568

The Naval & Military Press Ltd
www.nmarchive.com
Published in association with The National Archives

Published by

The Naval & Military Press Ltd

Unit 10 Ridgewood Industrial Park,

Uckfield, East Sussex,

TN22 5QE England

Tel: +44 (0) 1825 749494

www.naval-military-press.com

www.nmarchive.com

This diary has been reprinted in facsimile from the original. Any imperfections are inevitably reproduced and the quality may fall short of modern type and cartographic standards.

© Crown Copyright
Images reproduced by permission of The National Archives, London, England, 2015.

Contents

Document type	Place/Title	Date From	Date To
Heading	39th Division. 'A' & 'Q' Branch Mar 1916-Jly 1919		
War Diary	Witley Camp	01/03/1916	07/03/1916
War Diary	Havre	04/03/1916	08/03/1916
War Diary	Havre.	05/03/1916	09/03/1916
War Diary	Blaringhem.	06/03/1916	28/03/1916
War Diary	Lestrem.	28/03/1916	31/03/1916
Miscellaneous	Order Of Embarkation Of 39th Division For Havre. Appendix A.	18/02/1916	18/02/1916
Miscellaneous	Move Of The 39th Division. Appendix B.		
Miscellaneous	Casualties-39th Division March, 1916. Appendix C.		
War Diary	Lestrem.	01/04/1916	16/04/1916
War Diary	Locon.	17/04/1916	30/04/1916
Miscellaneous	Casualties Officer And Other Ranks Killed April 1916. Vol.2		
Miscellaneous	Casualties Officers April 1916 Killed.		
Miscellaneous	Total Casualties Killed April 1916		
Miscellaneous	Casualties Officer And Other Ranks Wounded April 1916		
Miscellaneous	Casualties Officers April 1916. Wounded.		
Miscellaneous	Died of Wounds (Included in figures Shown on Statement of "Killed").		
Miscellaneous	Total Casualties Wounded April 1916		
Miscellaneous	D.A.G., 3rd Echelon, Base.	05/06/1916	05/06/1916
War Diary	Locon.	01/05/1916	31/05/1916
Heading	Casualties May. 1916. Killed Officer Appendix 'A'.		
Miscellaneous	Others.		
Miscellaneous	Other Ranks.		
Heading	Casualties-May 1916. Wounded Officers And Other Ranks. Appendix 'A'.		
Miscellaneous	Others.		
Miscellaneous	Other Ranks.		
Miscellaneous	D.A.G., 3rd Echelon, Base. 39/1197/A.	13/07/1916	13/07/1916
War Diary	Locon.	01/06/1916	30/06/1916
Heading	Casualties June 1916. Wounded Others And Other Ranks.		
Miscellaneous	Officer Wounded And Missing.	31/05/1916	31/05/1916
Miscellaneous		31/05/1916	31/05/1916
Miscellaneous	Missing Other Ranks June 1916		
Heading	Casualties June 1916 Field Officer Other Ranks.		
Miscellaneous	Killed on Died of Wounds to 31.5.16. Officers.	31/05/1916	31/05/1916
Miscellaneous	Dated of Casualties. 30.6.16	30/06/1916	30/06/1916
Miscellaneous			
Heading	War Diary July 1916. A & Q Soeff 39 Division Original 2 Copy. Vol. 5		
War Diary	Locon.	01/07/1916	07/07/1916
War Diary	Locon to Bethune.	08/07/1916	08/07/1916
War Diary	Bethune.	09/07/1916	14/07/1916
War Diary	Bethune To Locon.	15/07/1916	15/07/1916
War Diary	Locon.	16/07/1916	31/07/1916

Miscellaneous	Corps Routine Orders By Major-General Colin Mackenzie, C.B. Commanding XI Army Corps.	31/07/1916	31/07/1916
Heading	Killed July 1916 Officer Other ranks Appendix. "B".		
Miscellaneous	Officers.		
Miscellaneous			
Heading	Casualties July. 1916 Wounded Officers And Other Ranks. Appendix. 'B'.		
Miscellaneous	Officers.		
Miscellaneous			
War Diary	Locon.	01/08/1916	11/08/1916
War Diary	Locon to Roellecourt.	12/08/1916	12/08/1916
War Diary	Roelle Court.	13/08/1916	23/08/1916
War Diary	Roellecourt to Bus-Les-Artois.	24/08/1916	24/08/1916
War Diary	Bus.	25/08/1916	27/08/1916
War Diary	To Acheux.	27/08/1916	27/08/1916
War Diary	Acheux.	27/08/1916	31/08/1916
Operation(al) Order(s)	39th Division Administrative Order No. 1	07/08/1916	07/08/1916
Miscellaneous	Supply And Transport Table.		
Operation(al) Order(s)	39th Divisional Administration Order No. 2	09/08/1916	09/08/1916
Miscellaneous	Supply And Transport Table.		
Miscellaneous	39th Divisional Administrative Instructions. No. 3	21/08/1916	21/08/1916
Miscellaneous	Supply And Transport Table.		
Miscellaneous	Supply And Transport Table.	22/08/1916	22/08/1916
Miscellaneous	39th Divisional Administrative Instructions.	22/08/1916	22/08/1916
Heading	Casualties August 1916 Killed Officers And Other Ranks.		
Miscellaneous	Officers.		
Miscellaneous			
Heading	Casualties, August 1916. Wounded Msg Officers and Other Ranks.		
Miscellaneous	Officers.		
Miscellaneous			
Miscellaneous	Missing.		
Heading	39th. Division A. & Q. 39th. Division September 1916		
War Diary	Acheux.	01/09/1916	30/09/1916
Heading	Casualties September 1916. Killed Officers And Other Ranks.		
Miscellaneous	Officers.	31/08/1916	31/08/1916
Miscellaneous			
Heading	Casualties September 1916 Wounded Officers And Other Ranks.		
Miscellaneous	Officers	31/08/1916	31/08/1916
Miscellaneous	Officers Killed: Operations 2/3rd September, 1916	02/09/1916	02/09/1916
Miscellaneous	Officers Wounded 2/3rd September 1916	02/09/1916	02/09/1916
Miscellaneous	Officers Missing-Operations 2/3rd September 1916	02/09/1916	02/09/1916
Miscellaneous	Other Ranks-Killed, Wounded, Missing, During Operations 2/3rd Sept.	02/09/1916	02/09/1916
Miscellaneous			
Miscellaneous	Missing.	31/08/1916	31/08/1916
War Diary	Acheux.	01/10/1916	01/10/1916
War Diary	Acheux To Hedauville.	02/10/1916	02/10/1916
War Diary	Hedauville.	03/10/1916	06/10/1916
War Diary	Bouzincourt Camp.	07/10/1916	31/10/1916
Heading	Casualties October 1916. Killed Officers And Other Ranks.		
Miscellaneous	Casualties, October, 1916. Officers Killed.		

Miscellaneous			
Heading	Casualties October 1916. Wounded Officers And Other Ranks.		
Miscellaneous	Casualties, October, 1916. Officers, Wounded.		
Miscellaneous			
War Diary	Bouzincourt Camp.	01/11/1916	15/11/1916
War Diary	Doullens.	16/11/1916	17/11/1916
War Diary	Esquelbecq.	18/11/1916	30/11/1916
Heading	Casualties. November 1916 Killed Officers & Other Ranks.		
Miscellaneous	Officers (Killed).	31/10/1916	31/10/1916
Miscellaneous			
War Diary	Esquelbecq.	01/12/1916	14/12/1916
War Diary	St. Sixte Convent.	14/12/1916	31/12/1916
Heading	Casualties December 1916. Killed. Officers And Other Ranks.		
Miscellaneous	Officers.		
Miscellaneous			
Heading	Casualties December 1916. Wounded. Officers And Other Ranks.		
Miscellaneous	Officers Wounded Missing.		
Miscellaneous			
War Diary	St. Sixte Convent.	01/01/1917	15/01/1917
War Diary	A.25.d.2.6. Hamhoek Camp.	15/01/1917	15/01/1917
War Diary	Hamhoek Camp.	16/01/1917	31/01/1917
Heading	Casualties January 1917 Killed Officers Other Ranks.		
Miscellaneous	Officers.		
Miscellaneous			
Heading	Casualties Jan 1917 Wounded Officers & Other Ranks.		
Miscellaneous	Officers Wounded Missing.		
Miscellaneous			
War Diary	Hamhoek Camp A.25.d.2.6	01/02/1917	18/02/1917
War Diary	Esquelbecq	19/02/1917	27/02/1917
War Diary	Reninghelst.	27/02/1917	28/02/1917
Miscellaneous	Funeral of General Bagnani. 'A'.	09/02/1917	09/02/1917
Heading	Casualties February 1917. Killed Officers And Other Ranks.		
Miscellaneous	Officers.		
Miscellaneous			
Heading	Casualties February 1917. Wounded Officers And Other Ranks.		
Miscellaneous	Officers:- Wounded And Missing.		
Miscellaneous			
War Diary	Reninghelst G34 B.3.0. Sheet 28	01/03/1917	08/03/1917
War Diary	Reninghelst.	08/03/1917	31/03/1917
Heading	Casualties March 1917. Killed Officers And Other Ranks.		
Miscellaneous	Officers.		
Miscellaneous			
Heading	Casualties March 1917. Wounded Officers And Other Ranks.		
Miscellaneous	Officers:- Wounded And Missing.		
Miscellaneous			
Heading	HQ A & Q 39 D Apl. Vol.14		
Heading	On His Majesty's Service. Secret.		
War Diary	Reninghelst.	01/04/1917	29/04/1917

War Diary	A.30.b.3.6. (Sheet-28) D Camp.	30/04/1917	30/04/1917
Heading	Casualties April 1917. Killed Officers And Other Ranks.		
Miscellaneous	Officers.		
Miscellaneous Heading	Casualties April 1917. Killed Officers And Other Ranks.		
Miscellaneous	Officers.		
Miscellaneous Heading	Casualties April 1917. Wounded Officers And Other Ranks.		
Miscellaneous	Officers Wounded And Missing.		
Miscellaneous Heading	Casualties April 1917. Wounded Officers And Other Ranks.		
Miscellaneous	Officers. Wounded And Missing.		
Miscellaneous War Diary	A.30.b.45 Sheet 28 N.W. D Camp.	01/05/1917	31/05/1917
Heading	Casualties. May 1917. Killed. Officers And Other Ranks.		
Miscellaneous	Officers.		
Miscellaneous Heading	Casualties. May. 1917. Killed. Officers And Other Ranks.		
Miscellaneous	Officers.		
Miscellaneous Heading	Casualties. May. 1917. Wounded. Officers And Other Ranks.		
Miscellaneous	Officers. Wounded And Missing.		
Miscellaneous Heading	Casualties. May 1917. Wounded. Officers And Other Ranks.		
Miscellaneous	Officers Wounded And Missing.		
Miscellaneous War Diary	Border Camp (A.30.b.35) Sheet 28	01/06/1917	06/06/1917
War Diary	Border Camp.	07/06/1917	30/06/1917
War Diary	Border Camp (A.30.d.45) Sheet 28	01/07/1917	03/07/1917
War Diary	C Camp.	04/07/1917	10/07/1917
War Diary	C Camp (G.6.b.19 Sheet 28)	11/07/1917	15/07/1917
War Diary	C. Camp.	16/07/1917	31/07/1917
Miscellaneous	Casualties. Officers Killed.		
Miscellaneous Miscellaneous	Casualties Officers Wounded And Missing.		
Miscellaneous Miscellaneous	Casualties Officers Killed.		
Miscellaneous Miscellaneous	Casualties Officers Wounded And Missing.		
Miscellaneous War Diary	C Camp.	01/08/1917	06/08/1917
War Diary	Meteren.	07/08/1917	14/08/1917
War Diary	Westoutre	15/09/1917	30/09/1917
Heading	Casualties August 1917. Wounded. Officers And Other Ranks.		
Miscellaneous	Officers. Wounded And Missing.		
Miscellaneous Miscellaneous	Missing. O.R.		

Heading	Casualties. August. 1917. Killed Officers And Other Ranks.		
Miscellaneous	Officers:- Killed.		
Miscellaneous			
Heading	Casualties. August. 1917. Killed. Officers And Other Ranks.		
Miscellaneous	Officers Killed.		
Miscellaneous			
Heading	Casualties. August 1917. Killed. Officers And Other Ranks.		
Miscellaneous	Officers.		
Miscellaneous			
Miscellaneous	Officers. Wounded And Missing.		
Heading	Casualties August. 1917. Wounded Officers And Other Ranks.		
Miscellaneous	Missing. O.R.		
Miscellaneous			
Heading	Casualties August 1917 Wounded. Officers And Other Ranks.		
Miscellaneous	Officers Wounded And Missing.		
Miscellaneous			
War Diary	Westoutre	01/09/1917	12/09/1917
War Diary	Dezon Camp.	13/09/1917	27/09/1917
War Diary	St Jans Cappel.	28/09/1917	30/09/1917
Miscellaneous	Officers.		
Heading	Casualties September 1917. Killed Officers.		
Miscellaneous	Officers. Wounded And Missing.		
Heading	Casualties September 1917. Wounded Officers.		
Miscellaneous	Officers.		
Miscellaneous	Officers. Wounded And Missing.		
Miscellaneous	Vol.1 W. 76		
Miscellaneous	Officers. Wounded And Missing.		
Heading	Casualties November 1916 Wounded Officers And Other Ranks.		
Miscellaneous	Officers (Wounded Missing).		
Miscellaneous			
Miscellaneous	Or Missing To 31.x.16. 1408 Missing November 1916 Total Missing To 30.11.1916	30/11/1916	30/11/1916
War Diary	St. Jans. Cappel.	01/10/1917	16/10/1917
War Diary	Dezon Camp.	17/10/1917	31/10/1917
Miscellaneous	October 1917 Officers Killed.		
Miscellaneous	Officers:- Wounded And Missing.		
War Diary	Dezon Camp.	01/11/1917	01/11/1917
War Diary	La Clytte.	01/11/1917	05/11/1917
War Diary	Dezon Camp.	06/11/1917	10/11/1917
War Diary	Westoutre	18/11/1917	26/11/1917
War Diary	Steenvoorde.	27/11/1917	30/11/1917
Miscellaneous	Officers Killed.		
Miscellaneous	Officers:- Wounded And Missing.		
Miscellaneous			
War Diary	Steenvoorde.	01/12/1917	10/12/1917
War Diary	Nielles-Lez Blequin.	10/12/1917	30/12/1917
War Diary	Border Camp.	31/12/1917	31/12/1917
War Diary	Steenvoorde.	01/12/1917	10/12/1917
War Diary	Nielles-Lez Blequin.	10/12/1917	30/12/1917
War Diary	Border Camp.	31/12/1917	31/12/1917

Miscellaneous	D.A.G., 3rd Echelon, G.H.Q.	17/05/1918	17/05/1918
Miscellaneous	Reference Adendum No. 2 to 39th Division Order No. 199	07/12/1917	07/12/1917
Miscellaneous	Administrative Instructions No. 2 Issued With Reference To 39th Division Order No. 199 Dated 5.12.17	06/12/1917	06/12/1917
Miscellaneous	Administrative Instructions 10.2 Issued With Reference To Divisional Operation Order.199 Dated 5.12.17	05/12/1917	05/12/1917
Miscellaneous	Train Table.		
Miscellaneous	5th (London) Division.	05/12/1917	05/12/1917
Operation(al) Order(s)	Addendum No. 2 To 39th Division Order No. 199	07/12/1917	07/12/1917
Operation(al) Order(s)	After Order 39th Division Order No. 199	06/12/1917	06/12/1917
Operation(al) Order(s)	Addendum To 39th Division Order No. 199	05/12/1917	05/12/1917
Miscellaneous	Table To Accompany Addendum To 39th Division Order No. 199. (D.o.199/1.).		
Operation(al) Order(s)	39th Division Order No. 199	05/12/1917	05/12/1917
Miscellaneous	To Accompany 39th Div. Order 199. Appendix "A".		
Miscellaneous	Table To Accompany 39th Division Order No. 199		
Miscellaneous	VIII Corps Administrative Instructions No: 2	04/12/1917	04/12/1917
Operation(al) Order(s)	VIII Corps Order No. 84	04/12/1917	04/12/1917
Miscellaneous	March Table To Accompany VIII Corps Order No. 64		
Operation(al) Order(s)	To Accompany VIII Corps Order No. 64		
Operation(al) Order(s)	Administrative Instructions In Connection With 39th Divisional Order No. 203		
Miscellaneous	Appendix "A".	22/12/1917	22/12/1917
Miscellaneous	March Table For Transport. Appendix "B".		
Miscellaneous	Appendix "C".		
Miscellaneous	Appendix "D" II Corps Circular Memorandum No. 36	09/12/1917	09/12/1917
Miscellaneous	Appendix "E". Employed Officers And Men.		
Miscellaneous	Amendment To 39th Divisional Administrative Instructions-Appendix 'C' Dated 26.12.17	27/12/1917	27/12/1917
Miscellaneous	Entraining Arrangements.	27/12/1917	27/12/1917
Miscellaneous	Entraining Table. Table A.		
Miscellaneous	Detail of Omnibus Train 29th Dec. Table "B".		
Miscellaneous	Lorry Programme.		
War Diary	Canal Bank Ypres.	01/01/1918	22/01/1918
War Diary	Couthove.	23/01/1918	23/01/1918
War Diary	Chateau.	24/01/1918	24/01/1918
War Diary	Mericourt Sur-Somme.	25/01/1918	02/02/1918
War Diary	Nurlu.	04/02/1918	12/03/1918
War Diary	Haut-Allaines.	13/03/1918	23/03/1918
War Diary	Clery-Sur-Somme.	23/03/1918	23/03/1918
War Diary	Frise.	23/03/1918	24/03/1918
War Diary	Chuignes.	25/03/1918	26/03/1918
War Diary	Chuignes. Proyart Hamel.	26/03/1918	27/03/1918
War Diary	Hamelet.	27/03/1918	27/03/1918
War Diary	Fouilloy.	28/03/1918	28/03/1918
War Diary	Domart-Sur La Luce.	29/03/1918	29/03/1918
War Diary	Boves.	29/03/1918	30/03/1918
Miscellaneous	Funeral of the Late Brigadier-General G.A.S. Cape, C.M.G. Royal Artillery, C.R.A., 39th. Division-on Wednesday 20th. March, 1918	19/03/1918	19/03/1918
Diagram etc			
Heading	39th Divisional Administrative A. & Q. 39th Division April 1918		
War Diary	Guignemicourt.	01/04/1918	01/04/1918
War Diary	Belloy St. Leonard.	02/04/1918	02/04/1918

War Diary	Oisemont.	03/04/1918	06/04/1918
War Diary	Gamaches.	07/04/1918	09/04/1918
War Diary	Cocove Chateau.	10/04/1918	11/04/1918
War Diary	Eperlecques.	12/04/1918	29/05/1918
War Diary	Eperlecques. N Of St Omer.	01/06/1918	04/06/1918
War Diary	Wolphus	07/06/1918	28/07/1918
War Diary	Walphus (Calais Sheet).	01/08/1918	21/08/1918
War Diary	Varangeville Dieppe.	22/08/1918	31/08/1918
War Diary	Verangeville.	01/09/1918	28/09/1918
War Diary	Verangeville. Dieppe Sheet.	01/10/1918	29/10/1918
War Diary	Verangeville Dieppe.	01/11/1918	16/11/1918
War Diary	Verangeville Dieppe.	01/11/1918	27/12/1918
War Diary	Varengeville.	01/01/1919	04/03/1919
War Diary	Rouen.	05/03/1919	31/03/1919
Heading	War Diary Of 39th Division ("A" & "Q" Branch) 1st To 30th April, 1919. Vol.38		
War Diary	Rouen.	01/04/1919	30/04/1919
Heading	War Diary Of 39th Division. ("A" & "Q" Branch). 1st To 31st May, 1919. Vol.39		
War Diary	Rouen.	01/05/1919	31/05/1919
Miscellaneous	Presentation Of Colours Major-General H.C.C. Uniacke, C.B., C.M.G.	02/05/1919	02/05/1919
Miscellaneous	18th Bn. Northumberland Fusiliers.		
Miscellaneous	16th Bn. Sherwood Foresters.		
Heading	War Diary Of 39. Division (Administrative Branch) June 1919. HQ A.A.Q. 39 D Vol.40. June.		
War Diary	Rouen.	01/06/1919	30/06/1919
Heading	War Diary Of 39th Division (Administrative Branch) 1st To 10th July. HQ A.R.Q. 39D. Vol.41		
War Diary	Rouen.	01/07/1919	10/07/1919

39TH DIVISION

'A' & 'Q' BRANCH

MAR 1916-JLY 1919

WAR DIARY / INTELLIGENCE SUMMARY

Army Form C. 2118

A. and Q. 39th Division. Asst. Qr.

Instructions regarding War Diaries and Intelligence Summaries are contained in F.S. Regs., Part II. and the Staff Manual respectively. Title Pages will be prepared in manuscript.

(Erase heading not required.)

Place	Date 1916	Hour	Summary of Events and Information	Remarks and references to Appendices
WITLEY CAMP	1st March	—	39th Division ordered to stand-to; entraining and embarkation delayed	
"	2nd March	—	Entrainment and Embarkation delayed.	
"	3rd March	—	Entrainment & Embarkation commenced from SOUTHAMPTON	vide Appendix A
"	4th March	—	2nd day of Entrainment and Embarkation at SOUTHAMPTON	— " —
"	5th March	—	3rd day of Entrainment and Embarkation at SOUTHAMPTON	— " —
"	6th March	—	4th day of Entrainment and Embarkation at SOUTHAMPTON	— " —
"	7th March	—	5th day of Entrainment and Embarkation at SOUTHAMPTON	— " —
HAVRE	4,5,6,7,8,9 March	—	Disembarkation of Division; units proceeded to rest CAMPS	vide Appendix B
HAVRE	5,6,7,8,9 March	—	Entrainment of Division for concentration area.	

WAR DIARY

A. and Q.

39th Division. Head Qrs.

INTELLIGENCE SUMMARY

(Erase heading not required.)

Army Form C. 2118

Place	Date	Hour	Summary of Events and Information	Remarks and references to Appendices

The chief points which are worthy of notice from the standpoint of A. & Q. branches of the Staff, concern the arrangements made on mobilization in:—

(a) These arrangements worked with extraordinary smoothness in spite of the delays it was known at would be experienced in the Division, owing to the fact of units being quartered in so many different points of entrainment in England.

(b) The furore of the Staff at Pm. of the Division the day & night & night arrangements have specially selected, & may have been sensibly said to have attained the maximum of perfection attainable at the time of arrival in the area of concentration.

(c) The absence of French inhabitants at the town of concentration was noticed at the commencement, but the cause of this in connection with an — from the civilian point of view was of the great benefit to the G.O.C. & his hastily assembled Staff, to enable them to make good the services of the members of the Division, & to obtain a knowledge of the existing local conditions.

(d) It would undoubtedly are [?] Staff Officers or C in C— arrived in area of concentration if a course could be attended for the first few days — such a course would probably be found fully remunerative to Army or Corps Headquarters if the day of officers, but little opportunity becoming [?] available.

Army Form C. 2118

A. and Q.
39th Division Hqrs.

WAR DIARY
INTELLIGENCE SUMMARY
(Erase heading not required.)

Instructions regarding War Diaries and Intelligence Summaries are contained in F.S. Regs., Part II. and the Staff Manual respectively. Title Pages will be prepared in manuscript.

Place	Date 1916	Hour	Summary of Events and Information	Remarks and references to Appendices
BLARINGHEM	6/3		Units as per programme attached arrived and detrained in good order. Proceeded to camp and billets	
"	7/3		ditto	
"	8/3		ditto	
"	9/3		ditto	
"	10/3		ditto	
"	11/3		116 Infantry Brigade marched to 8th Division for instruction in the trenches: also 2ng Field Coy RE	
"	12/3		184th and 186th Brigades RFA marched to 34 and 8 Divisions respectively for instruction.	
"	13/3		117 Infantry Brigade and 234 Field Coy RE marched to 8th and 34 Divisions respectively for instruction.	
"	14/3		Nothing to record affecting 'A' 'Q' branch.	
"	15/3		Inspection of 118 Infantry Brigade by General SIR C.C. MONRO. KCB O.C. 1st ARMY	

1875 Wt. W593/826 1,000,000 4/15 J.B.C. & A. A.D.S.S./Forms/C.2118.

Army Form C. 2118

WAR DIARY
~~INTELLIGENCE SUMMARY~~

A. and Q.
39th Division. A & Q dqrs

(Erase heading not required.)

Instructions regarding War Diaries and Intelligence Summaries are contained in F.S. Regs., Part II. and the Staff Manual respectively. Title Pages will be prepared in manuscript.

Place	Date 1916	Hour	Summary of Events and Information	Remarks and references to Appendices
BLARINGHEM	16/3		Nothing to record affecting 'A' & 'Q' Branch	
"	17/3		"	
"	18/3		"	
"	19/3		Ammunition column of 184 Brigade RFA proceeded to 34th Division for attachment.	
"	20/3		Nothing to record affecting 'A' & 'Q' Branch	
"	21/3		"	
"	22/3		"	
"	23/3		"	
"	24/3	10 am	The 39th Division is transferred to XI Corps. Following moves took place. 'E' Squadron SOUTH IRISH HORSE to LA HAYE; Div Cyclist Company to LES AMUSOIRES; 118 Infantry Brigade 227 and 234 Field Coys RE to LES LAURIERS area between LA MOTTE and MERVILLE.	
"	25/3		The 174, 179 & 186 Brigades RFA and DAC moved to 33rd Divisional Area. The 184 Brigade RFA moved to 38 Divisional Area W of ST VENANT — Troops in 33rd Div area administered by 33 Div and 184 Bde RFA & all administered by 38 Div. The 225 Field Coy RE and 116 Inf. Bde moved from trenches to billets at LA GORGUE and MERVILLE and will be in reserve to NEUVE CHAPELLE sector.	

1875 Wt. W593/826 1,000,000 4/15 J.B.C. & A. A.D.S.S./Forms/C. 2118.

Army Form C. 2118

WAR DIARY or INTELLIGENCE SUMMARY

A. and Q. 39th Division Asadops.

(Erase heading not required.)

Instructions regarding War Diaries and Intelligence Summaries are contained in F.S. Regs., Part II. and the Staff Manual respectively. Title Pages will be prepared in manuscript.

Place	Date 1918	Hour	Summary of Events and Information	Remarks and references to Appendices
BLARINGHEM	26/3		184 Bde RFA is attached to 58 Division for instruction only; 225 Field Coy RE joining 19th Div. for training only; the 13th (S) Bn. Gloucestershire Regt. (Pioneers) moved from RUE DE BRUGES, LA ROBECQ area; 133 Field Ambulance to CALONNE.	
"	27/3		Inf. Bde moved from Trenches to ESTAIRES area from attachment to 38 Div Division; 134 Field Ambulance moved from ESTAIRES to ZELOBES for attachment to 19th Division; 132 Field Ambulance moved from MORBECQUE to MANQUEVILLE; 39th Div Sanitary Section (No. 27) to CALONNE; 227 Field Coy RE from LES LAURIERS to BETHUNE area for attachment to 33 Div for instruction; 234 Field Coy RE from instruction attachment to 38 Div for instruction; reorganisation of 134 Field Coy RE received orders from 35 Division for employment under orders of O.C. 29 Siege Battery R.G.A. — Mobile Vet. Section to LE SART. Orders re 227 Field Coy RE antedated. Command Refreshment points HQ hosts to R.T.F.WITTES; 118th Rde from LA MOTTE ROAD; 116th Bde same; odd units - HAVERSKERQUE. 117 Inf. Bde is attached to 33 Division for instruction in the Field. — 39 Div H.Q. Report centre closed or BLARINGHEM at 11am and re-opens at same hour at LESTREM.	
"	28/3	11AM	Divisional H.Q. opened at LESTREM, move from BLARINGHEM. GLESART H.Q. Coy & Train move from L'ECLEME to L'EPREOL 227 Field Coy RE move from L'ECLEME to BETHUNE 16th (S)Bn Sherwood Foresters 16(S)Bn Rifle Bde come to BETHUVE under orders of G.O.C. 33RD DIV.	

Army Form C. 2118

WAR DIARY
INTELLIGENCE SUMMARY
(Erase heading not required.)

A. and Q. 39th Division A&QMG

Instructions regarding War Diaries and Intelligence Summaries are contained in F.S. Regs., Part II. and the Staff Manual respectively. Title Pages will be prepared in manuscript.

Place	Date 1916	Hour	Summary of Events and Information	Remarks and references to Appendices
LESTREM	28/3		Repelling Troops: Div Troops HAYERS KER QUE: 116[?] Bde[?] goes to LA MOTTE - MERVILLE ROAD; remainder of units at H.A. 33 Div. for administration.	
LESTREM	29/3		16th Sherwood Foresters came under orders of G.O.C. 19th Bde for training by rotation — in the AUCHY SECTION. 16R Rifle Bde. Came under orders of G.O.C. 98 Bde for training by rotation in the CUINCHY SECTION.	
LESTREM	30/3		Nothing to record.	
LESTREM	31/3.		Two Battalions 118 Inf Bde marched to PONT DU HEM and RITZ BAILLEUL. Summary of Casualties for March 1916 attached.	ref. to Appendix C

J. M. Bernardiston —
Major Genl.
Commanding 39th Div.

Programme 28.

SECRET

Appendix A

238/1

ORDER OF EMBARKATION OF
39th DIVISION for HAVRE.

Index No.	UNIT.

1st DAY, 3rd MARCH. 1916.

IV	13th Batt: Gloucester Regt:
V	174th Bde. R.F.A.
VI	225th Field Coy, R.E.
VII	132nd Field Ambulance.
VIII	56th Field Bakery.
IX	37th Field Butchery.
X	Nos. 333-337 Depot Units of Supply.
XI	H.Q. &. No.1.Sec. Div: Signal Company
XII	H.Q. &. H.Q.Coy, Div: Train.
XIII	39th Div: Cyclist Coy.

2nd DAY, 4th MARCH.

XIV	Divisional Headquarters.
XV	H.Q. Divisional R.A.
XVI	179th Brigade, R.F.A.
XVII	(H.Q. 116th Infantry Bde.
	(Section Signal Coy.
	(285th Coy. Divisional Train.
XVIII	11th Batt: R.Sussex Regt.
XIX	12th Batt: R.Sussex Regt.

3rd DAY, 5th MARCH.

XX	13th Batt: R.Sussex Regt.
XXI	14th Batt: Hampshire Regt.
XXII	186th Bde, R.F.A. (How)
XXIII	H.Q. Division R.E.
XXIV	227th Field Company. R.E.
XXV	133rd Field Ambulance.

4th DAY, 6th MARCH.

XXVI	(H.Q. 117th Infantry Brigade.
	(Section Signal Company.
	(286th Coy. Divisional Train.
XXVII	16th Battalion, Notts & Derby Regiment.
XXVIII	17th Battalion do.
XXIX	184th Brigade, R.F.A.
XXX	134th Field Ambulance.

5th DAY, 7th MARCH.

XXXI	17th Batt: K.R.R.C.
XXXII	16th Batt: Rifle Brigade.
XXXIII	Divisional Ammunition Col:
XXXIV	234th Field Coy; R:E:
XXXV	Cable Section (A.Z)
XXXVI	82nd Sanitary Section.
XXXVII	50th Mobile Veterinary Sec:
XXXVIII	Infantry Base Depot.

War Office (Q.M.G.2.)
    18th February, 1916.

Appendix 3

MOVE OF THE 39TH DIVISION. (Sheet No: 1.)

No: of Train.	Serial Number.	Bde.	UNIT.	Marche. W.T.	Havre dep.	St Omer. arr.	DETRAIN AT.	arr.
					5.3.16.	5.3.16.		5.3.16.
1.	3940 41	174th.	Bde. Headquarters.) 'A' Battery.)	9.	4.19.	21.05.	STEENBECQUE.	22.05.
2.	04		13th S.Bn. Glosters (P'oers).	15.	8.19.	6.3.16. 0.55.	THIENNES.	6.3.16. 2.15.
3.	05. 84.		39th Divl. Cyclists.) 225th Fld. Coy. R.E.)	17.	10.39.	3.15.	STEENBECQUE.	4.15.
4.	91.		132nd Field Ambulance.	19.	11.59.	4.55	THIENNES.	6.10.
5.	45.	174th.	Bde. Ammunition Column.	21.	13.19.	6.15.	STEENBECQUE.	7.15.
6.	06. 87.		H.Q. Div. Sigs. & No: 1 Sec.) H.Q. & H.Q. Coy. Div. Train.)	27.	17.39.	9.55.	THIENNES.	11.10.
7.	42.	174th.	'B' Battery.	1.	21.19.	13.55.	STEENBECQUE.	14.45.
8.	43.	"	'C' Battery.	3.	22.19.	15.15.	THIENNES.	16.30.
9.	44.	"	'D' Battery.	5.	23.59.	16.55.	STEENBECQUE.	17.55.

B.

Appendix 3

M O V E of the 39TH DIVISION. (Sheet 2).

No of Train.	Serial No.	Brigade.	UNIT.	HAVRE. dep. 5.3.16.	ST OMER. arr. 7.3.16.	DETRAINING STN.	arr. 7.3.16.
10.	3911	116th	11th S.Bn.Royal Sussex Reg:	8.19.	0.55.	STEENBECQUE	1.55.
11.	50	179th	Brigade Headquarters)	10.39.	3.15.	THIENNES	4.30.
	51	179th	"A" Battery)				
12.	01	116th	Divisional Headquarters)	11.59.	4.55.	STEENBECQUE	5.55.
	10		Brigade Headquarters)				
	15		No.2 Section Signal Co.)				
	88		No.2 Coy: Divisional Train)				
13.	02	179th	H.Q.Divisional Artillery)	13.19.	6.15.	THIENNES	7.30.
	52		"B" Battery)				
14.	12	116th	12th S.Bn.Royal Sussex Reg:	17.39.	9.55.	STEENBECQUE	10.55.
15.	55	179th	Brigade Ammunition Column	18.39.	11.15.	THIENNES	12.30.
16.	53	179th	"C" Battery	21.19.	13.55.	STEENBECQUE	14.55.
17.	54	179th	"D" Battery	22.19.	15.15.	THIENNES	16.30.

Appendix 3

MOVE of the 39th DIVISION. (Contd: sheet No: 3.)

No: of train.	Serial No:	Bde.	UNIT.	Marche. W.T.	HAVRE. dep,	ST OMER. arr.	DETRAIN AT.	arr.
					7.3.16.	8.3.16.		8.3.16.
18.	3913.	116th.	13th S.Bn. R. Sussex Rgt.	15.	8.25.	0.55.	STEENBECQUE.	1.55.
19.	3970. 3971.	186th. "	Bde. H.Q.) 'A' Battery.)	17.	10.39.	3.15.	THIENNES.	4.30.
20.	3992.		133rd Fld Amb.	19.	11.59.	4.55.	STEENBECQUE.	5.55.
21.	3983. 3985.		H.Q. Div. R.E.) 227th F. Co RE)	21.	13.19.	6.15.	THIENNES.	7.30.
22.	3914.	116th.	14th S.Bn.) Hants Rgt.)	27.	17.39.	9.55.	STEENBECQUE.	10.55.
23.	3955.	179th.	Bde Ammn Col.	29.	18.39.	11.15.	THIENNES.	12.30.
24.	3972.	186th.	'B' Battery.	31.	20.19.	12.55.	STEENBECQUE.	13.55.
25.	3973.	"	'C' Battery.	3.	22.19.	15.15.	THIENNES.	16.30.
26.	3974.	"	'D' Battery.	5.	23.59.	16.55.	STEENBECQUE.	17.55.

Appendix B

MOVE of the 39th DIVISION. (Contd: sheet No 4.)

No: of train.	Serial number.	Bde.	UNIT.	Marche. W.T.	HAVRE. dep.	ST OMER. arr.	DETRAIN AT.	arr.
					8.3.16.	9.3.16.		9.3.16.
27.	3921.	117th.	16th S. Bn. Notts & Derbys.	15.	8.25.	0.55.	STEENBECQUE.	1.55.
28.	3960. 3961.	184th. "	Bde. Headquarters. 'A' Battery.	17.	10.39.	3.15.	THIENNES.	4.30.
29.	3920. 3925. 3989.	117th. "	Bde. Headquarters. No: 3 Section Signals. No: 3 Coy. Divl. Train.	19.	11.59.	4.55.	STEENBECQUE.	5.55.
30.	3962.	184th.	'B' Battery.	21.	13.19.	6.15.	THIENNES.	7.30.
31.	3922.	117th.	17th S. Bn. Notts & Derby.	27.	17.39.	9.55.	STEENBECQUE.	10.55.
32.	3965.	184th.	Bde. Ammunition Column.	29.	18.39.	11.15.	THIENNES.	12.30.
33.	3963.	184th.	'C' Battery.	31.	20.19.	12.55.	STEENBECQUE.	13.55.
34.	3993.		134th Field Ambulance.	3.	22.19.	15.15.	THIENNES.	16.30.
35.	3964.	184th.	'D' Battery.	5.	23.59.	16.55.	STEENBECQUE.	17.55.

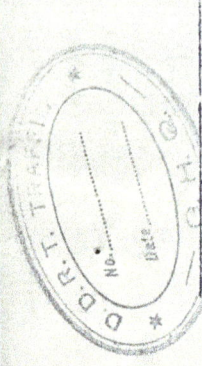

Appendix B

E.B.

MOVE of the 39th DIVISION. (Contd: sheet No. 5).

No. of train.	Serial number.	Bde.	UNIT.	Marche. W.T.	HAVRE. dep.	ST OMER. arr.	DETRAIN AT.	arr.
					9.3.16.	10.3.16.		10.3.16.
36.	3923.	117th.	17th. S. Bn. K.R.R.C.	15.	8.25.	0.55.	THIENNES	2.15.
37.	3979.		D.A.C.No.1 Section (2/3rds)	17.	10.39.	3.15.	STEENBECQUE	4.30.
38.	(3986. (3994. (3995. (—		234th Field Coy: R.E. 82nd Sanitary Section. 50th Mobile Vet: Section Cable Section.	19.	11.59.	4.55.	THIENNES	6.15.
39.	3980.		D.A.C.No.2 Section (2/3rds)	21.	13.19.	6.15.	STEENBECQUE	7.30.
40.	3924.	117th.	16th S.Bn. Rifle Bde.	27.	17.39.	9.55.	THIENNES	11.15.
41.	3981.		D.A.C.No.3 Section (2/3rds)	29.	18.39.	11.15.	STEENBECQUE	12.30.
42.	(3980.A. (3981.A.		D.A.C.No.2 Section (1/3rd) D.A.C.No.3 Section (1/3rd)	1.	21.19.	12.55.	THIENNES	14.15.
43.	(3978. (3979.A.		D.A.C. Headquarters D.A.C.No.1 Section (1/3rd)	3.	22.19.	15.15.	STEENBECQUE	15.15.

ALL UNITS COMPLETE.

CASUALTIES - 39th DIVISION

March, 1916.

Date of casualty.	Unit.	Name of Officer.	Nature of casualty	Remarks.
13.3.16.	11th Bn Royal Sussex	Major the Hon N. Lytton.	Wounded.	
"	" " " "	Captain H.M. Tyler	"	
"	14th Bn. Hants.	Lieut. L. Langdon.	"	Died of Wounds 14.3.16.
22.3.16.	13th Bn. Gloucesters	Lieut G.S.D. Hillier.	"	
26.3.16.	1/6th Bn. Cheshires.	Lieut. C.R. Norman	" acc.	

Date of casualty.	Unit.	Number of casualties	Nature of casualty.	Remarks.
12.3.16.	11th Bn. Royal Sussex.	1 O.R.	Killed.	
13.3.16.	" " " "	4 O.R.	"	
"	" " " "	1 O.R.	Died of Wounds. 13.3.16	
"	" " " "	8 O.R.	Wounded. 2 Died of Wnds. 14.3.16.	
"	" " " "	1 O.R.	Wounded at duty.	
"	12th " " "	3 O.R.	Wounded.	
"	13th " " "	1 O.R.	"	
14.3.16.	12th " " "	1 O.R.	" acc.	
15.3.16.	11th " " "	3 O.R.	Wounded.	
"	13th " " "	1 O.R.	"	
"	14th Bn. Hants	1 O.R.	"	
16.3.16	11th Bn Royal Sussex	2 O.R.	"	
"	12th Bn Royal Sussex	2 O.R.	"	1 Died of Wounds. 18.3.16.
17.3.16	11th Bn Royal Sussex	2 O.R.	"	
"	12th " " "	2 O.R.	"	
"	13th " " "	1 O.R.	"	
"	17th Bn Notts & Derby	1 O.R.	"	
18.3.16.	12th Bn Royal Sussex	2 O.R.	"	
"	13th " " "	1 O.R.	"	
19.3.16	12th " " "	1 O.R.	Killed.	
"	" " " "	2 O.R.	Wounded.	
"	17th K.R.R. C.	1 O.R.	Killed.	
"	" " " "	1 O.R.	Wounded.	
20.3.16.	11th Bn Royal Sussex	1 O.R.	"	
"	" " " "	1 O.R.	" acc.	
"	16th Notts & Derby	1 O.R.	"	
"	17th " " "	1 O.R.	"	
"	17th Bn K.R.R. C.	1 O.R.	"	

Cont.

Two.

CASUALTIES - 39th DIVISION (Cont.)

Date of casualty	Unit.	Number of Casualties.	Nature of casualty.	Remarks.
20.3.16.	16th Rifle Brigade	3 O.R.	Wounded	
21.3.16	12th Bn Royal Sussex.	3 O.R.	"	1 Died of wnds. 22.3.16.
"	16th Bn Notts & Derby	1 O.R.	"	
"	" "	1 O.R.	" at duty.	
"	17th Bn K.R.R. C.	1 O.R.	"	
"	13th Bn Gloucesters	1 O.R.	" acc.	
22.3.16	14th Bn Hants	2 O.R.	"	
23.3.16	17th Bn Notts & Derby	1 O.R.	"	Died of Wounds 23.3.16.
"	17th Bn K.R.R. C	1 O.R.	Killed.	
"	16th Bn Rifle Brigade	1 O.R.	Wounded acc.	
26.3.16	1/6 Bn Cheshires	1 O.R.	" "	

SUMMARY.

OFFICERS.	KILLED.	Nil.	
"	WOUNDED.	(X) 4.	(X) includes one died of wounds.
"	WOUNDED (acc)	1.	

OTHER RANKS.	KILLED	8.	
"	WOUNDED	(X)49.	(X) includes six died of wounds.
"	WOUNDED (acc)	5.	
"	WOUNDED (at duty)	2.	

"A" + "Q" 39th Division.

WAR DIARY

~~INTELLIGENCE SUMMARY~~

(Erase heading not required.)

Army Form C. 2118.

Instructions regarding War Diaries and Intelligence Summaries are contained in F. S. Regs., Part II. and the Staff Manual respectively. Title pages will be prepared in manuscript.

Place	Date	Hour	Summary of Events and Information	Remarks and references to Appendices
LESTREM	1916 1/4		Two Battalions of the 118 Infantry Brigade left PONT DU HEM and RITZ BAILLEUL for the trenches. Two Battalions 118 Inf Bde left area near MERVILLE for PONT DU HEM and RITZ BAILLEUL. This Brigade will relieve the 57 & 58 Inf Bde in the MOATED GRANGE SECTION from 1st April to the 7/8 of April and during that period be under command of the G.O.C. 19th Division.	
	2/4		All detached units of the Division fed by sending lorries from our Railhead - MERVILLE - to the train to bring to their refilling Point after which Divisional Coy Train proceeds.	
	3/4		G.O.C. XI Corps inspected 116 Infantry Brigade after Ladies and a Lecture at MERVILLE given to Officers by the War and Staff European attendance.	

Army Form C. 2118.

D. A. & Q. 39th Division

WAR DIARY

~~INTELLIGENCE SUMMARY~~

(Erase heading not required.)

Instructions regarding War Diaries and Intelligence Summaries are contained in F. S. Regs., Part II. and the Staff Manual respectively. Title pages will be prepared in manuscript.

Place	Date	Hour	Summary of Events and Information	Remarks and references to Appendices
LESTREM	4/4		G.O.C. XI Corps inspected 17th Ryl. Sherwood Foresters and 17th Bn. K.R.R.C. left to rejoin 117th Inf. Bde.	
LESTREM	5/4		Conference at Headquarters 1st Army. Local Purchasing discussed. S.A.A.Q. M.G. attends	
LESTREM	6/4		Nothing to report	
LESTREM	7/4		Railway guide by X I Corps regarding Transport of a Territorial Infantry Brigade to the effect that the establishment was the same for all Infantry Brigades in the Army where armed with LEWIS guns	
LESTREM	8/4		Conference at Divisional Headquarters	
LESTREM	9/4		G.O.C. 1st Army inspects 179 & 184th Brigades R.F.A.	

"A" + "Q" 39th Division

WAR DIARY

~~INTELLIGENCE SUMMARY.~~

(Erase heading not required.)

Army Form C. 2118.

Place	Date	Hour	Summary of Events and Information	Remarks and references to Appendices
	1916			
LESTREM	10/4		G.O.C. XI. Corps inspects 116th & 38th Reserve Forestry and 16th British Rifle Brigade	
"	11/4		Nothing to report.	
"	12/4		G.O.C. XI. Corps inspects 2 Battalions of the 118 Inf. Bde.	
"	13/4		G.O.C. XI. Corps inspects last 2 Battalions of the 118 Inf. Bde.	
"	14/4		116th and 118th Infantry Brigades move to the 38th (Welsh) Divisional Area.	
"	15/4		116th Inf.13 Bde. moved into the forward line relieving 113th Bde. Brigade of the 38th Div'n and the 9th Corps R.A. to 38th Div. R.A. relieves the 38th Div. R.A. on the GIVENCHY — FESTUBERT fronts.	

Army Form C. 2118.

"A" "Q" 30th Division

WAR DIARY

~~INTELLIGENCE SUMMARY~~

(Erase heading not required.)

Instructions regarding War Diaries and Intelligence Summaries are contained in F. S. Regs., Part II. and the Staff Manual respectively. Title pages will be prepared in manuscript.

Place	Date	Hour	Summary of Events and Information	Remarks and references to Appendices
	1916			
LESTREM	16/4		The 118th Inf. Bde relieved the 114th Infantry Brigade of the 38th Division and moved into the FESTUBERT Section.	
LOCON	17/4	8am	39th Divisional Headquarters moved to LOCON in relief of the 38th Division.	
LOCON	18/4 to 23/4		Nothing to report.	
LOCON	24/4		The 117th Infantry Brigade relieved the 118th Infantry Bde: the former Brigade moving into the FESTUBERT Section and the latter into Divisional Reserve. Divisional Battle opened.	
LOCON	25/4 to 30/4		Nothing to report.	
			List of Battle Casualties for April 1916 attached.	A.

A.H. Murray(?)
Major Genl.
Command 30th Div.

Casualties   Officers and Other Ranks

Killed

April 1916

Casualties — Officers — April 1916.
Killed

Rank & Name	Unit	Nature of Casualty	Date
Lt. W.W. Park	1st Bn. Herts	Killed	2.4.16
2/Lt. G.F. Lambert	1st Bn. Herts	Died of wounds	15.4.16
2/Lt. F.W. Battley	11th Bn. Sussex	Killed	21.4.16
Lt. F.C.H. Gilbert	14th Bn. Hants	Killed	24.4.16

Total Casualties — Killed — April 1916

Unit	1st	2nd	3rd	4th	5th	6th	7th	8th	9th	10th	11th	12th	13th	14th	15th	16th	17th	18th	19th	20th	21st	22nd	23rd	24th	25th	26th	27th	28th	29th	30th	Total
11th Bn. Rl Sussex Regt.																1				2	2		1								6 ?
12th " " "																4	3	1				2		1			1				11
13th " " "				1												1	1	1					2	1					1		8
14th Bn. Hampshire Regt.		1																								4	1				9
16th Bn. Notts & Derby Regt			1																							1			1		3
17th " " "													1			3				1											7
17th Bn. Kings Royal Rifle Corps													1																1		2
16th Bn. Rifle Brigade																															1
11th Bn. Cheshire Regt.				1										1							1										3
14th Bn. Black Watch							1																								1
11th Bn. Cambo Regt.																						1									1
1st Bn. Herts Regt																															1
13th Bn. Gloucester Regt.																					1			1					1		3
Royal Army Medical Corps																															
Royal Engineers								1																							1
Army Service Corps																															
Royal Artillery																															
"E" Squadron, South Irish Horse																															
Divl. Cyclist Coy.																															
Total	1	2	2	1			1	1			1		2	1		9	4	1	1	4	3	3	3	2		5	2		3	3	55
Total Killed	1	2	2	1			1	1			1		2	1		9	4	1	1	4	3	3	3	2		5	2		3	3	55

Casualties — Officers and Other Ranks.

Wounded

April 1916.

Casualties — Officers — April 1916
Wounded

Rank & Name	Unit	Nature of Casualty	Date
2/Lt. C.F. Lambert	1st Bn Herts	Wounded (since died of wounds)	1.4.16
Lt. Col. G.L. Archer	1/1st Bn Cambs	" at duty	2.4.16
Rev. J. Howse C of E	A.C. Dept. 1/1st Cambs	" " "	2.4.16
2/Lt. H.L. Morell	16th Notts & Derby	"	2.4.16
Lt. W.W. Fitzherbert	13th Ryl. Sussex	"	16.4.16
Lt. A.J. Warner	12th " "	"	16.4.16
2/Lt. D. St H. Lamer	Instr L.T.M. Batty. attch 116th J. Bde	"	17.4.16
2/Lt. C.G. Vandyk	174 Bde R.F.A.	"	19.4.16
Lt. H.Q.K. Mullineaux	12th Rl. Sussex	"	19.4.16
2/Lt. W.R. Benner	17th Notts & Derby	" acc. (at duty)	21.4.16
2/Lt. J.W. Husband	14th Black Watch	"	22.4.16
2/Lt. J.C. Prain	118th Bde M.G. Coy.	"	23.4.16
Lt. A.C. Tayler	13th Rly Sussex	"	24.4.16
Lt. C.A.G. Burgess	11th Rly Sussex	"	29.4.16
2/Lt. Temp. Capt. J.A. St L. Fredennick	Seaforths employed with 12th Sussex Regt	"	30.4.16

Died of Wounds (Included in figures shown on Statement of "KILLED")

Date	Unit.	Number.
3.4.16	16th Notts & Derbys.	One
3.4.16	1/6th Cheshire Regt.	One
7.4.16	1st. Cambridgeshire Regt.	One
17.4.16	13th Royal Sussex Regt.	Three
17.4.16	14th. Hants. Regt.	One
19.4.16	14th Hants. Regt.	One
20.4.16	12th R. Sussex Regt.	One
20.4.16	1st. Herts. Regt.	One
21.4.16	1st. Herts. Regt.	One
22.4.16	12th R. Sussex Regt.	One.

Total casualties — Wounded — April 1916

Unit	1st	2nd	3rd	4th	5th	6th	7th	8th	9th	10th	11th	12th	13th	14th	15th	16th	17th	18th	19th	20th	21st	22nd	23rd	24th	25th	26th	27th	28th	29th	30th	Total
11th Bn. Royal Sussex Regt																			5	1	2		2					3	8	1	23
12th " " "																2	5		6	3	1	4	2	5	1	1		2	5		27
13th " " "															1	14	2	1	3	1	1			1	2	1		1		1	30
14th " Hampshire Regt.			6	1					2	1				3		2	1			1	1		3	1	1		1	1	1		22
16th " Bn. Notts & Derby Regt	4							5	1														1		1	6		1	2		18
17th " " "							1																						2		16
17th " Kings Royal Rifle Corps	1											1	1	3		2				1						1					12
16th " Rifle Brigade		9	6	5	8							2	2						1					3		1					27
11th " Cheshire Regt			2	1		2	1						1																		12
11th " Black Watch				1		2		5									2	2				4									12
11th " Bombs. Regt.				1													5	3													10
1st " Herts Regt.				1						1										1	1	1	3	3							12
13th " Gloucester Regt																												2	2		4
Royal Army Medical Corps																															
Royal Engineers			1	1														1	1							1				1	6
Army Service Corps																											1				
Royal Artillery								1							2			2													5
"E" Sqdn. South Irish Horse																															
Bn. Cyclist Bn.																															
Total	1	15	16	10	8	4	1	7	3	2	1	4	4	3	3	20	13	6	17	7	7	10	15	9	6	11	3	8	20	2	236
254 Tunnelling Coy R.E.																		1	1		1										3
39th Bde attd X 39 Bde (TM)																								1							1
118 Bde M.G. Coy																				1											1
Bur. 255 Tunnelling Coy R.E.																															
Total Wounded	1	15	16	10	8	4	1	7	3	2	1	4	4	3	3	20	13	6	18	9	8	10	15	9	7	11	3	8	21	2	242

CONFIDENTIAL

39/1197/A.

D.A.G.,
3rd Echelon,
Base.

Herewith War Diary for "A" and "Q" branches of this Divisional Staff for the month of May, 1916.

Will you kindly acknowledge receipt.

Major-General,
Commanding 39th Division.

5.6.16.

Army Form C. 2118.

VOL 3

"A" and "Q" STAFF
39ᵗʰ DIVISION

WAR DIARY
or
INTELLIGENCE SUMMARY.
(Erase heading not required.)

Instructions regarding War Diaries and Intelligence Summaries are contained in F. S. Regs., Part II. and the Staff Manual respectively. Title pages will be prepared in manuscript.

Place	Date	Hour	Summary of Events and Information	Remarks and references to Appendices
	1916			
LOCON.	1/5.		118 Infantry Brigade relieved 116 Infantry Brigade in 'B' (GIVENCHY) Section; the latter Brigade coming into Divisional Reserve.	
"	2/5 3/5 4/5		Nothing to report.	
"	5/5.		The Commander-in-Chief visited Divisional Headquarters; did not stay long. 117 Infantry Brigade carried out Battalion relief in 'C' Section and 118 Infantry Brigade in 'B' Section.	
"	6/5.		A.A. & Q.M.G. put the a conference attended by the Staff Captains T.A. and Infantry Brigades: administrative matters brought up at Corps Conference are discussed.	

Army Form C. 2118.

WAR DIARY
or
INTELLIGENCE SUMMARY.

(Erase heading not required.)

Instructions regarding War Diaries and Intelligence Summaries are contained in F.S. Regs., Part II. and the Staff Manual respectively. Title pages will be prepared in manuscript.

Place	Date	Hour	Summary of Events and Information	Remarks and references to Appendices
	1916			
LOCON	7/5		Nothing to report	
	8/5			
-,,-	9/5		The M.G.C. inspected 'E' Sqn & Hen S.I.H. and 39th Divisional Cyclist Company prior to them leaving the Division.	
-,,-	10/5		E Squadron S.I.H. and 39th Divisional Cyclist Company leave to join the II Corps 1st Army and XV Corps 4th Army respectively. These Divisional troops to much felt.	
-,,-	11/5		Nothing to report.	
	12/5			
-,,-	13/5		116 and 118 Infantry Brigades lost carried our Battalion reliefs in 'C' and 'B' Sectors respectively.	
-,,-	14/5		Nothing to report.	

T2134. Wt. W708-776. 500000. 4/15. Sir J. C. & S.

WAR DIARY or INTELLIGENCE SUMMARY.

Army Form C. 2118.

(Erase heading not required.)

Place	Date	Hour	Summary of Events and Information	Remarks and references to Appendices
LOCON	15/5	9.0	17th L.E. infts to the 17 (S) Bn K.R.R.C. Orders received for reorganisation of Royal Artillery. Each Brigade will now consist of 3 Batteries of 18 Prs. and 1 Battery of 4.5 (Howitzer). The four Brigade Ammunition Columns are abolished & Reserve Brigade Ammunition Columns with HQ and 3 Sections = A Echelon & D.A.C. reorganised with HQ and 3 Sections = A Echelon and one Section 'B' Echelon. 'A' Echelon will always be with the Division while B will act as Corps Reserve. It is not yet clear how the 3 sections of 'A' Echelon will provide for the 4 Brigades.	
		14.5	Hostile aeroplane dropped 6 bombs in the vicinity of Div. H.Q. no damage was done as the bombs fell in a field.	
		14.13	17 Infantry Brigade relieved 118. J.B. in 'B' GIVENCHY section. 116 J.B.de carried on our trenches in relief.	

Army Form C. 2118.

WAR DIARY
or
INTELLIGENCE SUMMARY.
(Erase heading not required.)

Instructions regarding War Diaries and Intelligence Summaries are contained in F. S. Regs., Part II. and the Staff Manual respectively. Title pages will be prepared in manuscript.

Place	Date	Hour	Summary of Events and Information	Remarks and references to Appendices
LOCOR	1916			
	17/5		Headquarters 186 Brigade R.F.A. relieved HQ 179 Brigade R.F.A. in command of "C" group Area	
	18/5		Nothing to report.	
	19/5		Lecture on "NEUVE CHAPELLE" delivered to the Division by Brigadier General W.H. ANDERSON. General Staff (x 11 Corps). Arrival of 116 and 117th Brigade Machine Gun Companies from England. They are billetted at LE VERT ANNOY and LE HAMEL respectively.	
	20/5		Nothing to report.	
	21/5		Strong evidence of lachrymatory gas at DHQ. & officers on leave from S.E. and left at 3 Section Head quarters.	

T 2134. Wt. W 708—776. 50000. 4/15. Sir J. C. & S.

Army Form C. 2118.

WAR DIARY
or
INTELLIGENCE SUMMARY.
(Erase heading not required.)

Instructions regarding War Diaries and Intelligence Summaries are contained in F. S. Regs., Part II. and the Staff Manual respectively. Title pages will be prepared in manuscript.

Place	Date	Hour	Summary of Events and Information	Remarks and references to Appendices
	1916			
LOCON.	22/5		Divisional Gas School starts its first course.	
LOCON.	23/5		Three officers 68th Division arrived from England for 3 days attachment: one Brigade Commander attached to 117 Inf Bde, CRE and DAA & QMG.	
LOCON.	24/5		Twenty cadets from 9 HQ. School for Cadets arrived for 48 hours instruction in the trenches: 10 Inf & each Section.	
LOCON.	25/5.		118th Inf Bde relieved 116th Inf Bde in FESTUBERT Section. Captain V. B. Ramsden S.W.B. vacated appointment of GSO 3. He was relieved by Captain M. W. PAUL 1th The Duke of Cambridge's Own Middlesex Regt from 33rd Division.	
LOCON.	26/5		Fifty O.R sent to join the 3rd AUSTRALIAN Mining Coy.	

Army Form C. 2118.

WAR DIARY
or
INTELLIGENCE SUMMARY.
(Erase heading not required.)

Instructions regarding War Diaries and Intelligence Summaries are contained in F. S. Regs., Part II. and the Staff Manual respectively. Title pages will be prepared in manuscript.

Place	Date	Hour	Summary of Events and Information	Remarks and references to Appendices
LOCON	1916 26/5		Normal routine being found by the 3 Infantry Brigades.	
LOCON	27/5		Orders received from XI Corps to be prepared to carry out changes in the Div. front in connection with change of Corps front in the Lt. front. To provide a reserve which should be available to counter the I Corps on our right in the event of a hostile attack against LOOS. Infantry Brigades are now to move RA, RE, & ambulances to remain unchanged. moves to be as follows. 116 Bde (in Div. Reserve) to take over CUINCHY Section from 98 Bde 33 Div. 7. 105 — 135 Div to take over FESTUBERT Section from 118 Bde 118 Bde after relief to form 39 Div. Reserve near GORRE & ESSARS. Motor Ambce Resvt. in the area.	
LOCON	28/5		Orders received for moves detailed above to be carried out tonight. Allotment of 183 Bde 61st Div DIV Cavalry — 2 Battalions of 182 Bde to be taken in hand and trained in CUINCHY Section.	

T.J.134. Wt. W708—776. 50000. 4/15. Sir J. C. & B.

Army Form C. 2118.

WAR DIARY
or
INTELLIGENCE SUMMARY.
(Erase heading not required.)

Instructions regarding War Diaries and Intelligence Summaries are contained in F.S. Regs., Part II. and the Staff Manual respectively. Title pages will be prepared in manuscript.

Place	Date	Hour	Summary of Events and Information	Remarks and references to Appendices
	1915			
LOCON	29/5		Relief carried out last night. The Div. Sector now consists of the CUINCHY and GIVENCHY Sections — astride the LA BASSEE canal.	
LOCON	30/5		305 Bde RFA (1st Div) attached to our Div RA 2/2 Field Coy RE (—") " " " RE 2/7 Warwicks 1/8 Bde (—") " " " 116 Inf Bde " " 8 " " " " 116 Inf Bde	
LOCON	31/5		G.O.C. 1st Army inspects Divisional Bombing School A list of Casualties (killed & wounded) is attached	A

B.E. Dixon Ma?
F Major General
Cmdg 39th Division.

Appendix 'A'

Casualties May. 1916.

Killed

Officers and Other Ranks

Officers.

Rank + Name	Unit	Casualty	Date
Lieut. T. W. Coles	18th Bde R.F.A.	Acc. Killed	1.5.16
2/Lt. E.G. Westacott	16" Rifle Bde	Wounded & Died of Wounds	19.5.16
" G.E. Elliot	13" R. Sussex Regt	" 20.5.16 Died of Wounds	21.5.16
" R.H. Lifetree	16" Notts & Derbys	Killed	21.5.16
Lt. Y. L. Ellis	14" Hants	"	29.5.16
2/Lt. J. Cornwall	13" Sussex Regt	"	30.5.16

Other Ranks

Unit	1	2	3	4	5	6	7	8	9	10	11	12	13	14	15	16	17	18	19	20	21	22	23	24	25	26	27	28	29	30	31	Total	
11th Bn R. Sussex Regt	1																															4	
12" " "											3*			1			2					1				1						8	x 1/ATTd 255 T.Cy RE.
13" " "											1		2																	2	1	7	
14th Bn Hampshire Regt							1	2				1						1	4x	1									1			8	x Include 4 acc. drowned
15" Bn R. Derby Regt																					1	3	2	3	1	1	1		1	3		12	
17" " "												1								1										2	1	10	
17 " King's Royal Rifle Corps																								3	1							4	
16" " Rifle Bde.				1			1			2					1	1							2			3			1			6	
1/6" " Cheshire Regt																1	1							3	1	1				1		9	
1/5 " Royal Highlanders																2																1	
1/1 " Cambo Regt								1		2				1	1		1				1						3					7	
1/1 " Scots "																					1						3	1				6	
Div. Artillery																																1	
" Engineers																																1	
Army Service Corps																																	
Royal Army Med. Corps									1																								
13 Bn R. Lanc. Regt (Pioneers)																								1			1					2	
X. 39 Tn Battery attd 39 DAC																																1	
Total	1	2		2	1	2	2	3		5	5	1	3	2	1	4	3	1	4	1	4	6	6	7	2	6	5	2	2	8	1	86	
25th Tunnelling Cy R.E.																															1	1	
Grand Total	1	2		2	1	2	2	3	1	5	5	1	3	2	1	4	3	1	4	1	4	6	6	7	2	6	5	2	2	8	1	87	

APPENDIX 'A'

Casualties - May 1916.

Wounded.

Officers and Other Ranks.

Officers.

Rank & Name	Unit	Casualty	Date
2/Lt. F. Yorke	1/6 Cheshires.	Wounded	2.5.16
" C. Chantler.	"	" at duty.	"
" R.C. Osborne	4/5 Royal Highlanders.	"	8.5.16
" (Temp. Capt) R.G. Wood.	1/1 Cambs.	" at duty.	9.5.16
" W.J. Dean.	254 Tunnelling Coy R.E.	"	"
" A.T. Ogle.	1/1 Herts.	"	10.5.16
Lieut. T. Roberts.	17 Notts & Derbys attd 118 T.m.B	"	12.5.16
2/Lt. R.G. Caldecott.	12 Sussex	"	14.5.16
" W.J.O Raines.	1/1 Cambs	"	"
Lt. J.H. Shield.	16 Rifle Bde.	" at duty.	20.5.16
2/Lt. A.L. Crockford.	13 Glosters	"	21.5.16
" E.D. Smythies.	17 K.R.R. Corps	"	23.5.16
Capt. A.S. Bates.	1/1 Cambs	"	24.5.16
Lt. R.R. Tattersall.	16 Rifle Bde	"	26.5.16
2/Lt. G.K. Foster.	1/6 Cheshires.	"	27.5.16
" A.D. Parkin	16 Notts & Derbys.	"	28.5.16
" G.E. Odom.	16 Kings Liverpools attd.	"	29.5.16
	118 Bde m.G. Coy.	"	

Other Ranks.

Unit	1	2	3	4	5	6	7	8	9	10	11	12	13	14	15	16	17	18	19	20	21	22	23	24	25	26	27	28	29	30	31	Total	
11" Bn R. Sussex Regt					2							6	1		2	4	2	1	1		2	1	2	2						1		27	
12" "						1					2	1			4	5	1						1			2		1				20	
13" "		1		2			1	1			2	2	4			1			2	1	3									6	18	41	abs 1 man missing 12/16
14" Hampshire Regt										8	2	3		1	2		2	2	2	2	5					2	2	7	9	8	3	38	
16" " D.o.b Derby Regt	1						2		3		2				4				6	7	2	1	2	2	1	10			3	3	1	49	
16" " "			4					5	1						5		4			4	1	7	8	11		3		2	2		3	39	
17" King's Royal Rifle Corps								7												3	5		4	25	9				4		3	55	
17" Rifle Brigade							2	2	3	4		1		4		6	4	5	2	4		7	7			11		2		6		45	
16" Cheshire Regt		11			2								1																			22	
H/5 Black Watch (Royal Highrs)																																19	
1/1 Cambs Regt		8						2																								33	
1/1 Scouts												1											1				2	3				30	abs 2 men missing 27/16
Divisional Artillery												1									1									1		1	
" Engineers																																11	
Army Service Corps												1																				1	
Royal Army Med. Corps										2		2								1	1										2	15	
13' Bn Alberta Regt (Canada)																																	
Total =	3	10	4	5	8	4	4	15	6	17	10	23	7	5	11	19	9	8	13	22	22	17	18	41	10	29	5	17	19	27	32	449	
25" Tunnelling Coy R.E.									5	1									3	1						1	1					14	
118 Bde H.Q.																																1	
x/39 T.M Battery also D.A.C (39)																																1	
N/39 - 174 Bde (3.A																																1	
Grand Total =	3	10	5	5	10	7	4	15	11	18	10	23	7	5	12	19	9	8	16	23	22	17	18	41	10	30	7	17	19	27	32	466	

CONFIDENTIAL.

D.A.G.,
   3rd Echelon,
      Base.

39/1197/A

      Herewith War Diary for "A" and "Q" branches of this Divisional Staff for the month of June, 1916 (original and copy).

      Will you kindly acknowledge receipt.

                      Major-General,
               Commanding 39th Division.

13.7.16.

SECRET

"A" & "Q" Branches 39th Division

WAR DIARY
or
INTELLIGENCE SUMMARY.
(Erase heading not required.)

Army Form C. 2118.

Place	Date	Hour	Summary of Events and Information	Remarks and references to Appendices
LOCON	1916 June 1st 2nd 3rd		Nothing to report	
"	4th		Small raid by 16th (S) Bn the Sherwood Foresters in GIVENCHY Section	
"	5th		General Officers Commanding First Army and XI Corps visited Divisional Headquarters and new officers who were about to rain a major-General N.W. BARNARDISTON M.V.O. left for England. Brigadier General G.G.S. CAREY. C.B. took over command of the 39th Division.	
"	6th		Small raid carried out by the 13th (S) Bn the Sussex Regt: yielded successful; on completion slightly orders were received to our original etc 118. Infantry Brigade relieves 117 Infantry Brigade in GIVENCHY	

Army Form C. 2118.

A + "Q" Branches, 39th Division

WAR DIARY
or
INTELLIGENCE SUMMARY.

(Erase heading not required.)

Place	Date	Hour	Summary of Events and Information	Remarks and references to Appendices
LOCON	1916 June 7th		Small raid carried out by 14 R(S)Br the Hampshire Regt. 116 Infantry Brigade moved from CUINCHY Section Division Reserve at LOCON. 117 Infantry Brigade moved from Division Reserve to FESTUBERT. News received of the death of FIELD MARSHAL LORD KITCHENER Secretary of State for War. Brigadier General R. DAWSON C.B. arrived to take over command of the 39th Division.	
-"-	8/6		Nothing to report	
-"-	9th & 10th			
-"-	11th		116 Infantry Brigade relieved by 98 Brigade 33rd Div: in CUINCHY Section 106 " " " 117 " 39th Div in FESTUBERT "	

"A" & "Q" Branches 39th Division

Army Form C. 2118.

WAR DIARY
or
INTELLIGENCE SUMMARY.

(Erase heading not required.)

Place	Date	Hour	Summary of Events and Information	Remarks and references to Appendices
LOCON	1916 June 12th		61st Division took over FAUQUISSART – MOATED GRANGE SECTOR from 38th Division who proceeded to XVII Corps Battle Practice under the orders of APM XI Corps to test Battle Stops and capture huts.	
"	13th		Memorial service for the late Field Marshal Lord KITCHENER held in the Divisional arrangements.	
"	14th		Twice advanced one hour to a later time as directed by recent decree of the French government. 11 a.m. became midnight.	
"	15th		Nothing to report.	
"	16th		The 116th Infantry Brigade took over FERME DU BOIS Section, relieving 15th & 17th H.I. Infantry Brigade 35th Division during the night of 16/17th June.	

Army Form C. 2118.

A"" Branches 39th Division

WAR DIARY
or
INTELLIGENCE SUMMARY.
(Erase heading not required.)

Instructions regarding War Diaries and Intelligence Summaries are contained in F. S. Regs., Part II. and the Staff Manual respectively. Title pages will be prepared in manuscript.

Place	Date 1916	Hour	Summary of Events and Information	Remarks and references to Appendices
LOCON.	June 16th.		The 117 Infantry Brigade took over FESTUBERT Section; 1/3 d. GLOSTERS moved from ESSARS to LACOUTURE relieving 1/9 d. Northumberland Fusiliers 35 Div. 9 d. Infantry Brigade 33rd Division took over GIVENCHY Section in relief of 118 Infantry Brigade.	
---	17th		GIVENCHY Sector came under command of G.O.C. 33rd Division. 118 Infantry Brigade from Brigade in 39 th Div. Reserve Div. area in LA CHAPELLE - LÉTOURET area. DIVISIONAL SECTOR embraces FESTUBERT and FERME DU BOIS Sectors.	
	18th 19th 20th		Nothing to report.	
LOCON.	21st 22nd		Relinquishing any remains of former 1/2 d. 1/3 d. RS men 1/5 received. 1/2 R 1/3 R 1/5 moved Feb 16 J/5 to moved to fields about YPRES CHAPELLE and LES LOGES.	

Army Form C. 2118.

"A" Branches 39th Division

WAR DIARY
or
INTELLIGENCE SUMMARY.
(Erase heading not required.)

Instructions regarding War Diaries and Intelligence Summaries are contained in F. S. Regs., Part II. and the Staff Manual respectively. Title pages will be prepared in manuscript.

Place	Date	Hour	Summary of Events and Information	Remarks and references to Appendices
	1915			
LOCON	22/6		"Battle practice" to test mobile posts, stragglers posts in the supervision of A.T.M. XI Corps.	
	23/6		Nothing to report.	
	24/6			
	25/6		A detachment of 13th Gloucestershire Regt (Pioneers) strength about 290 officers and men, and 2 sections of 234 Field Coy R.E. move to GRACAUT for training and steering operations under G.O.C. 116 Infantry Brigade.	
			Supply RAILHEAD moved to BETHUNE	
	26/6		Nothing to report.	
	27/6		39 Divisional Supply Column moves from CHOIVE to BETHUNE	

Army Form C. 2118.

"A" Brigade, 39th Division

WAR DIARY
or
INTELLIGENCE SUMMARY.
(Erase heading not required.)

Instructions regarding War Diaries and Intelligence Summaries are contained in F. S. Regs., Part II. and the Staff Manual respectively. Title pages will be prepared in manuscript.

Place	Date	Hour	Summary of Events and Information	Remarks and references to Appendices
	1916			
LOC IV 28/6	28/6		Nothing to report.	
–"–	29/6		Operations by 11th, 12th & 13th Battalion Royal Sussex Regiment HAMPSHIRE RGT. 13th Bn Royal Sussex Regiment and 234 Field Company R.E. against the BOAR'S HEAD.	14th
	30/6		12th and 13th Bns Royal Sussex Regiment moved to billets at VIEILLE CHAPELLE and LES LOBES and formed part of the Brigade in Divisional Reserve (118 Infantry Brigade).	'A'
			A list of Casualties for the month of June 1916 is attached	

M.C.Dogn Lt.Col
Major General
Cmdg 39 Division

T.J.134. Wt. W708—776. 50000. 4/15. Sir J. C. & S.

Casualties - June 1916.

Wounded.

Officers and Other Ranks
———————————— 1

Wounded to 30.5.16 = 36
Missing to 31.5.16 = Nil

Officers - Wounded and Missing.

Rank	Name		Unit	Casualty	Date
T. 2 Lt	Turnbull	C.L.	17° Bn K.R.R. Corps	Wounded	3. 6.16
"	Davies	R.E.	16° Notts Derbys	"	5th
T. Lt	Brook	G.H.	11th Sussex	"	5th
T. 2 Lt	Hanby	J.J.	12th "	"	5th
"	MacRoberts	D. de P.	13th "	"	7th
T. Lt	Sprigg	G.A.R.	11th Hants	"	8th
2 Lt	Lloyd	C.B.	1/6th Cheshires	"	8th
Lt	Trimbel	T.H.	1/1st Cambs	"	8th
T. Lt	Kelcher	R.R.	11th Sussex	"	9th
T. Capt	Watt	A	4/5 Rl Stafors	"	11th
T. 2 Lt	Reece	G.	17° Notts Derbys	"	15th
"	Holland	A.L.	16° "	"	16th
2 Lt	Rigby	D.M.	1/6th Cheshires	"	17th
T. 2 Lt	Rigby	W.J.E.	"	"	18th
"	Sargent	E.J.	17° K.R.R.Corps	"	19th
T. Lt	Janes	C.V.	13th Sussex	"	21st
"	Laws	P.J.	16° N.+Derbys	"	24th
T. 2 Lt	Rayner	L.V.	16° T.M Battery.	on duty.	27th
Lt	Stracchie	T.H.	179 Bde R.F.A	"	27th
T. 2 Lt	Scragg	A	16° N.+Derbys	accidently	27th
"	Delph	Leo	39° Dn Signal Coy R.E.	"	28th
"	Dixon	K.	17° K.R.R.Corps	"	28th
T. Lt	Roberts	R.T.	Artists Rifles attd 17 KRRC	"	28th
2/Lieut.	Hunter	J.K.	57 Bde R.F.A 35 Brigade	"	30th

Unit	Total to 31.5.16	1	2	3	4	5	6	7	8	9	10	11	12	13	14	15	16	17	18	19	20	21	22	23	24	25	26	27	28	29	30	Total to 30.6.16	Remarks
11th Sussex	49	1	1	5	1	37	1		1	5	2	2		1						1			1		2	4	4				95	238	
12th "	62		2	3	2	9				5	2	2							4	3		3	7		2			2		1	230	332*	
13th "	75	3						4	5												5	4	4	4							219	327	
14th Hants	63	2		2	3	6	6	14				1			1					4	3		1	1	2		1		8	5	54	162	
16th R.W. Surreys	69				2	23			5	4	1		3	3	2	4	2	1	2	4		2	2	1	2	2	1		1	2	6	124	
17th K.R.R.Corps	59	0		7	2	5				3			3	1	1	3			4	3	1		4	3	1	2	1	3	1	2	4	104	
17th Rifle Brigade	73	7		1		5		1	4	4	1	5			7	4	2	2	2		1	2	2		2	2	1	5	12	3	11	140	
16 Cordubria	55						5		6	3	2	3	3	3		7	1	3			1		3	1		2	1					97	
11/5 Black Watch	31				1			4	1		4	6			1		1	8													17	62	
1/1 Cambs	43			2		2		1			2		2		1		2			1	1						1					55	
1/1 Herts	42				1						2				1	1	1	3	7		1	2			3		1	1	1			67	
12th Rifles	20	1							1	1		1					2						1									31	61	
5th Antrim	6																															7	92	
5th Tinnaghead	17	2																														31	7	
A.S.C.	1																																31	
25th R.Iny R.E.	17			1				1		1	1										1		1						1			23	
116 Bole ag Cay(m)	2																														11	13	
8 "	2																														3	5	
X/39 T.M. Battery					2																					1			1		2	4	
Y/39 "																														1	1	2	
118/2 T.M. Battery	1																													11	11	
R.A.M.C.																																	
Total	463	26	4	21	17	90	12	12	17	18	16	19	10	9	7	14	9	17	17	12	17	13	23	13	12	10	15	14	24	13	714	1928	
O.sec 255 T.M. Cy. R.E.	1							1																								1	
2/1st Wessex 61st Divn					2	4	9	1																								18	
4th L.N. Lancs att.2/7 Worc R.						1																										1	
9 R. Hampshire																																1	
2/5 Warwick 61st Divn																1																1	
Grand Total	464	27	4	23	19	100	13	25	17	18	16	19	10	9	7	14	9	17	17	12	17	13	23	13	12	10	15	14	24	13	719	2000	

Missing. — Other Ranks — June 1916.

Unit.	Total to 31.5.16	4.6.16	30.6.16	Total to 30.6.16
11th Sussex	1		8	9
12th "	-		120	120
13th "	1		148	149
16th Sherwood Foresters		5		5
1/1st Herts.	2			2
13th Rifle Brig.			13	13
231 Fd. Coy. R.E.			4	4
116th M. G. Coy.			1	1
14th Hants			3	3
Total	4	5	297	306

Casualties - June 1916

Killed

Others Other Ranks

Killed or Died of Wounds } 9   Officers
to 31.5.16

Rank	Name		Unit	Casualty	Date
T. 2/Lt	Richards	R.A.	11" Sussex	Killed	3rd June 16
T. Lt.	Boyd	A.G.	12" "	"	5th
Lieut.	Wise	G.C.J.	2/7 Warwicks 61st Div attd	"	5th
2/Lieut.	Vaughan	H.J.	1/1 Cambs.	"	8th
T. Capt	Gillespie	T.J.	13" Sussex	Wounded 18/6 Died of Wounds	19th
Lieut	Wilkinson	J.B.	225 Field Coy R.E.	" 23/6/16 "	23rd
T. Capt	Humble-Crofts	C.W.	13" Sussex	Killed	30th
T. 2nd Lt	Schubart.	H.	"	"	"
—	~~Spencer~~	~~H~~	~~" Starks~~	—	—
T. 2nd Lt	Tenrow	S.P.	116" L.T.M. Battery	Killed	30th
"	Miles	A.O.	13" Sisters	"	"
T. Lieut	Sparks	C.	12" Sussex	"	"
T. 2nd Lt	Jesshope	R.J.	"	"	"
"	Moody	L.L.	"	"	"
"	~~Rason~~	~~J.A.~~	"	~~Missing believed Killed~~	"
T. Capt	Cotton	A.D.	"	Killed	"

Date of Casualties.
30.6.16.

Rank.	Name.	Unit.	Casualty.
T. Captain	Cassels E.	11th Bn. R. Sussex Rgt.	Wounded.
T. Lieut	Lewis H.S.	-do-	-do-
T. 2/Lieut	Chalk A.	-do-	-do-
T. 2/Lieut.	Jones E.B.T.	-do-	-do-
T. Lieut-Col.	Impey G.H.	12th Bn. R. Sussex Rgt.	-do-
T. Lieut	Robinson H.C.T.	-do-	-do-
T. Lieut	Boys S.C.	-do-	-do-
T. 2/Lieut	Ambler G.	-do-	-do-
T. 2/Lieut	Dorman C.C.B.	-do-	-do-
T. 2/Lieut	Mercer J.	-do-	-do-
T. Captain	Hughes S.	13th Bn. R. Sussex Rgt.	-do-
T. Captain	Makalua M.J.M.	-do-	-do-
T. 2/Lieut.	Turner L.B.	-do-	-do-
T. 2/Lieut	Sparkes E.	-do-	-do-
T. Lieut.	Allen E.M.	14th Bn. Hampshire Rgt	-do-
T. 2/Lieut	Dorrity G.O.	116th M.G. Company	-do-
T. Lieut	Titley R.K.	116th T.M. Battery	-do-
T. Lieut	Nivin E.F.	132nd Field Ambulance	-do-
2/Lieut	Bull L.R.	117th Bde M.G. Company	-do-
2/Lieut	Hunter J.S.K.	157 Bde R.F.A. ∅	-do- ∅ 35 Div.
T. 2/Lieut	Sangster H.P.	14th Bn. Hampshire Rgt.	-do- att. 39
T. Lieut	Fitzherbert W.W.	13th Bn. R Sussex Rgt.	-do- Div. Arty.
T. 2/Lieut	Mason F.A.	12th Bn. R Sussex Regt	-do-

T. 2/Lieut	Grisewood F.	11th Bn. R. Sussex Rgt.	Missing.
T. 2/Lieut	Cushen A.C.	-do-	-do-
T. Captain	Cotton A.N.	12th Bn. R. Sussex Rgt	-do-
T. 2/Lieut	Swallow S.H.	-do-	-do-
T. 2/Lieut	Arkcoll F.T.	-do-	-do-
T. 2/Lieut	Ardill J.R.	-do-	-do-
T. 2/Lieut	Moyle F.W.	-do-	-do-
T. 2/Lieut	Hanby F.J.	-do-	-do-
T. 2/Lieut	Salberg J.B.	-do-	-do-
T. Captain	Whittaker R.D.A.	13th Bn. R. Sussex Rgt	-do-
T. 2/Lieut	Oliver H.P.G.	-do-	-do-
T. 2/Lieut	Morgan D.N.	-do-	-do-
T. 2/Lieut	Prior L.A.	-do-	-do-
T. 2/Lieut	Dudley E.W.	-do-	-do-
T. 2/nd Lt.	Diggens M.C.	-do-	-do-
T. Lieut	Wild R.P.	13th Bn. Gloucester Rgt	-do-
T. Lieut	Langley-Smith N.H.	-do-	-do-
T. 2/Lieut	Collins L.K.	-do-	-do-
T. 2/Lieut	Mason F.A.	12 Bn. R Sussex Regt	-do-

Unit	Total 1/5/16	1	2	3	4	5	6	7	8	9	10	11	12	13	14	15	16	17	18	19	20	21	22	23	24	25	26	27	28	29	30	Total 1/6/16	Remarks
11th Suss	31	2	5	1	3	6	1	1				1											1			1					24	55	
12th "	20			3	1	2	1	3															4								41	86	
13th "	15																			1											50	71	
14th Hants	17		2	1	4		1	1	1															4	1			1			6	33	
16th R.S. Doubts	15		1	1	1	6	1	3					1	1		2		1		1	2		1	2					1	3			22	30	
17th "	17		2			6														1			1						2		1		25	
17th K.R.R Corps	8		1		1														1					1								1	11	
16th Rfl Bde	7						1												1														9	
1/4 Cheshire	9										2										1				1×							3	x accidentally
4/5 Argyllse	2							1		1									1	1	2	1	1	1									13	
1/1 Combo.	8		2		1				1				1						1														14	
1/1 Hunt	11		1											1																	10		13	
13th Cheshire	2						1																										2	
Artillery	-				1															2													3	
Engineers	2																					1											3	
25th Tun. Coy R.E.	1																																1	
X/39 T.M. Batty	-			1	1																		1										1	
Y/39 "	1																															3	4	
116th MGC Coy	-																																1	
118/2 T.M. Batty																																		
Total	150	3	8	8	16	31	4	5	2	3	2	2	1	2		2		1	4	2	5	7	8		1	1	1	3	3	156	400	
2/17 Bunners 61st Div attached						1																											1	
Grand Total	150	3	8	8	31	4	9	2	3	2	2	1	2	1	2	1	4	2	5	7	8	1	1	1	3	3	156	400					

SECRET

39/ VOL 5 WA69

July

WAR DIARY
July 1916

A & Q. Staff. 39 Division
original & copy.

SECRET A + Q Branches

WAR DIARY
or
~~INTELLIGENCE~~ SUMMARY.
(Erase heading not required.)

Army Form C. 2118.

Page 1

Place	Date	Hour	Summary of Events and Information	Remarks and references to Appendices
	1916			
LOCON	1/7		The 118th Infantry Brigade relieved the 116th Infantry Brigade in the FERME DU BOIS Section. The latter Brigade became the Brigade in Divisional Reserve.	
LOCON	2/7		Nothing to report.	
LOCON	3/7		Lt-General Sir R. Hacking Comdg XI Corps inspected "remnants" of the 12th & 13th Bns. Royal Sussex Regt's, the detachments 234 Field Coy. R.E. and 13th Gloucestershire Regt. (Pioneers) and Trench Mortar Batteries who took part in the operations at the BOAR'S HEAD. Place of parade R.34.c.9.9. (BÉTHUNE Contoured Sheet) Raid against the German trenches by the 1st Rifle Brigade 117 Inf. Bde.	
LOCON	4/7 5/7		Nothing to report.	
LOCON	6/7		Orders received for 39th Div. to hold CUINCHY, GIVENCHY and FESTUBERT	

SECRET

A/Q Branches

WAR DIARY
or
~~INTELLIGENCE SUMMARY.~~

Army Form C. 2118.

Page 2

Place	Date	Hour	Summary of Events and Information	Remarks and references to Appendices
	1916			
LOCON	6/7		Sections with all 3 Bdes in the line and Corps Cavalry Regt and 1 Sect N°. 5 M.M.G. Battery in Div.L. Reserve. 61st Div. taking over from 39 Div. the FERME DU BOIS Section.	
LOCON.	7/7.		116 Inf. Bde moved from VIEILLE CHAPELLE area to BETHUNE – BEUVRY area in relief of 100 L. Bde 33rd Div. last night. 118 Inf. Bde were relieved by 184 Bde 61st Div. in FERME DU BOIS Section last night and moved to VIEILLE CHAPELLE area.	
LOCON TO BETHUNE	8/7.		116 Inf. Bde with 13th Gloucesters attached took over CUINCHY Section leaving from 98 Bde 33rd Div. — 118 Inf. Bde hastily relieved 19 Bde 33rd Div. in GIVENCHY Section — remain in Brigade Group. Divisional Headquarters moved to BETHUNE arriving at 10am and took over offices of 33rd. Div. — the Divisional Reserve comprising 8 Xt Cyclo. Co. Regt. 1 Sect. N°. 5 M.M.G. Batty. located at ESSARS. LT-COLONEL L.ST. HALLIDAY V.C. C.B. R.M.L.I. 9 SO.1. admitted to hospital.	

SECRET   "A" & "Q" Branches.

WAR DIARY
or
INTELLIGENCE SUMMARY.
(Erase heading not required.)

Army Form C. 2118.

Page 3

Place	Date	Hour	Summary of Events and Information	Remarks and references to Appendices
BETHUNE	1916 9/7		Nothing to report.	
"	10/7			
"	11/7		German aeroplane dropped several small bombs near BETHUNE railway station about 4.30 a.m. one killed and 2 wounded in 39 D S.C. slight damage done to one or two huts. Divisional.	
"	12/7		Small raids were carried out by the 16th Sherwood Foresters & 17 KRRC. 117 Infts de Marini/W Major General R. DAWSON. C.B. handed over command of the Division to Major General G.J. CUTHBERT. CB. CMG and proceeded to England. Lt Colonel F.W. GOSSET. DSO. (R.A.) arrived and assumed duties of C.S.O.I. vice Lt Colonel L.ST. HALLIDAY V.C. C.B. sick	
"	13/7		First Army Commander General Sir. C.C. MONRO G.C.M.G. K.C.B inspected at X.22.d.2.a. at 3 P.M. 17th Sherwood Foresters 17th KRRC & 16th RFles Brigade	

SECRET

"A" & "Q" Branches.

WAR DIARY
or
INTELLIGENCE SUMMARY.

Army Form C. 2118.

Page 4

Place	Date	Hour	Summary of Events and Information	Remarks and references to Appendices
	1916			
BETHUNE	13/7		Wholed recently made rivets. Brigadier Genl. E.H. FINCH HATTON DSO. THE BUFFS. took over command of 118th Bde vice B/gdr. T.T. BARRINGTON, returned home sick.	
"	14/7		Orders received for 39 Div. to take over FERME DU BOIS Section as before.	
BETHUNE to LOCON.	15/7	10AM	Divisional Headquarters moved to LOCON.	
LOCON	16/7		Corps offensive operations starting—bombardment of GIVENCHY and CUINCHY fronts at 7.2 noon until 4 P.M. Main operations postponed owing to bad weather.	
"	17/7		Further postponement of operations owing to weather being bad.	
"	18/7		Nothing to report.	

SECRET   A.-Q. Branches   Army Form C. 2118.

Page 5

WAR DIARY
or
INTELLIGENCE SUMMARY.
(Erase heading not required.)

Place	Date	Hour	Summary of Events and Information	Remarks and references to Appendices
	1916			
LOCON	19/7		Cmdr. offensive structures Givenchy.	
"	20/7		Raid by 1/6 Cheshire, 1/1 Herts and 1/1 Cambridgeshire Regts. Identification was of Ft. 2 & 1 31st Regt. 53rd R. Div, XXVII Reserve Corps captured by 1/6 Cheshire Regt. last night.	
"	21/7		117 Inf. Bde. relieved in the FERMÉ DU BOIS section by 116 Inf. Bde.	
"	22/7		Nothing to report.	
"	23/7		Orders received for 118 Inf. Bde. to move back into GIVENCHY section 1/6 West FESTUBERT and 117 into Divisional Reserve. Raid by 1/6 Cheshire Regt.	
"	24/7		Raid by 1/1st Bn Royal Sussex Regt. last night.	

SECRET 'A' Branch
WAR DIARY
or
INTELLIGENCE SUMMARY
(Erase heading not required.)

Army Form C. 2118.
Page 6

Place	Date	Hour	Summary of Events and Information	Remarks and references to Appendices
	1916			
LOCON	25/7	10 AM	The G.O.C. 39 Div. assumed command of the new Divisional Sector – GIVENCHY and FESTUBERT Sections: 2 Bdes in line and 1 Bde in Div. Reserve. After several moves the Division resumes its original Sector as taken over from 38th (Welsh) Div. on 17th April 1916.	
"	26/7		12 & 13 Ln Bns Royal Sussex Regt. received drafts of 300 men 15 being these are first draughts since the Losses of these Bns. attaching on the BJARS HEAD on the 29/30th June.	
"	27/7		Presentation of the Ld. rifleship to G.O.C. First Army General Sir C.C. MONRO G.C.M.G. K.C.B. in the Square at MERVILLE at 3 PM. Brigadier General and Band furnished by G.O.C. Div. A List of recipients is attached. Felve by Lt. Colonel F.W. GOSSET, D.S.O. (9.20) in his address to the SOMME. 14th Hampshire Regt. captured a wounded prisoner in No MAN'S LAND in FESTUBERT SECTION. He is an "Offizier-aspirant" of 243 Res. Regt.	Appendix A

SECRET

"A" (i) Branch
WAR DIARY
or
INTELLIGENCE SUMMARY.
(Erase heading not required.)

Army Form C. 2118.

Page 7

Place	Date	Hour	Summary of Events and Information	Remarks and references to Appendices
LSCOV	1916 28/7 29/7		Nothing to return.	
-"-	30/7		One company of the 14th Hampshire Regt 116 Inf Bde attempted a raid upon the German trenches in the FESTUBERT Section.	
-"-	31/7		Infliction of 1/1 Cambridgeshire Regt by M.G.C. 17th Sherwood Foresters 117 Inf Bde raided the German trenches at the GERMAN DUCKS BILL, and a long shaft dug from 252 Tunnelling Coy R.E.	
			A list of casualties for the month of July 1916 is attached	Appendix B.

B.C. Dogen KCB
Major General
Commanding 39th Division

CORPS ROUTINE ORDERS

BY

Major-General COLIN MACKENZIE, C.B.
Commanding XI Army Corps.

Headquarters,
31st July 1916.

---

434. IMMEDIATE REWARDS.

The General Officer Commanding, First Army, presented, on 27th instant, on parade, the ribands of the decorations recently awarded to the following Officers, W.Os., N.C.Os., and Men, for gallantry and devotion to duty in the field:-

THE MILITARY CROSS.

2/Lieut. D.I.EVANS,	251st Tunnelling Coy. R.E.
Captain O.C.K.CORRIE,	North Somerset Yeomanry (attached H.Q. R.A., 39th Division).
2/Lieut. H.E.O.ELLIS,	39th Divisional Signal Company.
Lieut. C.O.BOLTON	12th Bn Royal Sussex Regiment.
T.2/Lieut. G. AMBLER,	12th -do-
T.Lieut E.S.ELLIS,	13th -do-
2/Lieut. C.A.F.WHITLEY	13th -do-
2/Lieut. A.L.CROCKFORD	13th Bn Gloucestershire Regiment.
Lieut. H. QUEST,	14th Bn York & Lancaster Regt.
2/Lieut. H.R.CLASS,	2/5th Bn R.Warwick Regt.
Lieut. F.A.RIDLER,	2/4th Gloucestershire Regt.
No.3116 C.S.M. F.DANIELS,	2/5th Royal Warwick Regt.

THE DISTINGUISHED CONDUCT MEDAL.

874	Sgt. E.J.GREEN,	11th Bn Royal Sussex Regiment.
421	Sgt. P.W.HOLLOBONE,	12th -do-
2909	Cpl.C.FOWLER,	13th -do-
P.27	C.S.M. L.A.LUDGATE	16th Bn The Rifle Brigade.
S.13891	Rfn. F.G.RICHARDS	-do-

THE MILITARY MEDAL.

32387	Bombdr H.P.LAUNDER,	5th Siege Bty. R.G.A.
24664	Gunner B.KEIRAN,	100th Siege Bty. R.G.A.
64356	Bombdr R.T.PICKWORTH,	-do-
1823	Gunner G.A.ELLIOTT,	138th Heavy Bty. R.G.A.
1236	Gunner R.H.EPPS,	1/2nd London Heavy Bty. R.G.A.
1377	" G.F.NIXON,	-do-
61327	Sgt. W. KNIBBS,	39th D.A.C. att Z/39 M.T.M.Batty.
46032	Cpl. J.CROOKS,	39th D.A.C. att X/39 M.T.M. Batty.
101386	Cpl.G.RICHARDS,	39th D.A.C. att Y/39 M.T.M. Batty.
L.28566	Br. J. STEWART,	"B" Batty 174th Bde. R.F.A.
L.38237	Br. H.WOOD,	"C" Batty 184th Bde. R.F.A.
26791	Br. G.CHAPMAN,	"A" Batty 186th Bde. R.F.A.
L.31864	Br. C.CUTTS	39th D.A.C. att.Z/39 M.T.M.Batty.
41291	A/Br. T. FANNING,	"D" Batty. 174th Bde. R.F.A.
L.28593	Gr. L.C.PRAGNELL,	"C" Batty.174th Bde. R.F.A.
L.38160	Gr. F.W.CLAYDON	"B" Batty.186th Bde. R.F.A.
L.33496	Gr. G.R.ILES,	39th D.A.C. att Y/39 M.T.M. Batty.
59607	Gr. W. CROXON,	39th D.A.C. att X/39 M.T.M.Batty.

No.	Rank	Name	Unit
No.2223	Gunner	L.A. CHAPMAN,	"A" Batty 305th Bde. R.F.A.
No.2455	Gunner	R.L. WILLIAMS	"A" Batty. -do-
151632	Sapper	M. CARNEY,	251st Tunnelling Coy. R.E.
15585	"	J. MARTIN,	-do-
151533	Sergt.	A. REYNOLDS,	-do-
132313	Sapper	T.J. MILLETT,	-do-
136435	A/2nd Corpl.	H. POWELL,	-do-
132176	L/Cpl.	W.O. DUNSTAN,	-do-
87537	2/Cpl.	J. MASLIN,	39th Divisional Signal Company.
87321	Spr.	E.B. BEATON,	-do-
101810	Sgt.	H.J. WILKINSON,	234th Field Company.
13152	Spr.	A. WRIGHT,	-do-
131539	Pnr.	H. WARDLE,	-do-.
2517	Pte.	J. McWHINNIE,	2nd A.& S. Hdrs, attd. 251st Tunnelling Coy.R.E.
9484	"	P. TODD,	-do-
11072	"	J. McMILLAN	-do-
17166	"	E.C. MORRIS,	2nd Bn. S.Staffs Regt. attd. 251st Tunnelling Coy.R.E.
772	Sergt.	E.H. ENGLISH,	13th East Yorkshire Regt.
14/364	Pte.	A. RUSSELL,	14th York & Lancaster Regt.
876	Cpl.	S. NOAKES,	11th Bn Royal Sussex Regt. (attd.116th T.M.Bty).
1157	Pte.	E.J. BROWN,	11th Bn Royal Sussex Regt.
2213	Sgt.	G. ALSTON,	12th Bn Royal Sussex Regt.
2219	"	W.A. AUKETT,	12th -do-
1691	L/Cpl.	W.D. GRENYER,	12th -do-
1535	L/Cpl.	C.F. LASSETTER,	12th -do-
1559	L/Cpl.	H. WELLS,	12th -do-
1523	L/Cpl.	A. DRURY,	12th -do-
1409	Pte.	G. HILLS,	12th -do-
1830	Pte.	S.C. BAKER,	12th -do-
2689	L/Sgt.	W.P.G. HARROLD,	13th -do-
2641	L/Cpl.	G. CHAMBERS,	13th -do-
3521	L/Cpl.	C.E. BALL,	13th -do-
2896	Pte.	C. DAVIES,	13th -do-
3340	Pte.	R. EMSLEY,	13th -do-
2854	Pte.	A. BAILEY,	13th -do-
5095	Pte.	F.A. COOPER,	13th -do-
25812	Pte.	J. HUTCHINSON,	16th Bn Sherwood Foresters.
25863	Pte.	T.E. PEGG,	16th -do-
27846	L/Cpl.	E. CAWTHORNE,	17th Bn Sherwood Foresters.
717	Sgt.	L. PARKIN,	1/6th Bn Cheshire Regt.
1034	Sgt.	J. JACKSON,	1/6th -do-
1585	L/Cpl.	F. UTLEY,	1/6th -do-
1589	L/Cpl.	J. TITLEY,	1/6th Bn Cheshire Regiment.
3395	Sgt.	J. COLTART,	4/5th Black Watch.
4790	Cpl.	J. CASSIDY,	4/5th -do-
1693	Pte.	G. SMITH,	1/1st Bn. Cambridgeshire Regt.
1643	Pte.	G. JUGG,	1/1st Bn. -do-
19831	Cpl.	R.W. SMILES,	13th Bn. Gloucester Regt.
4314	Drummer	E. SPIERS,	2/5th Bn.R. Warwick Regt.
2831	L/Sergt.	H.W. MORGAN,	-do-
1333	Pte.	H.V. GARDNER,	1/7th Bn The Welsh Regt. attd. 2/4th Bn The Oxfordshire & Bucks L.I.
4520	Pte.	C. HUNT,	2/8th Bn. Worcestershire Regt. attd. 183rd T.M. Batty.
65884	L/Cpl.	E.T. FAIRBROTHER,	132nd Field Ambulance.

H C Holman
Brig-General,
D.A.& Q.M.G. XI Corps.

CORPS ROUTINE ORDERS

BY

Major-General COLIN MACKENZIE, C.B.

Commanding XI Army Corps,

Headquarters,
31st July 1916.

---

435. **IMMEDIATE HONOURS and REWARDS.**

1. Under authority delegated by His Majesty the King, the General Officer Commanding-in-Chief has awarded the MILITARY CROSS to the undernamed Officer for gallantry and devotion to duty in action :-

Date of award 29-7-16.

2nd Lieut. C.H. CORK, 16th (S) Bn King's Royal Rifle Corps.

2. Under authority delegated by the General Officer Commanding-in-Chief, the Corps Commander has awarded the MILITARY MEDAL to the undernamed N.C.O. and Men for gallantry and devotion to duty in action :-

Date of award 30-7-16.

No. 96028 L/Cpl. W.H. NEWBY, 222nd Field Company, R.E.
    96110 Sapper T. CHURCHWARD,   -do-
    96278 Sapper T. CARROL,   -do-
    84501 Sapper A. LEE,   -do-

Brig-General,
D.A. & Q.M.G. XI Corps.

Appendix "B"

Killed

July 1916

Officers & Other ranks.

Officers.

Rank & Name			Unit	Casualty	Date
T. Capt	Blunden	O.	16 Rifle Bde	Killed	4.7.16
T. 2/Lt	Butt	L.J.O.	"	"	"
T. Capt	Fleacher	S.W.	"	Wounded since died	"
T. 2/Lt	Henshaw	F.	17 Notts & Derbys	Killed	12.7.16
"	Dawson	N.B.	119 T.M.Battery	Wounded since died	"
"	Seabrook	H.S.	16 Notts & Derbys	Missing believed killed	"
"	Straker	F.	Y/39 T.M. Battery	Wounded since died	17.7.16
"	Day	P.O.J	17 KRRCorps	Killed	20.7.16
Lieut	Kerman	G.A.	1/1 Cambs	Missing	"
2/Lt	Hawkinson	G.E.	"	"	"
"	Jameson	A.B.	"	Killed	21.7.16
Lt	Scobie	James E.	225 Fd Coy R.E.	"	30.7.16
T. 2/Lt	Macnaghten	A.C.H	13 R. Sussex	"	31.7.16

Unit	July 1	2	3	4	5	6	7	8	9	10	11	12	13	14	15	16	17	18	19	20	21	22	23	24	25	26	27	28	29	30	31	Total
11" Sussex Regt									1	1	1		1											2	1							8
12" "																											1		2			4
13" "												1								1											2	4
14" Shark "	1									2													3	6							1	4
16" Nokka + Dokapo								1			2	3																				7
17" "			3	2	3			1					1				1		3					1					1			13
17" K.C.R Corps			2	1	2	1			2					1	2				3					1								15
16" 1 Afr Bde				3						1	1	1	1	1	2				3													13
16" Chaduma										1				5			1		4										1	2	1	14
4/5 R.A Nigh Bde @eu			2													1			1				3	1								8
1/1 Kamba																			1	2												3
1/1 Masai			1						1							1			3													9
13" Sluska Regt																													1		1	2
Artillery																		3														3
Engineers																										1						1
25th Punja. Reg K.S.											1				1																	1
39" Sm Supply Col																															1	1
11" F.W. Battery												2																				2
Total	1		6	5	7	2	1	2	4	4	6	8	3	8	6	3	3	5	15	1	1		8	10	2	1	2	3	3	1	3	126
2" Curl. Rifles (2S1.T.Cay KER) eta													1																			1
16S Bde Q3A (31st Bn) attacks.																				1								1				1
Enchanted Tomb January												2																				2
Grand Total	1		6	5	7	2	1	2	4	4	6	8	4	8	5	3	3	5	15	2	1		8	10	2	2	2	4	3	1	4	126

Appendix "B"

Casualties July. 1916

Wounded

Officers and Other Ranks.

Officers

Rank and Name	Unit	Casualty	Date

OFFICERS.

Rank.	Name.		Unit.	Casualty.	Date.
T. Lieut.	Wood	C.M.	17th N & D	Wounded	2.7.16.
T. 2/Lt.	Spencer	W.E.C.	13th Sussex	" acc.	3.7.16.
2/Lt.	Carette	R.H.	1/1 Cambs	"	"
Captain	Clerk	A.G.	1/1 Herts	"	"
2/Lt.	Drury	F.McR.	"	"	"
T./Lt.	Scott	L.K.	225F CoyRE	Missing	4.7.16.
T/2/Lt	Bullivant	A.J.	17th N & D	Wounded	"
T/Captain	Brickwood	R.	16th R.B.	"	"
T/Lt.	Salt	R.F.	"	"	"
T/2/Lt.	Lamb	R.P.	"	"	"
T/2/Lt.	Jones	R.V.	"	"	"
T/2/Lt	Finlay	E.N.A	"	Missing	"
T/Lt.	Fenton	G.F.R.	"	" blvd killd	"
T/2/Lt	Lawson	J.	17th N & D	Wounded	5.7.16.
T/2/Lt	Barnes	J.	13 Glostrs	" shell shck	6.7.16.
T/2/Lt	Dallas	C.B.	17 K.R.R.	"	7.7.16.
T/2/Lt	Doogan	G.W.	11th Sussx	"	10.7.16.
T/2/Lt	Darky	R.	117 MG Coy	" acc.	"
T/2/Lt	Hart	C.J.	16th N & D	"	12.7.16.
T/2/Lt	Cholerton	J.R.	"	"	"
T/2/Lt	Dixon	V.G.	17 K.R.R.C	"	"
T/2/Lt	Griffith	J.E.	184 BdeRFA	"	13.7.16.
T/Captain	Grice	W.L.	1/1 Herts	"	"
2/Lt T/Lt.	Gold	L.G.	"	"	15.7.16.
2/Lt	Smith	J.V.	4/8 Mdlsx attachd. 1/1 Herts	"	16.7.16.
T/2/Lt	Sierra	J.E.	Y39 T.M.B.	"	17.7.16.
Captain	Hacker	C.F.	R.A.M.C. att.1/1 Herts	" at duty	18.7.16.
Captain	Tibbutt	R.J.	1/1 Cambs	"	19.7.16.

Rank.	Name.	Unit.	Casualty.	Date.
Lt.T/Capt	Smith A.W.	1/6 Cheshires	Wounded at duty	20.7.16.
2/Lt	Looker A.W.	1/1 Cambs	"	"
2/Lt T/Lt	Loyd R.P.	1/1 Herts	"	"
2/Lt	Smith J.W.	"	"	"
2/Lt	Francis W.F.	"	"	"
T.2/Lt	Benner W.R.	17th N & D.	"	"
2/Lt.	McCurick C.S.	4/5th Rl. Hldr	"	21.7.16.
2/Lt.	Coltman F.T.	1/1 Cambs	"	"
Lt.T/Capt	Molony B.C.	1/1 Herts	"	"
Lt.T/Capt	Wallace T.	3rd Borderers att.11 Sussx	"	22.7.16.
Lt.T/Capt	Smith AW	1/6th Cheshires	"	23.7.16.
T/2/Lt	Carter N.C.	13th Sussex	"	"
T/2/Lt	Ashmore G.M.	14th Hants	"	"
T/2/Lt	Gammon K.W.	11th Sussex	"	24.7.16.
T/2/Lt	Allen C.A.	"	"	27.7.16.
Maj.(Bn. Lt-Col)	Beddington C	W & C Yeomanry att.14 Hants	"	"
2/Lt	Watts H.G.	3/5 Beds, att. 1/1 Herts	" acc.	"
T/Capt	Hulks H.J	17 K.R.R.C.	"	29.7.16.
T/Lt	Recordon D.A.	"	"	"
T/2/Lt	Harden E.J	13 Sussex	" at duty	31.7.16.
T/2/Lt	Meade J.W	14th Hants	"	"
T/2/Lt	Marshall C.T.	"	"	"

Unit	1	2	3	4	5	6	7	8	9	10	11	12	13	14	15	16	17	18	19	20	21	22	23	24	25	26	27	28	29	30	31	Total	Remarks
11 Bn R Sussex R.						2		3	2	7	3	3	5	2	4					2	7	3	4	4	1	1	1	1	2		1	55	
12 "												2	4							2	1					1				1	1	12	
13 "													6	4								1					1		1	1	7	23	
14 " Hampshire	3		1	1	5	3	2		1	5	2	4	1	4					1		1	1				1	8	8	1			64	
16 " Notts & Derby		1	1	16	5	7	3	3	3	3	2	5	2	2							3	1	5	14	1		3					58	
17 " "	1	1	1	3	1	4	3	2	3	2	2	3	2	2					3	1									2	2		66	
17 " KRR Corps		3	4	3	1			4	1	1	1	2	2	2	2	1				2							2	3	4	2	4	63	
16 " Rifle Bde	4	2	1	80		1	1	1	1	2	7	8	6	4	5	3				2	1						1	2		1	2	129	
16 Cheshire R.						1	1		2	1	2	1	1	9	12	9	11	7	6	9		4										72	
4/5 Black Watch			1	4	2	1	1		1	2	2	2	2	1	2				1													41	
11" Cameron	4								1				4				6	1	2	3		6	6	5	1							50	
9" Hants					2	1		1	1		1	5	6	1	1	1	1	2	1	7		2	1		3							52	
13" Gloster	3		1	1				1	1									2											2		1	15	
Artillery			1	2			1						1	1	1			4		1	2		1						1			13	
Engineers				2								1	3				2										1					11	
A.S. Corps																																2	
R.A.M.C.						1							2		1																	3	
Div. H.Q.																																2	
253 J Bry R.E.																	3															3	
118 2nd M.G.Bry																																4	
X/39 J.M.Battery													1									1										1	
148/2 S.M.I.Battery											1			1																		4	
116 M.G.Bry										2																						2	
39 Lin Supply Col											2	2																		2		4	
117 Field Amb												3																				3	
Total	16	19	9	112	14	20	11	13	10	24	24	47	32	31	21	17	20	17	38	25	16	23	27	10	5	14	8	16	5	26		747	
Less 253 JBry RE																											1						
2/24 SH 251 JBry RE																													2				
Grand Total	16	19	9	112	14	20	11	13	10	24	24	47	32	31	21	17	20	17	38	25	16	23	27	10	5	14	8	16	5	26		747	

SECRET

Army Form C. 2118.

Page 1

"A" + "Q" Branches, 39th Division

WAR DIARY
INTELLIGENCE SUMMARY
(Erase heading not required.)

Vol 6

Place	Date	Hour	Summary of Events and Information	Remarks and references to Appendices
	1916		August 1916.	
LOCON	1/8		116 Inf Bde relieved by 118 Inf Bde in FESTUBERT SECTION. XI Corps order No 62 received stating that the Division will be relieved in the line by 30th Div which commences to arrive about 4th Aug. 6. – 39 Div G.S.O.2 with Army Reserve has Gunnery South.	
"	2/8		STAFF Capt with Staff Capt 117 Inf ran proceeded to BRYAS area to find billets for the Division.	
"	3/8		XI Corps order received directing that 39 Div be relieved in the line and will be withdrawn to ALLOUAGNE – LOSINGHEM – AUCHEL by noon 10 Aug. 31st Div. to take over the FESTUBERT Section and 30th Div. GIVENCHY Section.	
"	4/8		Anniversary of declaration of war against Germany	

"A" H.Q. Branches 39th D.

Army Form C. 2118.

Page 2

WAR DIARY
~~INTELLIGENCE SUMMARY~~
(Erase heading not required.)

Place	Date	Hour	Summary of Events and Information	Remarks and references to Appendices
LOCON	4/8	1916	G.O.C. 39 Div. inspected 14th Hampshire Regt. at ECLUSE D'ESSARS	
"	5/8		Orders received for withdrawal of Div. from the line into Army Reserve and for relief by 12th Afj. Div. Genmore since GT BRYAS area. G.O.C. 39 Div. inspected 11th R Sussex Regt. at ECOLE DES JEUNES FILLES BETHUNE.	
"	6/8		117 Infantry Brigade relieved by 116 Infantry Bde in GIVENCHY Sector. Special Divine Service Paraded in the Grand Place. BETHUNE for the anniversary of 2nd year of the war. Attended by Maj Gen M.L. HORNBY, D.S.O. Comdr & all the troops in hand.	
"	7/8		BETHUNE shelled about Noon. Funded 38cm (15in). Shells but slight damage and casualties. Damage done was steel rail in GRAND PLACE marker day. 16 H Rifle Bde	

T2134. Wt. W708—776. 50C040. 4/15. Sir J. C. & S.

A.Q. Branches, 39th Div.

WAR DIARY
INTELLIGENCE SUMMARY

Place	Date	Hour	Summary of Events and Information	Remarks and references to Appendices
	1916			
LOCON	7/8		and a few districts of Reserve Bde in the town. Troops were for most of the time without sleep. Sue cas relatively low given.	
"	8/8		The d Army orders received stating Division will be concentrated in HUIVCHY — BRETON — ROELLÉCOURT area for training. DHQ to be at ROELLÉCOURT; Div. administered by XVII Corps.	
"	9/8		16th Stewart Fusrs & 117 IF Bde and 4/5 Black Watch arrived from LE HAMEL & BETHUNE and from LE TOURET to RIEZ DU VINAGE respectively. M.G.C. infection of 4th Stewart Fusrs at x 25 a centre (Maxime Cimetière street many).	
"	15/8		117 IF Bde arrived from BETHUNE to AUCHY area. 118 IF Bde	

Army Form C. 2118.

HQ Braydes, 39th Div.

Page 4

WAR DIARY
of
INTELLIGENCE SUMMARY.
(Erase heading not required.)

Place	Date	Hour	Summary of Events and Information	Remarks and references to Appendices
LOCON	1916 10/8		Relieved — FESTUBERT Section by 33rd Infantry 31 Div	
—	11/8		116 Infantry Bde relieved in GIVENCHY Section by 21st Infantry Bde 30th Div. 116 I. Bde marching to ALLOUAGNE area. 117 and 118 Inf. Bdes made to LA THIEULOYE and AUCHY areas respectively.	
LOCON TO ROELLE- COURT	12/8		Div. HQ moved to ROELLECOURT. The 39 Div. leaves XI Corps	
ROELLE- COURT	13/8		The Div. is now in GHQ reserve but comes under XVII Corps of the Third Army from the 12th inst. Third Army HQ at ST POL and XVII Corps HQ at AUBIGNY.	
—	14/8 15/8		Nothing to report	

A.Q Branches 39th Div

WAR DIARY
INTELLIGENCE SUMMARY

Army Form C. 2118.
Page 5

Place	Date	Hour	Summary of Events and Information	Remarks and references to Appendices
ROELLE-COURT	16/8		Nothing to report.	
	17/8			
	18/8		A.A. & Q.M.G. proceeded to ACHEUX to visit G.O.C. Div. when 3 Div relieves returning on the 19th Aug.	
	19/8		A.A. & Q.M.G. with Staff Captain 118 Inf. Bde. proceeded to ACHEUX to visit G.O.C. Div. returning on the 20th Aug.	
	20/8.		Orders received from Fourth Army for the Div. to move to MARIEUX area and to come under orders of Reserve Army. The Div. proceeds by route march via 3 Brigade Groups, viz one of 116 Inf. Bde. and 2 Bns 117 Inf. Bde. which are marked by Tactical trains.	
	21/8		Nothing to report for the move.	
	22/8		Nothing to report.	

Army Form C. 2118.

A.Q. Branch 39th Div

Page 6

WAR DIARY
INTELLIGENCE SUMMARY.
(Erase heading not required.)

Instructions regarding War Diaries and Intelligence Summaries are contained in F.S. Regs., Part II. and the Staff Manual respectively. Title pages will be prepared in manuscript.

Place	Date	Hour	Summary of Events and Information	Remarks and references to Appendices
ROELLE- COURT	1916 22/8		Nothing to report.	
-"-	23/8		Three Brigade groups marched from and South.	
ROELLECOURT TO BUS-LES- ARTOIS	24/8		Divisional HQ moved this morning to BUS-LES-ARTOIS and came under V Corps. DIV R.A. is at SARTON - THIEVRES - FAMECHON area	
BUS	25/8		Concentration of Div. in BUS - VAUCHELLES - WARNIMONT WOODS area	
-"-	26/8		118 Inf Bde took over locality from River Ancre to MARY REDAN from 18 Div & 6 Div.	
-"- TO ACHEUX	27/8		Div. HQ moved to ACHEUX. 116 Inf Bde moved up Mailly	

T2134. Wt. W708-776. 500040. 4/15. Sir J.C. & S.

"A" Branch 39 Div.

WAR DIARY
or
INTELLIGENCE SUMMARY

Army Form C. 2118.

Page 7

Place	Date	Hour	Summary of Events and Information	Remarks and references to Appendices
	1916			
ACHEUX	27/8		MAILLET works with Bde HO at VITERMONT.	
"	28/8		117 Inf Bde moves to BERTRANCOURT and BEAUSART.	
"	29/8		Very heavy thunderstorm during the afternoon	
"	30/8		Nothing to report.	
"	31/8		Return of Casualties for August 1916 attached	

A.C. Daly Major General
Comdg. 39 th Division

SECRET. Copy No. 7

39TH DIVISION ADMINISTRATIVE ORDER NO.1.

Ref. 1/100,000 Mnp

HAZEBROUCK & LENS Sheets
and BETHUNE Sheet 1/40,000

7/8/1916.

1. With reference to 39th Division Order No. 35 dated 6/8/1916.

2. Billeting Parties will proceed to the new areas at least six hours in advance of main bodies.

3. Supply arrangements will be carried out in accordance with the attached Supply and Transport Table.

4. Ordnance Stores will be delivered at Refilling Points at times stated on Supply and Transport Table.

5. All R.E. Stores and Material in excess of Units' scale, as laid down in their Mobilization Store Tables, are to be handed over to incoming Units.

   All clothing in excess of authorised scale, as laid down in G.R.O., will be handed over to the nearest Baths.

   All Salvage Stores will be handed over to the 116th, 117th and 118th Infantry Brigade Sections of the Divisional Salvage Company.

6. Headquarters of the Divisional Salvage Company will be at LOCON.

7. The Divisional Salvage Company will rejoin the Division after evacuating any Salvage Stores left behind.

8. Railhead will remain at BETHUNE for the present.

ACKNOWLEDGE.

B. P. Dwyer
Lieut-Colonel,
A.A. & Q.M.G.
39th Division.

Copies issued at .... to:-

G.O.C.	Divn. R.A.	Divn. Supply Col.
G.	Divn. R.E.	Camp Commandant.
A.Q.	116 Inf. Bde.	D.A.D.O.S.
A.D.M.S.	117 Inf. Bde.	
A.D.V.S.	118 Inf. Bde.	
A.P.M.	13/ Glouc. Regt.	
War Diary. ✓	Divn. Train.	
Signals.	S.S.O.	

SUPPLY AND TRANSPORT TABLE

Unit.	9th August.	10th August.	11th August.	12th August.	13th August.
H.Q. Group. H.Q. Coy. Train.	R.P. No Change.	R.P. No change. Time...7 a.m. 3 Batteries attachd. for supplies to No. 3 Coy Train	R.P. No Change. Time...7 a.m. Deliver supplies to RF. by 8 am.,& then despatch empty Supply Wagons to Billets at LILLERS	R.P. LILLERS for HQ Group at 8 am. HQ Train march to LILLERS with supplies for Div.HQ; RE,HQ; FA,HQ; 82 San. Sec; 50 Mobile Vet. Section	R.P.LILLERS for H.Q. Group less 1 Bde.RF. at 8 a.m.
116th Inf Bde. No 2 Coy Train	R.P. No Change.	R.P. No Change. Time...7 a.m.	R.P. No Change. Time 7 am.	R.P. No Change. March to ALLOUAGNE for 116 Inf. Bde. at 8 am. with supplies for 116th Inf Bde.	R.P. PONT DU NEVEILLON for 116 Inf. Bde. at 8 am. 132 Field Amb. Pioneers.
117th Inf. Bde. No 3 Coy. Train	R.P. No change.	R.P. No Change. Time...7 a.m. March to AUCHEL with supplies for 117 Inf. Bde; 3 Coys RE.; Pioneers; 132 & 134 Field Ambulances. Deliver supplies for 133 Field Amb. by 8 am, and take supply wagon to AUCHEL empty.	R.P. RAMBERT Time...7 a.m. for 117 Inf. Bde. 3 Coys.RE. 132 Field Ambulance 133 do. do. 134 do. do. Pioneers 3 Btys R.F.A.	R.P. RAMBERT. for 117th Inf.Bde 3 Coys.R.E. 132 Field Amb 133 do. Pioneers at 8 am.	R.P. RAMBERT. for 117 Inf Bde. 3 Coys R.E. 133 Field Amb. at 8 am.
118th Inf. Bde. No.4 Coy. Train	R.P. No Change.	R.P. No Change. Time...7 am. 1337.A	R.P. No change. Time...7 am. March to BULBULE.	R.P. BULBULE for 118 Inf.Bde 134 Field Amb. 1 Bde Amb. at 8 am.	R.P. BULBULE for 118 Inf. Bde. Group. 134 Field Amb. 1 Bde. R.F.A. at 8 am.

SECRET.

Copy No... 8

39th Divisional Administration Order No. 2.

Ref. 1/100,000 Map.
LENS & HAZEBROUCK Sheets.

9..8. 1916.

1. With reference to 39th Divisional Order No. 36 dated 9/8/1916.

2. Supply arrangements will be carried out in accordance with the attached Supply and Transport Table.

3. Ordnance Stores will be delivered at Refilling Points at times and places given.

E. F. Faukner

Major,
D.A.Q.M.G., 39th Division.

Copies issued at .10.... p.m. to.

G.O.C.	Divl. R.A.	Divl. Supply Col
"G"	Divl. R.E.	Camp Comdt.
A.Q.	116th Inf. Bde.	X1 Corps.
A.D.M.S.	117th Inf. Bde.	
A.D.V.S.	118th Inf. Bde.	
A.P.M.	13th Gloucester Rgt.	
D.A.D.O.S.	Divl. Train.	
War Diary.	S.S.O.	
Signals.		

SUPPLY and TRANSPORT TABLE.

UNIT.	10 August	11 August	12 August	13 August	14 August.
H.Q GROUP.	R.H. BETHUNE. R.P. No Change Time 7 a.m. 3 Bats.RFA attcd	R.H. BETHUNE. R.P. No change.7 a.m. Deliver supplies to RFA T.M. Bats & D.H.Q by 8 a.m. Proceed to ALLOUAGNE.	R.H. LILLERS. R.P. ALLOUAGNE. 7 a.m. Deliver supplies to D.H.Q. T.M. Bats & R.F.A. on arrival at Divl Troops area.	R.H. LILLERS R.P. OSTREVILLE 8 a.m. with supplies as on 12th.	R.H. TINQUES. R.P. OSTREVILLE with supplies as on 13th; also 134 Field Amb. 82 San. Sec. 50 Mob. Vet Sec. Pioneers.
H.Q. COY. TRAIN.	for supplies to No. 3 Coy.Train. Supply 2" T.M. Batteries.				
116 Inf. Bde.	R.H. BETHUNE. R.P. No Change 7 a.m.	R.H. BETHUNE. R.P. No Change 7.a.m. Deliver supplies to 116th Inf. Bde. before it marches.	R.H. LILLERS. R.P. No Change.7.30am. Proceed to ALLOUAGNE. 7.a.m. Take supplies for 82 San Section 50 Mob. Vet Sec.	R.H. LILLERS. R.P. ALLOUAGNE. 7.a.m. Proceed to 116 Inf Bde. Area. Supply units as on 12th August.	R.H. TINQUES. R.P. TINCQUETTE also supply 1 Coy.RE 132 Field Amb.
No.2 Coy TRAIN					
117 Inf. Bde.	R.H. BETHUNE R.P. No Change Time 7 a.m. Proceed to AUCHEL with supplies for 117 Inf Bde, 3 Field Coys,RE., 3 Bats.RFA, Pioneers, 132 & 134 Field Amb.	R.H. BETHUNE. R.P. LOZINGHEM.7.30am Proceed to MONCHY BRETON area with supplies for 117 Inf Bde,3 Field CoysRE, 3 bats.RFA, Pioneers 132 & 134 Field Amb	R.H. LILLERS. R.P. OSTREVILLE 7.30 a.m. Proceed to 117 Inf. Bde. area with supplies for same units as on 11th.	R.H. LILLERS. R.P. BAILLEUL-AUX)-CORMAILLES 8 a.m. Supply units as on 12th Aug	R.H. TINQUES. R.P. same as on 13th. also supply 1 Coy R.E. 133 Field Amb.
No.3 Coy. TRAIN					
118 Inf. Bde.	R.H. BETHUNE. R.P. No Change. 7 a.m.	R.H. BETHUNE. R.P. No Change.7.am Proceed to CAUCHY a la TOUR with supplies for 118 Inf Bde & 133 Field Amb.	R.H. LILLERS. R.P. CAUCHY a la TOUR 7 a.m. Proceed to 118 Inf Bde area with supplies for same units as on 11th.	R.H. LILLERS. R.P. VANDELICOURT 8 a.m. Supply units as on 12th Aug	R.H. TINQUES. R.P. same as on 13th also supply 1 Coy.,R.E.
No 4 Coy TRAIN.	Take over 133 Field Amb.				

V.T. Fairhead
Major-D.A.Q.M.g.
30th Division.

War Diary

SECRET.

Copy No. ...8...

39th DIVISIONAL ADMINISTRATIVE INSTRUCTIONS, NO.3.

Ref: 1/100,000 MAP
LENS Sheet.   21.8.1916.

1. With reference to 39th Division Order No. 38.

2. Two trains will be available for conveyance of four Battalions from MONCHY BRETON area to LUCHEUX area on the 24th August.

3. Entraining Station will be at LIGNY ST. FLOCHEL.
   Trains will leave at 10.59 and 11.44 hours.
   Detraining Station will be at BOUQUEMAISON.
   Trains will arrive at 13.15 and 13.45 hours

4. All Transport will proceed by road on the 23rd., and take over Rations for the 24th. from Train on arrival in Billets on evening of the 23rd.
   Transport of units proceeding by train will be in the BOUQUEMAISON area by 2 p.m., 24th., with rations.

5. Each train will take two Battalions (personnel only), and their Lewis Gun handcarts. The accommodation in each train is approximately 1,840.

6. Supply arrangements will be carried out in accordance with the attached Supply and Transport table.

7. Ordnance Stores will be delivered at Refilling Points.

S. F. Farmer

Lieut-Colonel,
A.A. & Q.M.G., 39th Division.

Copies issued at ... p.m. to

G.O.C. 1	War Diary 8	13th Bn. Gloucesters 15
"G" 2	Signals 9	Div. Train 16, 17, 18, 19, 20
"A" "Q" 3	Divisional R.A 10	S.S.O. 21
A.D.M.S. 4	Divisional R.E. 11	
A.D.V.S. 5	116 Inf. Bde. 12	
A.P.M. 6	117 " " 13	
D.A.D.O.S 7	118 " " 14	

SUPPLY and TRANSPORT TABLE.

UNIT	21 August	22 August	23 August	24 August	25 August
H.Q. Group H.Q. Coy Train	R.P. No change. R.H. PREVENT. H.Q. Coy will move under orders of the C.R.A. Transfer Supply Wagons for Div.HQ. H.Q., RE & 82 Sen. Sec. to No.3 Coy.	R.P. LUCHEUX area R.H. PREVENT H.Q. Coy move under orders of C.R.A.	Under Orders of C.R.A.	Under Orders of C.R.A.	Under Orders of C.R.A.
116 Inf. Bde. No. 2 Coy Train	R.P. No change. R.H. No change	R.P No change R.H. No change.	R.P. No change R.H. No change No 2 Coy moves to REBREUVE area & issues breakfast rations for 24th to two Bns. before leaving.	R.P. REBREUVE area R.H. No change No 2 Coy moves to LE SOUICH AREA.	R.P. LE SOUICH area R.H. BOUQUEMAISON
117 Inf. Bde. No 3 Coy Train	R.P. No change. R.H. No change	R.P. No change. R.H. No change.	R.P. No change R.H. No change. No 3 Coy moves to NUNCQ area and issues rations for 24th to DHQ & breakfast rations for 24th to 117 Inf Bde(less 2 Bns & Transport.) before leaving	R.P. NUNCQ area R.H. No change No 3 Coy moves to BOUQUEMAISON area	R.P. BOUQUEMAISON area R.H. BOUQUEMAISON
118 Inf Bde No 4 Coy Train	R.P. No change R.H. No change	R.P. No change R.H. No change	R.P. No change R.H. No change No 4 Coy moves to REBREUVIETTE area	R.P. REBREUVIETTE area R.H. No change No 4 Coy moves to LUCHEUX area	R.P. LUCHEUX area R.H. BOUQUEMAISON

SUPPLY and TRANSPORT TABLE.

UNIT	25 August	26 August	REMARKS.
H.Q. Group.	Under orders of C.R.E.	Under orders of Divisional Train.	
H.Q. Company Train			
116th Inf. Bde.	R.P. LE SONICH area R.H. BOUQUEMAISON.	R.P. LOUVENCOURT area R.H. BELLE EGLISE.	
No 2 Coy Train	No 2 Coy moves to WARNI-MONT WOOD area with supplies for 116 Inf Bde. 13th Gloucesters, 1 Field Coy. R.E., 132 Field Amb. 82 San Sec, 50 Mobile Vet. Section	No 2 Coy remain in WARNIMONT WOOD area	
117th Inf. Bde	R.P. BOUQUEMAISON area R.H. BOUQUEMAISON.	R.P. LOUVENCOURT area R.H. BELLE EGLISE.	
No 3 Coy Train	No 3 Coy moves to VAUCHELLES LES AUTHIE area with supplies for 117 Inf. Bde, 1 Field Coy R.E., 133 Field Ambulance and D.H.Q.	No 3 Coy remain in VAUCHELLES LES AUTHIE area	
118th Inf. Bde.	R.P. LUCHEUX area R.H. BOUQUEMAISON.	R.P. LOUVENCOURT area R.H. BELLE EGLISE.	
No 4 Coy Train	No. 4 Coy moves to BUS area with supplies for 118th Inf. Bde, 1 Field Coy., R.E. 134 Field Ambulance	No. 4 Coy moves to Ninel Billets & Bivouacs	

E.F. Pearson Major
for Lieut-Colonel,
A.A. & Q.M.G., 39th Div

22.8.1916.

SECRET.

Copy No. ...8.....

39th DIVISIONAL ADMINISTRATIVE INSTRUCTIONS

No. 4.

Ref. /100,000 MAP.
LENS Sheet.

22.8.1916.

1. With reference to 39th Divisional Order No. 39, dated 21.8.16.

2. Supply arrangements will be carried out in accordance with the attached Supply and Transport Table.

3. Ordnance Stores will be delivered at Refilling Points.

E. Ffalkner, Major
for Lieut-Colonel,
A.A. & Q.M.G., 39th Division.

Copies issued at 2 pm to

G.O.C.	D.A.D.O.S.	117th Inf Bde
"G"	WAR Diary	118th Inf Bde
"A" "Q"	Signals	13 Glostrs
A.D.M.S.	Divl. R.A.	Divl. Train
A.D.V.S.	Divl. R.E.	S.S.O.
A.P.M.	116 Inf Bde	Supply Col.

P.T.O

Casualties, August 1916

Killed

Officers and Other Ranks

Officers

Rank & Name		Unit	Casualty	Date
2/Lieut	Bolton G.G.	17 Notts & Derbys	Killed	1.8.16
T "	Dixon F.G.	"	"	"
T "	Langford A.H.A.	"	W. Since died of wounds	"
2/Lieut	Templar G.	179 Bde R.F.A.	Killed	8.8.16
T "	Davenport C.T.	14 Hampshires	Wounded since died of wounds	2.8.16
T "	Foley A.M.	10 Sussex attd 11 Surrey	Wounded 2.8.16 Died of wounds	3.8.16

Unit		1	2	3	4	5	6	7	8	9	10	11	12	13	14	15	16	17	18	19	20	21	22	23	24	25	26	27	28	29	30	31	1/32	Remarks
1st D.R. Cavalry		1						1		1																					1	3	6	
2nd R. Cavalry						1																											2	3	
3rd R. Cavalry																																		
4th Bn Hampshire			2	2					2																							2	4	
16th Div R Regt	5				1			2																									2	
4th Battle Battery	1							4																									1	
5th Bn R.R. Corps					2	2																											2	
1st R. Rifle Regt																																	4	
4th Bn Col. Regt						1																									1		4	
5th Bn Black Watch			2					1																									3	
4th Bn Gordon Regt				2			1																							2			4	
5th Bn H.L.Regt																														1			3	
6th Bn Gordon Regt	1							1																									2	
1st R Horse																																		
A S Corps																																		
R.A. M.C																																		
25th Inv Coy R E																																		
Ulsterville Coy																																		
Totals	8		4	4	3	3		8	2		1										1						1		2		5	8	53	
Independent Cambridge			1						1																									2	
Grand Total	6		2	2	3	3		8	3		1										1						1		2		5	8	55	

Casualties, August 1916.

Wounded & Msg

Officers and Other Ranks.

Officers

Rank	Name		Unit	Casualty	Date
T/Captain	Ludlow	J.B.	17 N. & Derbys	Wounded	1.8.16
T/2/Lt	Kent	M.A.	"	"	"
"	Flint	L.E.	"	"	"
"	Sheppard	F.W.	13' Sussex Regt	" acc	7.8.16
"	Kellaw	K.A.	13° "	" "	"
"	Edwardes	E.J.	13 Notts & Derbys / atta 117 T.M.B.	Wounded	8.8.16
T/Lieut	Sharpies	A.O.P.	18' Bde R.F.A.	"	"
T/2/Lt	Bakewell	J.A.	14 Hants Regt	"	9.8.16
"	Levy	M.P.	"	"	"
Lieut	Clements	D.F.	"	"	"
T/Capt	Fothergill	R.H.	13H' Field Amb	"	28.8.16
T/Lieut.	Connell	W.S.T.	R.A.M.C. atta H Sussex	"	31.8.16

Unit	1	2	3	4	5	6	7	8	9	10	11	12	13	14	15	16	17	18	19	20	21	22	23	24	25	26	27	28	29	30	31	Total	Remarks
11"Bn A Spearley	7								2	4																				1	4	12	
12"Bn A Lower Rfl	2					1	1		1	1									1		1											10	
10"Bn A Queen M		1							1		1																					3	
"Bn Stafordshire		1	6	1	7	2	1		1	3	1									1											5	12	
10"Bn Duke tth Rgts	48	1	2	4	3	2	1																									19	
25"Bn War Mrchrs	2	1	1	1																											3	63	
18"Bn K R Rif Corps	3	2		1			2	3		1		1																				11	
16"Bn Durlife Rtn							2																					4	6	7	8	29	
W.Br Cheshire Rg		1	1	7	1	3	2		1	2																			1	1		17	
4 Br Manchester			1	2	1	3	4	1													1							6	5	1	2	30	
H. Mans Regt		1	3	3	2	1	1	2																					1	7		22	
13"Bn Manchr Rg			1		1																									6		9	
Artillery							1	3	1	4																			1			10	
R. A. Corps				1		1			1																							1	
R. A. M. 6	4	1				1	1																									1	
23rd Bum Corps 8																															7	7	
No Bn M.G. Corps	1																														3	5	
Totals	73	8	15	18	15	9	11	13	10	12	10	1	1							2	1							11	12	12	38	272	
Attached to Cardoms & 2 Div Corps (Arty)				1			2																							6		4	
																																6	
Grand Total	73	8	16	19	16	9	11	15	10	12	10	1	1							2	1							11	12	12	44	282	

Missing

Unit	Total to 31-7-16	1-8-16	Total
11th Sussex	10		10
12th Sussex	120		120
13th Sussex	154		154
14th Hants.	6		6
16 Notts & Derbys	5		5
17 Notts & Derbys	2	12	14
17th KRRC	3		3
16 R.B.	25		25
1/6 Cheshires	1		1
4/5 Black Watch.			
1/1 Cambs			
1/1 Herts.	3		3
Engineers	7		7
13th Glosters.	13		13
116all G Coy.	1		1
A.S.C.			
Total	350	12	362

39th. DIVISION

A. & Q. 39th. DIVISION

S E P T E M B E R 1 9 1 6.

SECRET

ORIGINAL "A" J'Q
Page one
Vol 7

Army Form C. 2118.

WAR DIARY
INTELLIGENCE SUMMARY.
(Erase heading not required.)

Instructions regarding War Diaries and Intelligence Summaries are contained in F. S. Regs., Part II. and the Staff Manual respectively. Title pages will be prepared in manuscript.

Place	Date	Hour	Summary of Events and Information	Remarks and references to Appendices
	1916			
ACHEUX	1/9.		Preparations for the attack which is about to take place on Sept-3rd with zero hour at – 5.10 a.m. are continued. Anniversary of the formation of the 39th Division in 1915.	
ACHEUX	2/9.		116 and 117 Inf. Bdes take over the Battle front from 118 Inf Bde and unfold to complete arrangements for attack. 117 & 118 Inf Bde on 4/5. Inf Bde to be moved as the Divl. Reserve on attack into Divl. Reserve.	
ACHEUX	3/9.		116, 117 Inf. Bde and 4/5 Black Watch 118 Inf Bde attack the German trenches immediately North of the RIVER ANCRE, starting at – 5.10 a.m. The attack was in conjunction with an attack by the 49th Divn. on and across the left flank of the River Ancre — Immediately South of the RIVER ANCRE. 118 Inf. 2 Pn. 1/6 & 1/7 Inf. Bdes were withdrawn into Divl. Reserve with HQdrs ENGELBELMER and the Rue of Advanced	

T2134. Wt. W708–776. 500000. 4/15. Sir J. C. & 8.

Army Form C. 2118.

Page 2

WAR DIARY
or
INTELLIGENCE SUMMARY.
(Erase heading not required.)

Place	Date	Hour	Summary of Events and Information	Remarks and references to Appendices
	1916			
ACHEUX	3/9		Divl. HQ and 118 Bde took over the battle front. After the casualties in the action on 3rd were as follows:-	
			Killed Wounded Missing	
			OFFICERS 36 59 32	
			OTHER RANKS 234 1558 899.	
ACHEUX	4/9		Orders received to take over a further section of the line to the left of the HAMEL Section. 117 Bde. to be relieved to take over at this time: 116. Bde. to be in Divisional Reserve.	
ACHEUX	5/9		116. & 117. Inf. Bdes. re-organising.	
ACHEUX	6/9		Nothing to report.	
ACHEUX	7/9		ACHEUX and neighbourhood shelled during the night.	

Army Form C. 2118.

Page 3

WAR DIARY
INTELLIGENCE SUMMARY.
(Erase heading not required.)

Place	Date	Hour	Summary of Events and Information	Remarks and references to Appendices
	1916			
ACHEUX	8/9		A man of the 212 th Regt. taken prisoner by 2 Sergeants of the 4/5 Black Watch on the railway near the river.	
ACHEUX	9/9		Nothing to report.	
ACHEUX	10/9		116 Inf. Bde took over the section from BROADWAY to WATLING STREET from the 45 th Inf. Bde (4 8 Div N). All 3 Bdes are now in the line.	
ACHEUX	11/9 12/9 13/9		Nothing to report.	
ACHEUX	14/9		Special order received from Reserve Army Commander regarding the offensive on the 15 th: 14 & C. 39 Div N will regard as Reserve Army order.	

T2134. Wt. W708–776. 500000. 4/15. Sir J. C. & S.

Army Form C. 2118.

Page 4

WAR DIARY
or
INTELLIGENCE SUMMARY.
(Erase heading not required.)

Place	Date	Hour	Summary of Events and Information	Remarks and references to Appendices
ACHEUX	1916 15/9		16 Cheshire Regt. 118 Inf Bde carried out a raid against the German trenches just N. of the River ANCRE.	
" "	16/9 17/9 18/9		Nothing to relate.	
" "	19/9		16 Sh Bde took over REDAN sector from 54 Bde 2nd Divn. and still held AUCHONVILLERS sector. 118 Inf Bde took over Y RAVINE sector from 117 Inf Bde and also held HAMEL section. The latter Bde goes into Bullets in Div. Reserve.	
" "	20/9		117 Inf Bde took over SERRE and HEBUTERNE sections from 6th and 99 Inf Bdes. 2nd Divn.	
" "	21/9		Nothing to relate.	

Army Form C. 2118.

Page 5.

WAR DIARY
or
INTELLIGENCE SUMMARY.
(Erase heading not required.)

Instructions regarding War Diaries and Intelligence Summaries are contained in F. S. Regs., Part II. and the Staff Manual respectively. Title pages will be prepared in manuscript.

Place	Date	Hour	Summary of Events and Information	Remarks and references to Appendices
	1915			
ACHEUX	22/9		Nothing to report.	
" "	23/9		Raid by 11 Cambridgeshire Regt. upon German Trenches just North of River ANCRE.	
" "	24/9		Arrival of XIII Corps Cyclist Bn. who are allotted billets in MAILLY MAILLET.	
" "	25/9		Nothing to report.	
" "	26/9		Recd. log 16 Clubists Regt. upon German Trenches near to R. ANCRE.	
" "	27/9		Nothing to report.	
" "	28/9		16 Bn. of 115 Inf. Bde. also and 1 Coy of 117 Inf. Bde. relieved by 99th Inf. Bde.	

WAR DIARY
or
INTELLIGENCE SUMMARY.

Army Form C. 2118.

Page 6

Place	Date	Hour	Summary of Events and Information	Remarks and references to Appendices
ACHEUX	1915 30/9		117 St. Bde is withdrawn into Divisional Reserve with Bde HQ at BERTRANCOURT.	
			A list of Casualties for the month of September is attached.	

B.C. Dryer M.S.

Major General
Commanding 39th Division

Casualties September 1916.

Killed

Officers and Other Ranks.

Officers killed to 31-8-16 = 42.

Officers

Rank and Name		Unit	Casualty	Date
T 2nd Lt	Barrow L.A.H.	11th Sussex	Killed	1-9-16
T "	Hood O.	"	"	"
T Lt	Johns A.H.	12th "	"	"
T 2nd Lt	Black T	17th Sherwoods	"	17-9-16

Unit	Wgt Str	1	2	3	4	5	6	7	8	9	10	11	12	13	14	15	16	17	18	19	20	21	22	23	24	25	26	27	28	29	30	30+	Total	Remarks
11th Bn R. Sussex R.	69			9								1										2	1		1		1		1					15	
12th " "	93			3																														8	
13th " "	75			11											1							3					1	1						25	
14th Hants R.	51			23		1											2					2			1		1	1						30	
16th D.R.	31			12		1																			1									14	
17th " "	54			41						1							1												2					44	
17th H.R.R.C.	42			46			1										3					3								1				55	
16th Rifle Bde	28			31													3	1				3							2	3				41	
4th Berkshire R	27																					2							2					5	
4th Black Watch	144		1	31		6	1		1		3						1			1		1	5						2		5			43	
4th Camh R.	21			11	2												3						1	3							1			18	
4th Herts R	27		1	1	6																	1		1				3		1				15	
23rd Lond R	18	1		4	4																													9	
R.A.	7			1														1																2	
R.E.'s	4			—																															
J.S.C.	—																																		
11th A.M.C.	—			6	3																													9	
116 field Ay Coy	—			3																														3	
117 field Ay Coy	—			1																									1						
Y.39 T.M.B.	1																											1						1	
118 T.M.B.	1																												1					1	
Totals	561	1	1	234	9	6	1	2	1	—	—	4	1	1	—	1	10	1	1	—	9	12	4	12	1	2	8	4	5		339	
29th R.A. (att)	—		1																					1										1	
1st Central H.Q. Sig B	—																																1	
Grand Total	561	2	1	234	9	6	1	2	1	—	—	4	1	1	—	1	10	1	1	—	9	12	4	13	1	2	8	4	5		341	

Casualties September 1916

Wounded

Officers and Other Ranks

Officers wounded to 31-8-16 = 141
" missing " " = 20

Officers

Rank	Name		Unit	Casualty	Date
2nd Lieut	McPherson	J.	1/1 Cambs	Wounded	1-9-16
2nd Lieut	Eagle	L.P.	" attd 118 TMB	"	"
"	Lenton	S.H.	1/4 Northants attd 1/1 Cambs	"	"
"	Butler	E.A.	132 Bde RFA (attd)	"	"
T. Lt Col	Rudkin	C.M.G.	184 Bde RFA	" at duty	"
T. 2nd Lt	Odell	J.D.	186 Bde RFA	"	2-9-16
Capt	Kirk	N.	1/6 Cheshires	"	4-9-16
2nd Lt (T Capt)	Corfield	C.L.	1/1 Cambs	" at duty	"
2nd Lt	Bowers	C.H.	1/1 Cambs	"	"
2nd Lt	Symons	H.	1/1 Herts	"	"
T 2nd Lt	Bennett	R.	13th Glosters	Missing	"
Major	Nicholson	N.S.	186 Bde RFA	wounded at duty	5-9-16
2nd Lt	Robinson	W.E.E.	117 Bde " (attd)	wounded	6-9-16
Lt Col	Eardley-Wilmot	A.	179 Bde RFA	" at duty	"
T 2nd Lt	Staske	H.	13th Glosters	" (gas)	7-9-16
T. Lt	Pickett	S.R.	RAMC attd 17 KRRC	" (shellshock)	8-9-16
2nd Lt (T.Lt)	Adam	A.J.	1/1 Cambs	missing (wounded)	16-9-16
Lt (T. Capt)	Butler Sir H.J.J. Bt.		"	"	"
2nd Lt (T.Lt)	Shaw	W.	see opp. page	unofficially reported prisoner gassed & wounded	"
2nd Lt	Allpass	H.B.K.	" (1st Essex attd)	"	"
T 2nd Lt	Pratt	R.C.	117 M.G. Coy	Wounded	17-9-16
Capt (Bde Major)	Gunner	J.H.	116 Bde H.Q.	"	18-9-16
T. 2nd Lt	Page	R.	16 R.B.	"	"
T 2nd Lt	Butler	A.R.	15 Notts & Derbys	"	23-9-16
2nd Lt	Dove	N.J.	1/1 Cambs	" (gas)	"
2nd Lt	Gough	R.	179 Bde RFA	" "	24-9-16
"	Bunting	H.G.	1/1 Cambs	"	"
Lt	Green	J.E.S.	16 R.B.	"	27-9-16
Capt	Dadge	W.D.	1/6 Cheshires	"	"

OFFICERS KILLED: Operations 2/3rd September, 1916

Rank	and Name	Unit.	
2/Lt.	WALKER J.C.	1/1 Cambs. Regt.	
T.2/Lt	TATE T.C.	12th Sussex (10 Sussex, attd)	Died of Wounds
T.Lt.T.Capt	FABIAN A.S.	13th Rl Sussex Rgt	
T.Lt.	CHEAPE J. de C	13th Rl Sussex Rgt (8th Sussex, attd)	
T.2/Lt.	ORMSBY F.J.	13th Rl Sussex Rgt (14th Sussex, attd)	
T. Capt.	SKINNER F.T.	14 Bn. Hamps Rgt.	
T. Capt.	ROWSELL H.G.	"	
2/Lt.	DUNCAN W.B.	4/5th Rl.Highlanders	
2/Lt.	MILL R.C.K.	"	
T. Lt.	ROBERTSON W.S.	(10th R.H., attached)	
T. Major	ABRAHAMS M.N.	16th Bn. Rifle Bde	
T. Capt.	BROWN B.	"	
T. Lt.	RONALDSON C.R.	"	
T.2/Lt.	RAMSAY N.	"	
T.2/Lt.	Wegg-Prosser C.F.J.	(15 R.B., attd)	
T. 2/Lt.	GRANT H.E.	16th Bn. Rifle Bde. (17th R.B., attd)	
T.2/Lt.	THOMAS H.W.	16th Bn Rifle Bde (14th R.B., attd)	
T.2/Lt.	Pearce C.J.	117th M.G. Coy.	
T. Capt.	HECHT M.F.	17th Bn. K.R.R.C.	
T. Capt.	HULKS H.J.	"	
T.Lt.	EWEN P.K.S.	"	
T.Lt.	SPINNEY K.T.	"	
2/Lt.	BAILEY A.J.	"	
T.2/Lt.	SAUNDERS A.B.	"	.... Died of Wounds
T.2/Lt.	LACEY T.H.	"	.... Died of Wounds
2/Lt.	BUTCHER A.J.B.	" (6th Bn attd).	
T.2/Lt.	GOFFEY J.G.	" (23rd Bn attd)	
T. Major	STOLIARD G.S.	17th Notts & Derby	
T. Capt	Littlewood G.P	"	
T. Capt.	BROOKFIELD S.F.	"	
T. Capt	HOPEWELL R.G.	"	
T. Capt	SINGLETON F.C.	" (19th Bn attd)	
T. Lt.	WOODHOUSE L.D.	" (attd 117 T.M.B.)	
T. 2/Lt	Woolner S.H.	17 KRRC (23? Bn attd)	
T. Capt	Curtis A.J.R.		Died of wounds
T. Lt	Thomas S.E.B.	13 Sussex (16 Sussex attd)	

TOTAL KILLED 33.

OFFICERS WOUNDED   2/3rd September 1916.

RANK.	NAME.		UNIT.	
2/Lt.(T.Cap't)	CORFIELD.	C.L.	1/1st Cambs. Regt.	At duty.
2/Lt.	BOWERS.	C.H.	1/1st " "	
2/Lt.	SYMONS.	H.	1/1st Herts. Regt.	
2/Lt.	CHANTLER.	R.	1/6th Cheshire Regt.	
Capt.	KIRK.	R.	1/6th " "	
T.2/Lt.	KELIHER.	J.C.	11th R. Sussex Regt.	
T.2/Lt.	DOOGAN.	G.W.	11th " "	At duty.
T.2/Lt.	REDWAY.	W.R.	11th "(16th R.F.attd)	
T.2/Lt.	LIMBERY-BUSE.	R.G.K.	11th R.Sussex Regt.	Shellshock.
T.2/Lt.	ARKELL.	A.H.	12th "(19th Suss att)	
T.2/Lt.	GILL.	V.W.	12th "(16th R.F.att)	
2/Lt.	HODGE.	F.E.D.	12th "(3rd. Suss att)	
T/Lt.	ELPHICKE.	D.G.	13th R. Sussex Regt.	
T.2/Lt.	WILSON.	J.R.	13th "(10th Suss att)	
T.2/Lt.	BARTLETT.	C.	13th "(16th R.F.att)	At duty.
T.2/Lt.	HENNING.	S.	13th R.Sussex Regt.	
T.2/Lt.	MACLURE.	J.G.	13th " "	
T. Capt.	MOXLEY.	C.F.	14th Hants Regt.	
T.2/Lt.	McNAMARA	C.J.	14th " "	
T.2/Lt.	BARTLETT.	E.F.P.	14th "(16th Hants att)	
T.Lt & Adjt.	GOLDSMITH.	F.	14th Hants Regt.	At duty.
T.2/Lt.	GORMAN.	H.F.	14th "(1st Hants att)	
2/Lt(T/Capt) Staff Capt.)	WILL.	L.J.A.	116th. I.B. H.Q.	At duty.
Capt.	RETTIE.	J.L.	4/5th Royal Highldrs.	
Lt.	ROBERTSON.	W.L.	4/5th " "	
2/Lt.	GUTHRIE.	D.S.	4/5th " "	
2/Lt.	COX.	W.A.M.	4/5th " "	
T.2/Lt.	JAMES.	H.	4/5th "(Gordons att)	At duty.
T/Lt.	BROWN.	J.	16th Notts & Derbys.	
T.2/Lt.	BENNER.	W.	16th " "	
T.2/Lt.	HASTINGS.	W.J.	16th "(14th N&D att)	
T.2/Lt.	SIMPSON.	O.D.	16th "(4th " ")	
T.Capt.	BROCKLEBANK.	S.	16th Rifle Brigade.	
T.Capt.	RISLEY.	N.B.	16th " "	
T.Lt.	BARLOW.	J.H.F.	16th " "	
T.2/Lt.	CARTER.	C.A.	16th " "	
T.2/Lt.	CROSTHWAITE.	F.D.	16th " "	
T.Capt.	CURTIS.	A.J.P.	17th K.R.R.C.	
T.Capt.	TAYLOR.	R.G.	17th K.R.R.C.	At duty
T.Capt.	KIRK.	T.W.	17th K.R.R.C.	Shellshock.
T/Lt.	GIDNEY.	C.R.	17th " "	
T.2/Lt.	MONTGOMERY.	G.	17th "(23rd Bn,att)	
T/Lt.	BROWN.	R.L.	17th "(attd 117 M.G.Co)	
T/Lt.	ROSS.	B.J.	17th Notts & Derby R.	
T.Capt.	WIGHT.	R.S.	17th " "	
T.Capt.	TURNER.	F.R.	17th " "	
T/2/Lt.	BIRKIN.	W.N.	17th " "	
T. 2/Lt.	SALSBURY.	J.W.	17th " "	
T. 2/Lt.	NUGENT.	T.C.	17th "(19th Bn.att)	
2/Lt.	ARKILL-JONES.	E.T.	17th "(4th " ")	
T/Lt.	DUNNING.	J.B.	R.A.M.C.(M.O.13thSuss)	
T.Lt.	DARKE.	S.J.	" (M.O.16thR.B.)	
T. Lt.	TUCKER.	C.E.	132 Field Ambulance.	
T. Lt.	MITCHELL.	H.	134 "	
R.C. Chap.	NORTHCOTE.	P.M.	Army Chap.Dept.(attd.1/6 Cheshires	
T. Lt.	ELLEN.	C.W.	227 Field Coy. R.E.	
Maj.(T/Lt.Col)	SMITH D.S.O.	H.R.W.M.	132nd Bde R.F.A.(att)	
C.of E. Chap.	CRAWLEY	J.L.	A.C.D. attd 17 K.R.R.C.	
T.2/Lt.	STEWART.	C.A.	117th M.G.Coy(8th Wiltshires att)	

TOTAL WOUNDED - 59.

OFFICERS MISSING — OPERATIONS 2/3rd September 1916.

RANK	NAME		UNIT	
T.2/Lt.	BENNETT.	R.	13th Gloucesters.	
T.Capt.	PENRUDDOCKE.	C.	11th Sussex Regt.	
T.2/Lt.	VORLEY.	C.A.	11th " "	
T.Lt.	GROVES.	L.A.	11th " "	
T.2/Lt.	FISH.	B.E.	11th " "	
T.Capt.	NORTHCOTE.	E.S.	11th " "	
2/Lt.	MOLE.	H.P.	11th " (3rd Suss attd)	
T.2/Lt.	FRENCH.	A.A.	11th " (10th " ")	
T.Capt.	TUTTIET.	L.W.	12th Sussex Regt.	
T.2/Lt.	KENNEDY.	W.L.	12th " (10th Suss attd)	
T.2/Lt.	BARROW.	F.W.	13th " (14th " ")	
T.Lt.	THOMAS.	S.E.B.	13th " (10th " ")	
T.2/Lt.	HOPWOOD.	M.	13th " (" " ")	
T.Lt.	GREEN.	E.M.	14th Hants Regt.	
T.2/Lt.	ASH.	G.S.	14th " "	
T.2/Lt.	MAY.	W.G.	14th " (1st Garr.Bn.att)	
2/Lt	PEEL	C.N.	14th " (3rd Hants att)	
T.2/Lt.	BALL.	B.H.	14th " (13th " ")	
T.2/Lt.	HAYDON.	J.S.	14th " (" " ")	
T.2/Lt.	TEW.	D.Mc.L.	14th " (" " ")	
T.2/Lt.	RODGER.	J.A.V.	14th " (" " ")	
T.2/Lt.	SIMPSON.	R.	14th. " (" " ")	
T.2/Lt.	BEARN.	P.D.	14th " (" " ")	
T.2/Lt.	HIGGINS.	H.V.	116th M.G.Coy.	
T.2/Lt.	GREENE.	G.R.	116th " "	
2/Lt(T/Capt)	CUNNINGHAM.	R.C.	4/5th R.Highlanders.	
Lt.(T/Capt).	SHEPHERD.	E.A.	4/5th " "	
T.2/Lt.	CHAPPELL.	F.N.	16th Notts & Derbys.	Believed killed.
T.Capt.	HIELD.	J.H.	16th Rifle Brigade.	
T.2/Lt.	ROBERTS.	L.J.	16th " "	
T.2/Lt.	WOOLMER.	S.H.F.	17th K.R.R.C. (23rd Bn.att)	Wounded.
T.Capt.	WALTERS.	H.V.	17th Notts & Derbys.	"
T.Lt.	BUCK.	B.F.	17th " "	"
T.2/Lt.	ELLISSON.	M.A.	17th " "	
T.2/Lt.	PANTON.	A.W.	234 Field Coy. R.E.	

TOTAL MISSING. — 35.

OTHER RANKS - KILLED, WOUNDED, MISSING, during Operations 2/3rd Sept.

UNIT	Killed	Wounded	Missing.	Wounded since died of wounds.
11th Rl. Sussex Regt.	9	154	134	-
12th Rl. Sussex Regt.	-	46	37	3
13th Rl. Sussex Regt.	8	101	19	3
14th Hampshire Regt.	19	143	214	4
16th Notts & Derby Regt.	9	77	8	3
17th Notts & Derby Regt.	42	252	142	-
17th Kings Royal Rifle Corps.	43	177	98	3
16th Rifle Brigade.	31	240	176	-
1/6th Cheshire Regt.	-	19	-	-
4/5th Black Watch.	31	160	18	-
1/1st Cambridgeshire Regt.	11	46	1	-
1/1st Herts Regt.	1	5	-	-
29th Div. Artillery (attd)	-	4	-	-
39th Div. Artillery.	1	3	-	-
132nd Field Ambulance.	2	19.	-	-
133rd Field Ambulance.	-	9	26	-
134th Field Ambulance.	3	23	-	1
13th Gloster Regt.	4	21	3	-
39th Div. Engineers.	-	26	6	-
116th M.G. Company.	3	15	16	-
117th M.G. Company.	1	16	1	-
Y/39th T.M.Battery.	-	1	-	-
TOTAL.	218	1557	899	17

Unit	31/10	1	2	3	4	5	6	7	8	9	10	11	12	13	14	15	16	17	18	19	20	21	22	23	24	25	26	27	28	29	30	31	Total	Remarks
11"B. N Lanc Rgt	305	1	154					1				4	1			6	7	1	3				2	3	6	1			1			1	186	
12"B. N Stone Rgt	354		146					1	1				5	1										1	1	2	6		1		5		64	
12"Bn R Scots	353		101						1				5	1	3		3							2	7		4	1			1		133	
11"Dn N.Humberland	238		143				1				3					2	3	6	1	4	3			6	5	8	1	7	2		1	1	195	
6" Dn R Ir Rifles	201		77			2					6						1							1	4	1	4	1	2		1		101	
14"Bn Middx Regt	233		253	3		5		5					2	1		2	1		3				2	9	1	1	1	1		1	1	1	282	
14"Bn NIR Regt	214		177								2	2	1	1		1	10	1					9	1	1	1	1	1	1	3	4	1	211	
16"Bn Rifle Bde	237		240							2	1	2		1		2							1		2	1	4		6	1	3	3	275	
16"Bn Middx Regt	161	6	19	10	2	1		3			1		2			4	11	1						1	3	1			8	1	1		77	
1/5 Glouc West	116		160				1									17							2	2		3		3					179	
1/Welsh Regt	162	1	8	46	14	3	1	4						1			6	1					2	4	10	21	1		5	2	14	4	148	
1/Bn Sher Fors	135		5	5	11	3	4	2		5														1	2				2		1		42	
13"Bn Glouc Regt	116	1	4	21	20									1										1	4	1			4	1			58	
Artillery	30	2	2	3	1	2					1						1	1						1	1								20	
AS Corps	2																																1	
RAMC 6	14		51	26					1									1								1		1					78	
116 Div RE Coy	22	2	15																														18	
Royal Engineers	42	1	26			2							1		1		1									2	1		1				32	
Z 39 T M B		1																															2	
118 MG Coy			1		2																			2	2				2				6	
Y 39 T M B			1																									1					4	
17 M G Coy			16					1											5						5	1							29	
x 39 T M B																																		
Y 39 H T M B																	1												1				1	
Totals	2935	10	19	1534	77	21	8	21	14	4	1	22	12	4	5	30	19	36	16	5	8	19	29	28	49	23	14	39	9	30	15		2146	
2.2"? N.F. and 25, 27 64, 85	6	4	1	4	4	2																	1							1			2	
29" R.A (attd)	42		15																														15	
174 Fin By R.G.A		1																			6												6	
2"d Siege By R.A.F.C																								1								1	
1" Bougada Hd2 25T Boy RA																																		
25B Fin Boy RE																																1	
Grand Totals	2941	14	20	1538	81	23	8	21	14	4	1	22	12	4	5	30	19	36	16	5	14	21	30	28	50	23	14	40	10	30	15		2167	

Missing to 31-8-16 = 362. O.R.s

Missing

Unit	3-9-16	4-9-16	15-9-16	16-9-16	18-9-16	19-9-16	24-9-16
13th Glosters	3	3					
1/1 Cambs	1	2		1		1	
1/6 Cheshires			1				
16 R.B.	176				3	2	
11th Sussex	134						
12th Sussex	37						
13th Sussex	19						
14th Hants	214						
16th N.F.s	8						
17th N.F.s	142						
17th KRRC	98						
4/5. B Watch	18						
RAMC	26						
R. Engineers	6						
116 M.G.Coy.	16						
117 M.G.Coy	1						
Totals	899	5	1	1	3	2	1

Missing to 31-8-16 = 362. O.R.s

Missing

| Unit | 3-9-16 | 4-9-16 | 15-9-16 | 16-9-16 | 18-9-16 | 19-9-16 | 24-9-16 |

SECRET

Army Form C. 2118.

"A" + "Q" Branch.
WAR DIARY
—or—
INTELLIGENCE SUMMARY.
(Erase heading not required.)

Instructions regarding War Diaries and Intelligence Summaries are contained in F. S. Regs., Part II. and the Staff Manual respectively. Title pages will be prepared in manuscript.

Place	Date	Hour	Summary of Events and Information	Remarks and references to Appendices
ACHEUX	1916 1/10		Remainder of 117 Inf. Bde relieved by 6th H.L.I. R⁴ de 2ⁿᵈ Div. in SERRÉ and HÉBUTERNE Sections, and withdrawn to Div. Reserve with HQ at BERTRAM COURT. Summertime revealed as nothing save looting for	
ACHEUX TO HÉDAUVILLE	2/10	12 NOON	39 D.H.Q. moved to HÉDAUVILLE with Q. office situated in a field frequently used as a cinema. Very wet day	
HÉDAUVILLE	3/10		Div. Sector now extends from River ANCRE to WATLING STREET with 116 and 118 Inf Bdes in the line. This front is now held by II Corps. Orders received to relieve 18ᵗʰ Division in the SCHWABEN REDOUBT. Weather still very wet.	

T2134. Wt. W708—776. 500000. 4/15. Sir J. C. & S.

Army Form C. 2118.

A & Q Branch

WAR DIARY
INTELLIGENCE SUMMARY
(Erase heading not required.)

Page 2

Place	Date	Hour	Summary of Events and Information	Remarks and references to Appendices
HEDAUVILLE	1916 4/10		Divl. School closed at ACHEUX and moved to HEDAUVILLE. Weather still very wet.	
"	5/10		117 Inf. Bde reinforced by 11th Royal Sussex Regt, 116 Inf. Bde and 11 Cambridgeshire Regt. 118 Bde took over the THIEPVAL section from 55 Bde, 18th Divn & day three Brigades in the line again. Divn holds THIEPVAL, HAMEL, Y RAVINE and AUCHONVILLERS Sections being astride the river ANCRE.	
"	6/10		Orders received for Divn. HQ to move to camp near BOUZINCOURT	
BOUZINCOURT Camp.	7/10	8.30 am	Divn HQ moved to camp just N. of BOUZINCOURT HQ offices to be huts one hutted.	
"	8/10		Nothing to report	

"A" + "Q" Branch

WAR DIARY
or
INTELLIGENCE SUMMARY.

Army Form C. 2118.

Page 3

Place	Date	Hour	Summary of Events and Information	Remarks and references to Appendices
BOUZINCOURT Cont.	9/6			
"	9/10		117 Infy Bde carried out an attack against the N.W. face of SCHWABEN REDOUBT. 15th Bn: 116th Plan von Fusrs Rgt attacks this troops. Heavy casualties were inflicted on the Germans, our casualties were fairly heavy. No prisoners were taken.	
"	10/10		118 Infy Bde relieve the 117 Infy Bde in the THIEPVAL section	
"	11/10		Orders received for 118 Infy Bde to attack and take SCHWABEN REDOUBT: 13th Bn is the Left section.	
"	12/10		Nothing to report.	
"	13/10		Operations further : 1/1 Hertfordshire Regt capture 5/ his own in SCHWABEN REDOUBT area.	
"	14/10		Action of CAPTURE of SCHWABEN REDOUBT.	

Army Form C. 2118.

Page 4

WAR DIARY
INTELLIGENCE SUMMARY.
(Erase heading not required.)

Place	Date	Hour	Summary of Events and Information	Remarks and references to Appendices
	1916			
BOUZINCOURT Camp.	14/10		MAJOR E.T. de TENTITENY O'KELLY, ROYAL WELSH FUSILIERS posted as D.A.Q.M.G. 39 DIV vice MAJOR E F FALKNER Army Service Corps appointed D.A.Q.M.G. at Junior Staff School Cambridge	
"	15/10		Congratulatory messages received from Reserve Army, II and V Corps on success of SCHWABEN REDOUBT.	
"	16/10		11 Hertfordshire Regt. captured five prisoners who were the morning	
"	17/10		Nothing to report.	
"	18/10		" " " "	
"	19/10		" " " "	
"	20/10			
"	21/10		Our positions near the SCHWABEN REDOUBT were attacked at about 6am by the Germans who were repulsed by the 17th Sherwood Foresters	

Army Form C. 2118.

Page 5

"A" v "A" Branch

WAR DIARY
INTELLIGENCE SUMMARY
(Erase heading not required.)

Instructions regarding War Diaries and Intelligence Summaries are contained in F.S. Regs., Part II. and the Staff Manual respectively. Title pages will be prepared in manuscript.

Place	Date	Hour	Summary of Events and Information	Remarks and references to Appendices
	1916			
BOUZINCOURT CAMP	26/10		Headquarters shelled. Casualties 2 men killed & in ten wounded.	
BOUZINCOURT CAMP	21/10		Action at SCHWABEN REDOUBT. The Germans counterattacked at 4.45 a.m. but were driven off by 17 KRRC at about 5.50. Of the enemy we killed our own casualties were 2 officers & number including 2 officers killed and 2 wounded. 84 unwounded and 5 wounded other ranks of the Germans were taken prisoners. CAPTURE OF STUFF TRENCH by 116 & 117 Inf. Bdes. 1 officer and 87 O.R. of the enemy taken prisoners.	
BOUZINCOURT CAMP	22/10		Capture of positions in STUFF TRENCH consolidated by 116 Bde. 5th Bn. 15th Inf. 19 Division. relieved 116 Bde. in REDOUBT section, including STUFF TRENCH.	

Army Form C. 2118.

"A" ~ Q" Branch.

WAR DIARY
or
INTELLIGENCE SUMMARY
(Erase heading not required.)

Page 6

Place	Date	Hour	Summary of Events and Information	Remarks and references to Appendices
	1916			
BOUZINCOURT CAMP.	22/10		116. Inf. Bde. goes into Divn. Reserve. Army Commander conveyed his congratulations	
"	23/10		4/5 Black Watch relieved 17 K.R.R.C. in SCHWABEN REDOUBT. Very foggy day. Weather still very wet.	
"	24/10			
"	25/10		116. Infantry Brigade relieved 117 Infantry Brigade in the RIVER Section. G.O.C. Orders for General attack de ST PIERRE DIVION and ANCRE VALLEY received.	
"	26/10		Nothing to report except weather still wet but showing signs of clearing.	
"	27/10		117. Inf. Bde. relieved 116 Inf. Bde in the RIVER Section.	

Army Form C. 2118.

A. v.G. Beauchamp

WAR DIARY
INTELLIGENCE SUMMARY.
(Erase heading not required.)

Page 7

Instructions regarding War Diaries and Intelligence Summaries are contained in F. S. Regs., Part II. and the Staff Manual respectively. Title pages will be prepared in manuscript.

Place	Date	Hour	Summary of Events and Information	Remarks and references to Appendices
	1916			
BOUZINCOURT CAMP.	28/10		Visit by General Sir DOUGLAS HAIG G.O.C in C. 11 Herts and 4/5 R'le de Ward 118. Inf Bde handed at SERVIS.	
"	29/10.		118. Inf Bde relieves 117. Inf Bde in RIVER sector 4 day 24 hour guns to to the side	
"	30/10		116. Inf Bde relieves 118 Inf Bde in RIVER sector 4 day Very heavy rain	
"	31/10		Weather a little finer with almost a gale. A list of casualties for October 1916 is attached.	

B.C. Organ Lt. Col. 9k
Major General
Cmndg 39 Division

T2134. Wt. W708—776. 500000. 4/15. Sir J. C. & S.

Original

Casualties   October 1916.

Killed

Officers and Other Ranks.

CASUALTIES, OCTOBER, 1916.

OFFICERS KILLED.

Rank & Name.	Unit.	Casualty.	Date.
T/Lt. Hart C.J.	16th Notts & Derby	Killed	9.10.16
2/Lt. Godwin L.W.	"	"	"
T/2/Lt. Weeks R.S.	10th Mdlx.attd1/1Herts temp duty with 16thRB	"	10.10.16
Lt. Formby T.H.	1/1Cambs	"	13.10.16
2/Lt. Scott T.W.	" "	"	"
2/Lt. Drake P.A.	13th Gloucesters	"	"
Lieut(T/Capt)Lee E	1/1Herts	"	14.10.16
T/Lieut Barrie WCO	4/5th Black Watch	"	15.10.16.
2/Lt. Ferrier R.E.	" "	"	"
2/Lt. Vine R.S.	1/1 Cambs R.	"	"
2/Lt. Bowyer E.G.	" "	"	"
T/Lt. Bradford A.R.	" "	"	"
Lt. Holmes V.R.(MC)	1/6th Cheshires	"	"
Lt. Walker S.A.	RAMC.att.1/6th Ches.	"	"
2/Lt.Chattaway P.S.	1/6th Cheshires	"	"
2/Lt. Gibson C.M.	4/5th Black Watch	"	"
2/Lt. Smith W.T.	" "	"	"
T/2/Lt Coxon L.F.	12th R. Sussex	"	16.10.16.
T/2/Lt. Pearce CDF	14th Hamps.	"	18.10.16.
Lieut.Rawson L.R.	17th K.R.R.C.	"	24.10.16.
T/Capt.Kitchen E.H.	"	"	22.10.16.
T/2Lt.Honey GH.Le S	"	"	"
T/2/Lt.Doogan G.W.	11th R. Sussex	"	"
T/2/Lt. Salter F.H.	"	"	"
T/Capt.Warren F.R.F	12th "	"	"
T/2/Lt. Ivens F.H.H	11th "	"	"
T/Capt. Rees M.J.	132 Field Amb.	Wounded 22.10.16. D. of Wounds	30.10.16.

Unit	Total to 30/9/16	1	2	3	4	5	6	7	8	9	10	11	12	13	14	15	16	17	18	19	20	21	22	23	24	25	26	27	28	29	30	31	Total to 31/10/16	Remarks
11th Bn R. Sussex R.	2																															2	21
12th Bn R. Sussex R.								2	2	1	2	2	5				16			4		8					1					40	
13th Bn R. Sussex R.								2				1							1	1	1		23			4	3					34	
14th Bn Hampshire R.					2	2			1	1	1								1	10	1										1	30	
16th Bn Notts Derby R.						1		4	21									2														28	
17th Bn Notts Derby R.					2	1	1	11	10	4								2	2	4	9			1	3	1		1				53	
14th Bde H.Q. R.B.							1			1												20	2	1	1			4	2			44	
16th Bde Rifle Bde							1	5	4								5	6		1	1	25			1			1				46	
1/6 Cheshire Regt												2	3	4	3																	16	
4/5 Black Watch											1	2		24									2	1								41	
1/1 Camb's Regt						1					1			23	6										14							31	
1/1 Herts Regt												2		3	2															1	1	9	
13 Gloster									1														2	2	7							13	
RA																	1		1													1	
RE			1									1																				4	
A.S.C			1																1													1	
R.A.M.C.																						1										1	
X Y Z T.M. Btys	3																															3	
114 MG Coy							2						2																			2	
118 MG Coy										2																						4	
116 MG Coy													2																			2	
116 TMB																																	
Divl Hdqrs																						1										1	
Total		6	1	3	6	9	2	1	34	12	7	2	10	9	63	18	21	15	18	16	3	95	4	20	2	12	4	5	3	1	4	425	
Z 11 TM Bty										2																						3	
15th Machine at 39 Div																1																1	
Grand Totals		6	1	–	1	3	6	9	21	34	14	7	2	10	9	63	18	21	15	18	16	5	95	4	20	2	12	4	5	3	1	4	429	

Original

Casualties October 1916.

Wounded

Officers and Other Ranks.

CASUALTIES, OCTOBER, 1916.

OFFICERS, WOUNDED.

Rank and Name.	Unit.	Casualty.	Date.
T/2/Lt. Allen A.W.	1/1 Cambs. Rgt	Wounded	5.10.16
T2/Lt. Butler A.R.	16th Notts & Derby	"	7.10.16
T/Capt. King W.J.	" "	" S.A.D.	"
T/2/Lt. Pettigrew B. St.G.	17th "	"	8.10.16
T/Capt. Kenward S.	16th "	" S.A.D.	"
2/Lieut. Cooper G.C.	" "	"	"
T/2/Lt. Darke E.	" "	"	9.10.16
T/2/Lieut. Scragg A	" "	"	"
T/2/Lt. Copestake V.J.	" "	"	"
T/Capt. Stevens H.R.	117th T.M.B.	" at duty	"
T/Capt Hardy A.	16th Notts & Derby	"	"
T/Lieut Laws P.U.	" "	"	"
T/Lieut Lehfeldt W.R.A.	" "	"	"
T/2/Lt. Cooling A.E.	" "	"	"
T/2/Lt. Laws C.W.	" "	"	"
T/Capt Cook J.G.	" "	Missing	"
T2/Lt. Teahan J.P.	" "	"	"
T/2/Lt. Bayzand A.	" "	"	"
T/2/Lt. Ashworth C.H.	118th T.M.B.	Wounded	10.10.16
2/Lieut. Edwards A.L.	4/5th Black Watch	"	11.10.16
2/Lieut Bdll S.J.	1/1 Cambs R.	"	"
2/Lieut Brown G.	" "	"	13.10.16
2/Lieut Ashby H.R.	" "	"	"
Captain Miller S.	132 Field Amb.	" at duty	15.10.16
2/Lieut. Reid H.S.	234 Field Coy.R.E	"	"
Captain Moffat J.A.	4/5th Black Watch	"	"
Major Bowes-Lyon G.F.	" "	"	"
2/Lieut. Nelson W.	" "	"	"
2/Lieut. Dixon W.	" "	"	"
2/Lieut. Fergusson R.M.	" "	"	"
Lieut. Law I.M.	" "	"	"
2/Lt. Paterson I.S.	" "	"	"
2/Lt. Ross J.C.	" "	"	"
2/Lt. Nicoll M.W.	" "	"	"
Captain Field J.J.	132 Field Amb	"	"
T/Capt. Wood E.R.	1/1st Cambs R.	"	"
2/Lieut Fuggle A.J.T.ø	ø(3/7 Essex Attd))	"	"
2/Lieut Comer F.	1/1st Cambs R.	"	"
T/Capt Stickland J.R.	" "	"	"
2/Lt. Stanton E.V. ø	ø(4/Northants attd)	"	"
2/Lt. Bruce R.L.	1/1st Cambs R.	" shell shock	"
T/Lt.Col.Riddell E.P.A.	" "	"	"
T/ Major Few H.C.	" "	"	"
T/Capt. Corfield C.L.	" "	"	"
T/2/Lt. Brown F.L.	17th K.R.R.C.	Wounded.	"
T/2/Lt. Filtness D.	" "	"	"
2/Lt. Glover V.	118th M.G. Coy	"	"
2/Lt. Cunningham T.F.	" "	"	"
2/Lt. Reid J.A.J.	1/1 Cambs R.	"	"
T/2/Lt. Cotton R.B.	234 Field Coy R.E.	"	"
2/Lieut. Russell F.W.	1/6th Cheshires	"	"
2/Lieut. Booth R.W.	" "	"	"
2/Lieut Macaree A.J. ø	1/1 Cambs. R. ø 3/7 Essex attd.	"	16.10.16.
2/Lt. Palmer F.J.	118th M.G. Coy	"	"
2/Lieut Marchant W.S.	12th R. Sussex R	"	"
2/Lieut Fry C.R.M.	" "	"	"
T/2/Lt. Caffyn F.G.	17th Notts & Derby	"	17.10.16
T/2/Lt Appleby W,C.S.	12th R. Sussex	"	18.10.16
T/2/Lt. Smith Howard K.O.	" "	Missing	"

Continued.

CASUALTIES, OCTOBER, 1916.

OFFICERS, WOUNDED.

Rank & Name.	Unit.	Casualty.	Date.
T/Captain Kirlew T.O.	17th Notts&Derby	Wounded	19.10.16
T/2/Lieut. Hewat C.D.	" "	"	20.10.16
T/Captain. Bell J.J.J.	179th Bde., R.F.A	" at duty	21.10.16
T/2/Lt. Watson L.R.	17th Notts&Derby	"	"
T/2/Lt. Stott A.W.	17th K.R.R.C.	"	24.10.16
T/2/Lt. Coates P.	17th Notts&Derby	"	22.10.16
T/2/Lt. Turner W.R.	" "	"	"
T/2/Lt. Clifford J.S.	" "	"	"
Lieut. Haworth G.E.	1/6th Cheshires	"	"
T/2/Lt. Attwood H.A.	17th K.R.R.C.	"shell shock	22.10.16
T/2/Lt. Powers S.J.	" "	"	"
T/2/Lt. D'Ivernois VHB	11th R. Sussex	"	"
T/2/Lt. Booth L.P.	12th "	"	"
2/Lt. Grim R.A.	" "	"	"
T/2/Lt. Hole W.	" "	"	"
T/2/Lt. Boustead P.M.N.	" "	"	"
T/2/Lt. Hayes P.J.	11th "	"	"
2/Lt. Davison E. ∅	12th "	"	"
	∅ 3rd Sussex attd		
T/2/Lt. Langdale H.C.	13th R. Sussex	"	"
T/2/Lt. Wells G.A.	" "	"	"
T/2/ LT. Bartlett C.	" "	" at duty	"
2/Lieut. Box F.G. ∅	" "	"	"
	∅ 6th Sussex attd		
T/2/Lt. Wilson B.A.W.	14th Hants R.	" at duty	"
T2/Lt. Hutson G.T.	116th M.G. Coy	"	"
T/2/Lt. Platts J.R.A.	" "	" at duty	"
T/Lt. Brampton R.	116th M.G. Coy	" gas.	25.10.16
T/2/Lt Wise E.S.	V/39 T.M.B.	" gas	"
2/Lt. Heath M.B.	B/174 Bde.,R.F.A	"	27.10.16.

Unit	1	2	3	4	5	6	7	8	9	10	11	12	13	14	15	16	17	18	19	20	21	22	23	24	25	26	27	28	29	30	31	Total to date	Remarks
11th R Sussex R	7		1	1	1			3	1	2	6		1		4			1			1	118			1	1		4			11	161	
12th R Sussex R							5	5	1	4	2		5			46	42	23		4	42					3	19	2			3	191	
13 R Sussex R	2	2				5		3							1	4	9	2	5		48	7				19	11				1	135	
14 Hants Reg	1		4	5	2		9	32	25	28	1	3					32	50	8		2	1		1							1	122	
16 Notts Derby R							9	6	32	15	13		1		3	31	1	16	4	16	4	12		11	3	4		1	1			159	
17 Notts Derby R	1							6	7	1	4		1					16		6	87	1	29					1				148	
17 K R R C	1						15	16	2	4	2		3		3	2	32	2	1		112		5	5				16	1			195	
16 R Brigade										3	1		14		1	42	9	10			1	5	7	3								200	
1/6 Cheshire R	1	1	5	1		1		2				4	2	9	1	88			1					28	1					5		104	
4/5-13 Watch				1	3	3		3	6	3	2	5	1		14	3	12								5					1	8	194	
4/1 Herts R	4	1	4		3	3		3		1		16	7	11	14	6	1															72	
13 4 Leicester R	2		5	3	3			2							1	2	1	4	2	3	10	3										42	
RA	2						3								1	8		5			1	1	1									8	
RE									4							1					3											27	
ASC															5					5												15	
RAMC										3	1							1														15	
Y/39 HTMB	1				1																											1	
117 M G Coy	2							2	1	5	3				2	1						1										14	
R 2n Stradtong lec				1																												1	
X/39 TMB Y/39 TMB										2						1																2	
Z/39 TMB										2																						3	
112 M G Coy										1	1				11	2																24	
118 TMB															5	2																7	
116 M G Coy																				1	13			8								22	
Totals	19	8	11	12	13	34	69	94	122	52	29	23	41	26	45	59	121	57	83	62	52	13	488	14	81	21	32	11	19	4	6	25	2099
2 5 TMB 2 5 Div										2																						2
2 11 TMB 11 Div																	3															2
X/30 TMB 3 Canadian Div										3																						6
Z 130 TMB																	1															1
Grand Totals	19	8	11	12	13	34	69	94	122	57	31	23	41	26	45	59	124	61	83	62	52	13	488	14	81	21	32	11	19	4	6	25	2108

SECRET "A" T.q Brigades

WAR DIARY
or
INTELLIGENCE SUMMARY.
(Erase heading not required.)

Army Form C. 2118.

WO awQ 3 9
Page 1.
Vol A

Place	Date	Hour	Summary of Events and Information	Remarks and references to Appendices
	1916			
BOUZINCOURT CAMP.	1/11		116 Inf. Bde relieved by 118 Inf. Bde in the RIVER Section. Their Relief. F.C. TURNER C.M.G. Northumberland Fusiliers attd Hamilton Commandant 39 Div in Schools.	
BOUZINCOURT CAMP.	2/11		State of matin of rations postponed to Nov 7th. Very wet day.	
"	3/11		117 Inf Bde relieved 118 Inf Bde in the RIVER Section. Muddy and wet again.	
"	4/11		Owing to weather state of operations are indefinitely postponed.	
"	5/11		116 Inf. Bde relieved 117 Inf. Bde in RIVER Section. Very windy day.	
"	6/11		117 Inf Bde in Reserve 116 Inf Bde in RIVER Section.	

Army Form C. 2118.

Page 2

"A" H.Q. Braintree

WAR DIARY
INTELLIGENCE SUMMARY.
(Erase heading not required.)

Instructions regarding War Diaries and Intelligence Summaries are contained in F. S. Regs., Part II. and the Staff Manual respectively. Title pages will be prepared in manuscript.

Place	Date	Hour	Summary of Events and Information	Remarks and references to Appendices
BOUZINCOURT CAMP	1916 6/11		Zeppelin raid when the Fleet & on the SOMME front, started about 10.30 P.M. Kept being extinguished. Large ammunition dumps must of been hit as they have gone up.	
"	7/11		Operations again postponed indefinitely. Very heavy rain	
"	8/11		118 Inf Bde relieved 117 Inf Bde in the RIVER sector. Heavy showers	
"	9/11		Very fine day. Stronger westerly wind	
"	10/11		Orders received that our offensive will take place on Nov 13th.	
"	11/11		Major E.B. MATTHEW-LANNOWE the Queen's & 2nd Lt. DIXIE together with O/C TANKS. B.HQ and 12 Tanks proceeded to England on 12 Nov. but reporting at the War Office on arrival. 117 Inf Bde moved to 14 ARTILLERY, WOOD and SENLIS	

T2134. Wt. W708-776. 500000. 4/15. Sir J. C. & S.

"A" "Q" Branches.

Army Form C. 2118.

Page 3

WAR DIARY
of
INTELLIGENCE SUMMARY.
(Erase heading not required.)

Place	Date	Hour	Summary of Events and Information	Remarks and references to Appendices
BOUZINCOURT CAMP.	1916 11/4		118.Inf.Regt to move to AUTHUILLE BLUFFS and Huts in PIONEER ROAD. Misty day.	
"	12/4		Two prisoners of the 2nd Coy 1st Bn of 95th Regt. captured by 11th Royal Sussex Regt/116 Inf Bde last night. Captain R.H. OSBORNE 25th Huzzars joined 39 Divn as G.S.O.2.	
"	13/4		Offensive operations carried out by the Division. It attacked Castairn uts by the 118 Inf Regt to be with the 4th Hanstaini Regt 116 Inf Bde and 16th Notts & Derby Regt 117 Inf Bde all attain all objectives attained by 1st Division. 27 officers and 1,251 O.R. PRISONERS, passed through the 39th Divn cage up to 7pm.	
"	14/4		Orders received for the relief of 39 Divn by 19th Divn. 39 Divn to move to DOULLENS area.	

"A" HQ Branche.

Army Form C. 2118.

WAR DIARY
~~INTELLIGENCE~~ SUMMARY.
(Erase heading not required.)

Page 4

Place	Date	Hour	Summary of Events and Information	Remarks and references to Appendices
	1916			
BOUZINCOURT CAMP.	15/11		G.O.C. 39th DIVN. hands over command of the line to G.O.C. 19th DIVN. Divn HQ. remained at BOUZINCOURT CAMP.	
DOULLENS	16/11		Movement of the Division into DOULLENS area continued and completed. Divn HQ. closed at BOUZINCOURT CAMP at 11 am & opened same time at TOWN HALL DOULLENS. Orders received from VIII Corps for movement of DIVISION to POPERINGHE & ESQUELBECQ. Entrainment orders for the DIVISION from CANDAS and DOULLENS for the POPERINGHE and ESQUELBECQ area received.	
DOULLENS	17/11		Start of entrainment of 39th Divn less R.A. at CANDAS & DOULLENS stations of the "Yo-ho-chaem" of 39 Divn (39/1264/1Q) also received for Entrainment of 39 DIVN (39/1264/1Q).	
ESQUELBECQ	18/11	1130	Move of the DIVISION continues. Major of the Division VC MVO. Earl of DUMMORE. VC MVO. 16th Lancers joins the DIVISION as GSO.2. Vice Colonel R.H. Osborne posted to 1st ANZAC Corps. Report Centre opens at the ESQUELBECQ CHATEAU.	

"A" Branches.

WAR DIARY
INTELLIGENCE SUMMARY.

Army Form C. 2118.
Page 5

Place	Date	Hour	Summary of Events and Information	Remarks and references to Appendices
ESQUELBECQ	1918 19/11		Relief/entrainment of Divn completed.	
	M/20/11		39 R.A. withdrawn from line and moved to 'K' area.	
-	20/11		Nothing to report.	
-	21/11		39 R.A. moves into THIRD ARMY area.	
-	22/11		G.O.C. VIII Corps inspected 117 and 118 Infantry Brigades.	
-	23/11		Orders received that 118 Inf Bde will relieve 79th Territl (Fr[ench]) Regt. on night of Nov. 30th/1st Dec. G.O.C. VIII Corps inspected 116 Inf Bde.	
-	24/11		Major General G.J. Cuthbert CB CMG proceeds on leave to England. Brigadier General E.H. Finch HATTON. CMG DSO G.O.C. 118 Inf Bde assumed temporary command of 39 Division. 39 R.A. & FIRST Army area.	

Army Form C. 2118.

"A" H.Q. Branches

WAR DIARY
INTELLIGENCE SUMMARY.
(Erase heading not required.)

Page 6

Instructions regarding War Diaries and Intelligence Summaries are contained in F. S. Regs., Part II. and the Staff Manual respectively. Title pages will be prepared in manuscript.

Place	Date	Hour	Summary of Events and Information	Remarks and references to Appendices
ESQUELBECQ	19/6			
	25/6		Nothing to report	
	26/6		" " "	
"	27/6		HQ. 39 R.A. established at ESQUELBECQ. Brigadier General G. GILLSON DSO. CRA. 39 Divn assumed temporary command of Divn.	
"	28/6		118 Infantry Bde moved in under his setting up the line. 116 Brigade Hqrs to POPERINGHE. 1/1 Herts & Camb. J. 1/1 Cambridgeshire Rgt. to Camp J. 118 M.G. Coy and 118 T.M.B. to Camp.F: HQ 1/1 118 Infantry Bde & 4/5 Black Watch remained at WORMHOUDT 39 R.A. are situated as follows: 174,179 and 184 Bdes RFA at ARMEKE with 186 Bde at OCTEZEELE.	
"	29/6		118 Infantry Bde moved as follows: HQ 118 Infantry to ELVERDINGHE CHATEAU 4/5 Black Watch to Camp J: 116 Siebrue Rgt to West of ELVERDINGHE. 1/1 Cambridgeshire Rgt to ELVERDINGHE and to Defences. 118 M.G.C to the Tench. 118 T.M.B to Regina area W. of ELVERDINGHE. 1/1 Herts Rgt to Camp G. under G.O.C. 114 Infantry Bde 38th Welsh Divn.	

WAR DIARY
INTELLIGENCE SUMMARY

Army Form C. 2118.

Page 7

Place	Date	Hour	Summary of Events and Information	Remarks and references to Appendices
ESQUELBECQ	1916 30/11		13th Gloucestershire Regt (Pioneers) and 225 Field Coy RE relieve 19th Welsh Regt (Pioneers) and 221 Field Coy RE respectively of the 38th (Welsh) Division.	
			A list of casualties for the month of November is attached.	

B.C. Dugan Lt Col.
Major General
Comdg. 39 Division

17/12/1916.

Casualties.

November 1916.

Killed

Officers & Other Ranks.

Officers Killed to 31.10.16. = 108.

Officers (Killed)

Rank & Name		Unit	Casualty	Date
T. Lieut.	Harris H.J.L.	14th Bn. Hants Regt.	Killed	6:11:16
T. 2/Lt.	Fox F.D.	14th Notts & Derby Regt	"	5.11.16 (Reported 26.11.16)
T. 2/Lt.	Durant A.W.	184 Bde. R.F.A.	"	13:11:16
T. Lt.	Burch S.G.	16th Bn. Notts & Derby R.	"	"
T. 2/Lt.	Sewell H.V.	186 Bde. R.F.A.	"	"
Capt.	Kirk R.	1/6 Bn. Cheshire Regt	"	"
T. Capt.	Innes W.R.	" "	"	"
2/Lt.	Morrison R.C.	" "	"	"
2/Lt.	Sherriff L.F.D.	4/5 Bn. Black Watch	"	"

Total Killed to 30:11:1916 = 117.

Unit	1	2	3	4	5	6	7	8	9	10	11	12	13	14	15	16	17	18	19	20	21	22	23	24	25-26	27	28	29	30	Total to	Remarks
11th Bn R. Sussex Reg!	105	1									1		2																	109	
12th Bn R. Sussex Reg!	141	3	1								1		3																	149	
13th Bn R. Sussex Reg!	134					1																								135	
14th Bn Hampshire Reg	111	2				5																								118	
16th Bn Middx R'duksh!	43												5																	48	
17th Bn Middx R'duksh!	151			1	1								1																	154	
14th Bn K.R.R.C.	141						3																							144	
16th Bn Rifle Bde.	115			1		6																								122	
1/6 Bn Cheshire Reg!	48												26	1																75	
4/5 Black Watch	98									1			8	1																108	
110r Lancs Reg!	70	1							1	1			10																	83	
110r Hants Reg!	51												12	4																40	
13 Bn Glo'ster Reg!	40																													40	
Royal Artillery	10												2																	12	
Royal Engineers	8																													8	
A.S.C.	1																													1	
R.A.M.C.	10																													10	
X/39 T.M.B (Y.2)	4																													4	
114 M.G. Coy	3																													3	
118 M.G. Coy	4																													4	
116 M.G. Coy	5																													5	
Div. H.Q.	1																													1	
118 T.M.B.	1																													1	
Total	1325	5	3	-	1	1	8	8	-	2	1	1	1	69	9															1434	
Total	1325	5	3	-	1	1	8	8	-	2	1	1	1	69	9															1434	

SECRET

HQ APO 39 Page 1
Vol 10

WAR DIARY
of
INTELLIGENCE SUMMARY.
(Erase heading not required.)

Army Form C. 2118.

Instructions regarding War Diaries and Intelligence Summaries are contained in F. S. Regs., Part II. and the Staff Manual respectively. Title pages will be prepared in manuscript.

Place	Date	Hour	Summary of Events and Information	Remarks and references to Appendices
	1916			
ESQUELBECQ	1/12		Corps Conference at Head quarters VIII Corps: AA & QMG attended	
"	2/12			
"	3/12		Nothing to report	
"	4/12		Major General E. J. Cuthbert CB CMG returned from leave and resumed command of the Division	
"	5/12		11/D(S) Bn. R. Sussex Regt moved by rail to MOULLE: orders for move issued by SA/QMG, who was acting AA & QMG.	
"	6/12		G.O.C. Second Army inspected 116 and 117 Inf Bdg areas on route march	
"	7/12		Nothing to report.	
"	8/12		G.O.C. VIII & Corps inspected 117th Inf Bde & 17th Bn Sherwood	

Army Form C. 2118.

Page 2

WAR DIARY
INTELLIGENCE SUMMARY.
(Erase heading not required.)

Place	Date	Hour	Summary of Events and Information	Remarks and references to Appendices
ESQUELBECQ	8/12 1916		Foresters at Second Army School at TATINGHEM: Scouts at VOLKERINCKHOVE.	
"	9/12		Orders received from VIII Corps for 39 Divn to relieve 38 (Welsh) Divn in the left Sector starting 11 Dec 1916. 116/Inf Bde of 38 Divn will relieve 118 Inf Bde in the BOESINGHE sector.	
"	10/12		Orders received for 39 Divn to relieve 38 Divn. SC VIII Corps will clear 39 Divn Artillery at ARMÉ.	
"	11/12		Nothing to report	
"	12/12		Moves in accordance with 39 Divn Order no. 86. Carried out.	
"	13/12		116th Inf Bde to relieve 115th Inf Bde in Right Sector. 117th Inf Bde to relieve 117th Inf Bde in Left Sector.	

Army Form C. 2118.

Page 3

WAR DIARY
or
~~INTELLIGENCE SUMMARY.~~
(Erase heading not required.)

Instructions regarding War Diaries and Intelligence Summaries are contained in F. S. Regs., Part II. and the Staff Manual respectively. Title pages will be prepared in manuscript.

Place	Date	Hour	Summary of Events and Information	Remarks and references to Appendices
	1916			
ESQUELBECQ	14/12	am 6	Inspection of 39th Div. Artillery by G.O.C. Second Army Schools	
ST. SIXTE CONVENT		11.AM	39th Div. H.Q. Close at ESQUELBECQ CHATEAU and reopens at ST SIXTE CONVENT at same hour. Relief of 38th Div. Artillery by 39th Div. Artillery starts	
ST. SIXTE CONVENT	15/12		118 R (S) Fn. Regt. Smoke Regt. rejoins 116 Inf Bde from MOULLE	
"	16/12		Relief of 38th Div. Artillery completed	
"	17/12		Nothing to report.	
"	18/12			
"	19/12			
"	20/12		17th Stewart Fusiliers rejoins 117 L. Inf Bde.	

T2134. Wt. W708—776. 500000. 4/15. Sr J.C. & S.

Army Form C. 2118.

Page 4

WAR DIARY
or
INTELLIGENCE SUMMARY.

(Erase heading not required.)

Instructions regarding War Diaries and Intelligence Summaries are contained in F. S. Regs., Part II. and the Staff Manual respectively. Title pages will be prepared in manuscript.

Place	Date	Hour	Summary of Events and Information	Remarks and references to Appendices
	1916			
ST SIXTE CONVENT.	21/12	2.30 p.m.	The Commandant-in-Chief watched 118 Inf Bde in Centia. The arrangements made for inspection of 118 Inf Bde cancelled owing to bad weather	
"	22/12		Nothing to report.	
"	23/12		Raid by the Enemy who succeeded in reaching our front line trench. Relief by 117 & 118 Inf Bde of 38th Divr on completion rate 2 OR killed 4 OR wounded 5 OR and missing 8 OR	
"	24/12		118th Inf Bde reviewed by 116 Inf Bde in the right sector	
"	25/12		A very wet CHRISTMAS DAY.	
"	26/12 27/12 28/12		Nothing to report.	

WAR DIARY

Army Form C. 2118.

Page 5

Place	Date	Hour	Summary of Events and Information	Remarks and references to Appendices
ST. SIXTE CONVENT	1916 29/12		39th DIVISIONAL REINFORCEMENT Camp formed at 'F' Camp. Major H A LEGGATT 16th Sherwood Foresters attached to command. All infantry reinforcements to be sent to the camp on arrival from Base. Battalions in divisions completed with equipment. If anything cannot be made good, after further training camp will be shot at 'Reserve Army Musketry Camp' at TILQUES. He Trained reinforcements will join units forthwith.	
"	30/12		16 Sh. Fus. Rd. relieves 115 Inf. Bd. (38th Welsh Divn.) in BOESINGHE Sector 113th Inf. Bd. (38 Welsh Divn) moves to D.E.P. and S. Camps and comes under the orders of G.O.C. 39 Divn. as a Tactical Reserve	
"	31/12		Nothing to report.	
			Summary of Casualties for December 1916 is attached.	

S.C. Owen Major for
Major General
Commanding 39 DIVISION

31/12/1916.

Casualties December 1916.
Killed.
Officers and Other Ranks.

Officers.

Rank & Name	Unit	Casualty	Date

Unit	1	2	3	4	5	6	7	8	9	10	11	12	13	14	15	16	17	18	19	20	21	22	23	24	25	26	27	28	29	30	31	Total to 31/1/24	Remarks
11 R Sussex Regt															1						1											2	
12 R Sussex Regt																								2								2	
13 R Sussex Regt																																	
Northamptonshire Regt																							1	1	3							5	
16 Notts & Derby Regt																		2							9							11	
17 Notts & Derby Regt																																	
12 KRRC Corps																1	2						3	1	1							8	
16 Middx Regt																																	
16 Cheshire Regt																																	
4/5 Black Watch																																1	
11 Camb Regt			4																													4	
14 Hants Regt																																	
13 Ch. of Essex Regt																																	
Royal Artillery																																	
Royal Engineers																																	
A S C																																	
RAMC																																	
X.Y.Z./39 TMbty																								1								1	
117 H.T. Coy																																1	
118 H.T. Coy																		1														1	
116 H.T. Coy																																	
Div. Hdqrs																																	
118 T.H.Bty																																	
Total			4												1	1	3	2			1			5	2	6	9					1	35	

Casualties December 1916.

Wounded.

Officers and Other Ranks.
===

Officers. Wounded & Missing

Rank	Name	Unit	Casualty	Date
2 Lieut	Hendry J.	4/5 Black Watch	Acc. Wounded	4.12.16.
Major	Bowes. G.B.	1/1st Cambs.	" "	12.12.16.
T 2/Lieut	Hill P.H.	12th Sussex	Wounded	15.12.16.

Unit	Total to 30/11/16	1	2	3	4	5	6	7	8	9	10	11	12	13	14	15	16	17	18	19	20	21	22	23	24	25	26	27	28	29	30	31	Total to 31/12/16	Remarks
11th R. Sussex R.																																		4	
12th R. Sussex R.																						3	2	1	4									8	
13th R. Sussex R.																																			
14th Hampshire R.																			3															3	
16th Notts & Derby R.																								13	2	7	1							22	
17th Notts & Derby R.																										1								1	
16 Rifle Brigade																								4	2	1	1	1						10	
17th Bn K.R.R. Corps																2					2	2				6	1							11	
1/6 Bn. Cheshire Rgt.																											4					1		5	
4/5 Bn. Black Watch																																			
1/1 Bn. Cambs. Rgt.																											1							1	
1/1 Herts R.							1																											1	
13 G Leaders Rgt.																																			
Royal Fd Artillery																								1	–									1	
Royal Engineers																																			
A.S.C.																																			
R. of A.M.C.											8																							8	
V/59 H.T.M. Bty.																																			
117th M.G. Coy.																																			
Div. Hdqts.																																			
X.Y.Z/59 T.M. Btys.																																			
118th M.G. Coy.																																			
118th T.M. Bty.																																			
116th M.G. Coy.																																1		1	
Totals.							1				8					2	2				5	2	5	20	8	8	13		1			1		76	

SECRET

"A"&"Q" Branches

WAR DIARY
INTELLIGENCE SUMMARY

Army Form C. 2118

Vol XI Page 1

Place	Date	Hour	Summary of Events and Information	Remarks and references to Appendices
ST. SIXTE CONVENT.	1917 1st Jan	10 AM	General Officer Commanding VIII Corps presents Montenegrin Decoration at VIII Corps Headquarters (CHATEAU. LOVIE) to Brigadier General GILLMAN D.S.O. C.R.A. 39 Division and H-Colonel F.W. GOSSET D.S.O. R.A. G.S.O.1 39 Division.	
		4.1 PM	The enemy attempted to raid one of our posts near FORWARD COT-TAGE in three succeeded in entering our trenches. If one was made two were brought to 9th Rifle Battn. In casualties were 4/5 R.A.R. 1 Other Rank wounded one O.R. killed, 1 Officer ranks wounded 1 Officer missing 13th Gloucester Regt. (Pioneers) O.R. one.	
	2nd		Weather fine, nothing further to report.	
	3rd do			
	4 do			
	5 do			
	6 do			

Army Form C. 2118.

Page 2

"A"/"Q" Branches
WAR DIARY
or
INTELLIGENCE SUMMARY.
(Erase heading not required.)

Place	Date	Hour	Summary of Events and Information	Remarks and references to Appendices
ST SIXTE CONVENT.	1917 7/1		A party of the enemy (estimated strength about 40) raided No. 6 post, succeeded in getting through on our right. Nos 4 & 5 posts — three of our garrison were taken prisoners and the remainder were wounded.	
"	8/1		Conference at VIII Corps H.Q. :— At 2 P.M. G.O.C. attended 39 Divn. Order No. 89 received directing following reliefs: 118 Inf. Bde in HILLTOP Section by 114 Inf Bde of 38 (Welsh) Divn 117 " " — " LANCASHIRE FARM " " 113 " " " " " " 116 " " — " BOESINGHE " " 115 " " " " " " Also further reliefs: 118 Inf Bde to relieve 165 Inf Bde of 55 Divn in WIELTJE Section 116 " " — " 164 " " — " RAILWAY WOOD " 17 Inf Bde were relieved to become Divisional Reserve and located at A.B.C. & D Camps (N.E. of POPERINGHE).	

T2134. Wt. W708—776. 50C000. 4/15. Sir J. C. & S.

Army Form C. 2118.

Page 3.

A.Q Branches

WAR DIARY

INTELLIGENCE SUMMARY.

(Erase heading not required.)

Place	Date	Hour	Summary of Events and Information	Remarks and references to Appendices
ST SIXTE CONVENT.	11/1 9/1 10/1 11/1		Nothing to report except weather unsettled	
"	12/1		Relief as ordered in S.O. 89. in progress.	
"	13/1		118 Inf. Bde relieved by 14 Inf. Bde 3Bde (Welsh)Division 166 Bde (55 Div) relieved by 118 Inf. Bde.	
"	14/1		117 Inf. Bde relieved by 113 Inf. Bde 3 Bde (Welsh) Div weather cold and fine.	
" A 25 d.2.6 HAMHOEK Camp	15/1	Am 10.15 Noon	G.O.C. 39 Divn hands over command of LEFT SECTOR VIII Corps Front G.O.C. 39 Divn takes over command of RIGHT Section VIII Corps Front from G.O.C. 55th (WEST LANCASHIRE) DIVISION	

WAR DIARY
INTELLIGENCE SUMMARY

Place	Date	Hour	Summary of Events and Information	Remarks and references to Appendices
HAM HOEK CAMP.	1917 16/1		116 Inf Bde relieved in the BOESINGHE Section by 115 Inf Bde. A cold day.	
"	17/1		Infantry reliefs completed; cold weather continues, with continuing snowing. 39 Divl Artillery start relieving 55 Divn Artillery.	
"	18/1		Snow continues. Artillery reliefs completed.	
"	19/1		Frosts and cold continues.	
"	20/1		" " "	
"	21/1		Frost and cold continue; two O.R. of a German patrol were surrendered.	
"	20/2		Colonel H.F. DAVIES M.C. of the Royal FUSILIERS Staff Captain 12 Infantry Brigade assumed duties of Deputy Assistant Quartermaster General 39th Divison, vice Major E.J. de PENTHENY O'KELLY. of the Royal WELSH FUSILIERS attached to 15th Battalion Royal WELSH FUSILIERS.	

"A" "Q" Branches
WAR DIARY
or
INTELLIGENCE SUMMARY

Army Form C. 2118.
Page 5

Place	Date	Hour	Summary of Events and Information	Remarks and references to Appendices
HAMHOEIR CAMP	1917 24/1		G.O.C. Second Army visits 117 Inf. Bde in Reserve Camp (ABCAD). Brevet Major A.E.S. CLARKE, M.V.O. D.A.A. & Q.M.G. 39th Division, assumed duties of Assistant Adjutant and Quartermaster General 39th Division, vice 2nd Lieut-Colonel B.C. DWYER, D.S.O., A.S.C., the Leicestershire Regt., who proceeded to England on leave.	
—	25/1		G.O.C. Second Army visits 39 Divn. H.Q. Conference at H.Q. VIII Corps. 117 Inf. Bde relieve 118 Inf. Bde in the WIELTJE Sector.	
—	26/1 to 31/1		Cold weather continues	

Summary of Casualties for Month of January 1917 attached.

R. Dick Major
for Major General
Commanding 39th Divn.
January 1917 attached.

Casualties

January 1917

Killed

Officers & Other Ranks.

Officers

Rank	Name	Unit	Casualty	Date
2/Lt (T/Capt)	Smallwood GF	1/Herts	Killed	7-1-17
T 2/Lieut	Thompson FD	17 KRRC	"	13-1-17
T 2/Lieut	Beale CE	16 High Lds	Wounded S. D/W	29-1-17
T/Major	Hagerty WS	13 Sussex	"	31-1-17

Unit	1	2	3	4	5	6	7	8	9	10	11	12	13	14	15	16	17	18	19	20	21	22	23	24	25	26	27	28	29	30	31	Total
11th Bn R. Innisk'g																							3									3
12th —do—																								1								1
13th —do—																														2	2	6
14th Bn Hamps R.							1																								1	1
16th Bn Midd'x Derbys							1								1																	1
17th Bn Midd'x Derbys															1																	1
14th Bn N.F.			1																													1
10th Bn R. Dub. Fus																																1
11th Bn R.I. Rif																																1
Hist Bn Donald			1										4									1										6
11 Bn Central			1										3																			1
11 Bn Herts Re							2																									6
13th Bn Glosters			1										2																			3
Royal Artillery														1																		1
Royal Engineers																																
QAD																																
AOMC																																
X/39 Y/39 Z/30 M.B.														1																		
117 m. G.C.																																
115 m. G.C.																															1	1
116 m. G.C.																																
DHQ																							1									
115 Tm. B																																
Totals	3	1				2	1			2			4	2	1							1	4							3	3	30

Casualties Jan 1917.

Wounded

Officers & Other Ranks

Officers Wounded & Missing

Rank	and Name	Unit	Casualty	Date
2/Lieut	Paul WB	4/5 Bl Watch	Wounded	1.1.17
T/Capt	Jones CWJ	Cam Batt of KRRC	" S at D	3.1.17
T/2/Lieut	Hallam JD	17th Notts & Derby	"	4.1.17
T/2/Lieut	Bowmer V	16th — " —	"	5.1.17
T/Lieut	Peterson GHJ	14th Hants	" accd	9.1.17
T/2/Lieut	Spreckley WM	16 Notts Derbys	"	14.1.17
2/Lieut	Dramant AW	174 Bde RFA	" S at D	13.1.17
2/Lieut	Yates HS	1/6 Chesh (5 Chesh atc)	"	24.1.17
2/Lieut	Pratt RM	" (1/4 Chesh atc)	"	"
Capt	Lilley CK	82 San Sec	"	26.1.17
T/Capt & Adjt	Coxhead RJ	13 Sussex	"	30.1.17
Maj (T/Lt Col)	Draffen JW	13 Sussex (Scots Rfls)	"	31.1.17

April	1	2	3	4	5	6	7	8	9	10	11	12	13	14	15	16	17	18	19	20	21	22	23	24	25	26	27	28	29	30	31	Totals
11th L Swaby R	1																			1	1				15	1	1			1		20
12th —do—																									4	1						7
13th —do—							1	1	1	1			1				1					1					1	1	10	1		24
14th Hawk R													2	2								1		1					4	2	1	15
16th Northern Derby	2					2	1			1	2	1		1					1			3										11
16th —do—													2													2			1			5
16th K.Al. Spkr	2					1			2		1	1														1			3	6		16
14th A R C															1							2										5
16 Archer L			1			2							2			1	1	1					2									7
145 Black Watch	11	1							1				2	4	2	2	1	2							2	1						31
71 Camb Regt		3				1										1	1															8
76 Rifle Brig	6		15											3																		30
134 Glosh Regt	3					1			12					2	4																	15
Royal Artillery						2	1							1				1					3	1								14
Royal Engineer																	1					3	1									2
B L E																																
104 N G													1																			1
V/39 H A.Inf B																																
111 M G C																																
10 R G																																
X Y Z Inf Bs						1																								1		
115 M G C	1																															1
115 Inf Bs																																
116 M G C									1																							2
Totals	3	25	3	3	1	20	5	6	4	16	3	12	4	9	6	3	2	4	3	2	4	4	24	5	2	2	2	18	19	215

SECRET

Army Form C. 2118.

"A" + "Q" Branches
WAR DIARY 39 Div

~~INTELLIGENCE SUMMARY~~

Vol 12 Page 1

Place	Date	Hour	Summary of Events and Information	Remarks and references to Appendices
HAMHOEK Camp. A.25.D.2.6.	1917 1/2		Enemy attempt to raid our line in the RAILWAY WOOD Section, Lt-----did not penetrate and portion of it. One man of the 163rd. Infantry Regt. taken prisoner by a listening patrol from 14 Hampshire Regt. Led by Captain GOLDSMITH. Our casualties were killed Officers 2 Wounded 1 other Ranks 7 --- 14.	
"	2/2		Nothing to report	
"	3/2		118 Inf Bde started to relieve 117 Inf Bde in METZE Section. 1 Battalion 116 Inf Bde relieved by 2 Battns of 117 Inf Bde in the RAILWAY WOOD Section.	
"	4/2		Completion of relief of 117 Inf Bde by 118 Inf Bde in METZE Section and 116 Inf Bde by 117 Inf Bde in RAILWAY WOOD Section.	

Army Form C. 2118.

Page

"A" Branch
WAR DIARY
INTELLIGENCE SUMMARY
(Erase heading not required.)

Instructions regarding War Diaries and Intelligence Summaries are contained in F.S. Regs., Part II. and the Staff Manual respectively. Title pages will be prepared in manuscript.

Place	Date	Hour	Summary of Events and Information	Remarks and references to Appendices
	1917			
HAZEBROUCK CAMP A25d 2.6	4/2		116 Inf Bde go into A.B.C.D. Camps as Divisional Reserve. A very cold day.	
"	5/2 6/2 7/2 8/2		Intensely cold. Our fine weather continues.	
"	9/2	10 am	Funeral of GENERAL BAGNANI attached Second Army Headquarters. Cortège left HÔTEL SAUVAGE CASSEL at 10 a.m. the following officers attended: Major D.C. OWEN, DAA & QMG; Lt Colonel S. PARSONS DSO, Commanding 39 Div Train and T/Major F.R. LEITH, ADC GOC 39 Div. A bitterly cold but fine day.	A

WAR DIARY

INTELLIGENCE SUMMARY

Army Form C. 2118.

Page 3

F.Q. Canadian

Place	Date	Hour	Summary of Events and Information	Remarks and references to Appendices
HAM H+ Etc Camp A25C 26	1919 10/2		Orders received for the relief by 39 Divn. by 55 Divn. on the 15, 16, 17 and 18 of Feb. inst. 39 Divn. is moving the relief with the requisite on ESQUELBECQ CHATEAU the Brigade in camp at POPERINGHE and one Brigade at BOLLDER.	
" "	11/2		Lt. Colonel A.F. STEWART to Suffolk Regt. assumes duties of A/A & QMG 39 Divn. A/Lt Col Y.O. 13th in agn for Col. A.E.S. CLARKE, Mjr. + Bt. Col. Chandler AA & QMG 39th Divn. sick.	
" "	NIGHT OF 12/2 13/2		Raid by 11 Hertfordshire Rgt.[T.F.] who lost 2 known [other ?] to 161st. Infantry Bgd.	
" "	13/2 14/2		Raid by 16th Rifle Bde : no known losses Weather continues fine	

F/O branch
WAR DIARY
INTELLIGENCE SUMMARY
(Erase heading not required.)

Army Form C. 2118.

Page 4.

Place	Date	Hour	Summary of Events and Information	Remarks and references to Appendices
HAMHOEK CAMP. A.25.d.26	1917 DEC 15/2		Relief of 39th Division by the 55th Division begins. Weather starts to break up.	
"	16/2		116 Infantry Brigade relieved by 164 Inf. Bde 55th Division. It forms move to the BOLLEZEELE area for ABCO camps. Personnel carried by Vienne trams from POPERINGHE CHEESE MARKET starting train-by-train at intervals. Provision for emergence of December 25th.	
"	17/2		118 Inf. Bde relieved by 166 Inf. Bde (55 Divn) to the MELTZE Sector, proceeded by L, Y, Z camps. 117 Inf Bde relieved by 165 Inf Bde (55 Divn) to Railway Wood Sector moved to D E G P camps, becoming Divl. Reserve. G 38 (Welsh) Divn. 13 th Gloucestershire Regt (Pioneers) relieved by 1/4 South Lancashire Regt, and entrained at POPERINGHE CHEESEMARKET station.	

Army Form C. 2118.

H.Q. Branch
WAR DIARY
or
INTELLIGENCE SUMMARY.
(Erase heading not required.)

Page 5.

Place	Date	Hour	Summary of Events and Information	Remarks and references to Appendices
HAMHOEK Camp A.25.d.2.6.(why)	1917 17/2		On received reinforcements for BEGGAR'S CAMP Billets were arranged in POPERINGHE for night of 16th/17th. The following for whole Battn.	
	18/2	7pm	39 DH.Q moves to ESQUELBECQ CHATEAU immediately 55 Divn	
ESQUELBECQ	19/2		Orders received for the relief of 23rd Divn	
" — "	20/2, 21/2, 22/2		Nothing to report except westerly mists and sleet.	
" — "	23/2	12 MID NIGHT	39 Divn passed from the command of VIII to X Corps.	
" — "	24/2		16/S/F/13 de moved by several trains from BOLLEZEELE area to camps in OUDERDOM Area, establishing Headquarters in POPERINGHE	

Army Form C. 2118.

Page 6

A.Q. Branch
WAR DIARY
or
INTELLIGENCE SUMMARY
(Erase heading not required.)

Place	Date	Hour	Summary of Events and Information	Remarks and references to Appendices
	1917			
ESQUELBECQ CHATEAU.	25/2		116 Inf Bde relieved by Inf Bde (23rd Divn) in the Right Section of the ex Corps LEFT Section: 39th DAC relieved 23rd DAC.	
" "	26/2		117 Inf Bde relieved 68 Inf Bde (23rd Divn) in the Left Section, 23rd Divn front.	
" "	27/2		118 Inf Bde moved from L of C camps in OUDEZEEM area with Headquarters at POPERINGHE.	
REMINGHELST		10AM	Headquarters 39 Divn moved from ESQUELBECQ CHATEAU to REMINGHELST, and G.O.C. 39 DIVN takes over command of the LEFT DINSMYRAL SECTOR of the x Corps from G.O.C 23rd DIVN.	
" "	28/2		39th Divnl Artillery relieves 23rd Divnl or Artillery	
			A Summary of Casualties for Feb. 1917 is attached.	

A. Stewart McDowel for Major General
Comdg 39th Divison

'A'

FUNERAL OF GENERAL BAGNANI.

1. On going to the Church from the Hotel Sauvage, the order of the procession will be :-

    Pall Bearers.
    Four on each side of the coffin.

    Mourners and Italian Representatives.

    Representatives from Armies, Corps, &c., who will form up in fours in order of seniority, with junior officers in front. Representatives from the French and Belgian Armies, Army Commander and representative of the Commander-in-Chief.

2. On arrival at the Church -

    Pall Bearers.
    Will walk on each side of the coffin up the aisle and remain standing each side of the coffin during the service.

    Representatives.
    Will sit behind the Mourners and Italian Representatives.

3. On leaving the Church -

    Pall Bearers.
    Will accompany the coffin as before.

    Representatives.
    Will follow out and form up outside the Church in the same order as previously mentioned.

4. The procession will move from the Church in the following order :-

    Band and Drums.
    One Company of Infantry.
    Priests.
    Pall Bearers.   Coffin.   Pall Bearers.
    Mourners.
    Italian Representatives.
    Representatives from Armies and Corps in fours.
    Belgian Representatives.
    French Representatives.
    Army Commander.   Commander-in-Chief's Representative.
    Officer Commanding Infantry Battalion.
    Three Companies Infantry Battalion.

5. On arrival at Cemetery -

    Pall Bearers.
    Will accompany coffin to side of grave and stand clear of Priests and Mourners.

    Representatives.
    Will follow behind the coffin to the grave and then group themselves, with senior officers in front.

    Hats will <u>not</u> be removed.

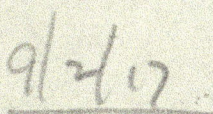

Original

Casualties
February 1917
Killed

Officers and Other Ranks

Officers

Rank & Name	Unit	Casualty	Date
T 2/Lieut Colebrook L.C.	14 Bn Hants R.	Killed	1.2.17
" Humphrey Davy I.H.W.	"	"	"
2/Lieut Turner R.S.	12 Bn R Sussex R.	"	3.2.17
T 2/Lieut Rowe A.H.	17 Bn Notts & Derby	"	4.2.17
T 2/Lieut MacLehose J.C.	11 Bn Rifle Bde	"	14.2.17
2/Lieut Carr C.J.	17 Bn Notts & Derby	Wd 14/2/17 Died of wounds 20/2/17	20.2.17

Unit	1	2	3	4	5	6	7	8	9	10	11	12	13	14	15	16	17	18	19	20	21	22	23	24	25	26	27	28	Total
11th Inf Swords Rgt				4																								4	
12th Inf Swords Rgt														4														4	
13th Inf Swords Rgt																												1	1
14th Inf Swords Rgt	1					1		2		1		2																7	
14th Inf Swords Bn								2	2			2	3	3	1	1									1			5	
14th Inf Arty Co					1						1			1														3	
16th Inf Cavalry Rgt													3		1													2	
16th Inf Black Watch								1		2					1														
17th Inf Combat Rgt								1					1															1	
11 Inf Regt Rgt										1	1																	1	
Bdyn Etobiledgt	4																											6	
Royal Artillery																												1	
Royal Engineers					1																								
1/39 Sm Bn																												1	
Total	11	—	4	—	1	1	3	3	—	—	5	3	2	15	1	1										2			53

"Original"

Casualties

February 1917.

Wounded

Officers and Other Ranks.

Officers :- Wounded and Missing.

Rank and Name.		Unit	Casualty	Date.
2nd Lt. (Acting Capt.)	Bircham. B.O.	14 Hants.	Wounded	1.2.17.
T. 2nd Lt.	Wentworth. C.J.	12 Sussex.	"	3.2.17.
Major (T. Lt. Col.)	Milward. H.M.	17 Notts & Derby.	"	4.2.17.
T. Lt.	Andrew. J.F.	4/5 Black Watch	" at duty	7.2.17.
Lt.	Ffrench. D.M.	4 Suffolks attd. 1/1 Cambs.	" "	9.2.17.
Lt. (A/Capt.)	Kil'Kelly. E.C.R.	186 Bde. R.F.A.	" S.a.d.	11.2.17.
2nd Lt.	Barnes. A.S.	" "	" "	"
2nd Lt.	Crowdy. E.J.	174 Bde. R.F.A.	" "	"
2nd Lt.	Leach. T.S.	14 Hants.	" acc.	12.2.17.
T. Capt.	Kenward. S.	16 Rifle Bde.	"	13.2.17.
T. Lt.	Robinson. G.M.	"	"	14.2.17.
T. 2nd Lt.	Wilson. A.	"	"	14.2.17.
2nd Lt.	Gordon. H.E.	"	"	14.2.17.
T. 2nd. Lt.	Dorg. D.S.	186 Bde. R.F.A.	" S.a.d.	13.2.17.
Lt. (Actg. Capt.)	Kil'Kelly E.C.R.	" "	"	"
2nd Lt.	Sketch. H.J.	277 Bde. R.A. attd. 39 R.A.	"	"
2nd Lt.	Keighley L.R.	1/5 Rl. Lancs. 55th Div. (attd)	"	16.2.17.
2nd Lt.	Hollis B.	4/5 Black Watch.	"	13.2.17.

Unit.	1	2	3	4	5	6	7	8	9	10	11	12	13	14	15	16	17	18	19	20	21	22	23	24	25	26	27	28	Total.
11th Bn. R. Sussex Regt.			1					3	3	2	1	1		4														1	12
12th do do		2	6							1				1															10
13th do do	3																									2	1		6
14th Bn. Hampshire Regt.	15																								1	2	3		21
16th Bn. Notts & Derby Regt.	1	2		1		2			1	5	8	1	3	6	1								3						34
17th do do	3	1					1			1	3	1	12	1	8	2										1			35
16th Bn. Rifle Brigade.	2			3					2	1			41	1	1	2													53
14th Bn. K.R.R.C.	3	1	1					1	2		4			3	1														18
1/6 Bn. Cheshire Regt.						1				2	5		2	7	1														18
4/5 Bn. Black Watch.						2	1		5	4	1		1	1	4											1			19
1/1 Bn. Cambs. Regt.						1			2		1	1	4	1	3	1													15
1/1 Bn. Herts. Regt.								1					4		1														6
13th Bn. Gloucester Regt.								1					1	1															3
Royal Artillery	1	4								1	1	3	1	2	6	2	1												22
Royal Engineers										2	1			1	1														5
Army Service Corps																													
Royal Army Medical Corps												1																	1
1/39 H.T.M. Bty.												1																	1
114 M.G. Coy.							1	4			1				1														6
X.Y.&Z/39 T.M.Btys																												2	2
118 M.G. Coy.													2		1														3
116 M.G. Coy.	1																												1
TOTALS	29	10	8	2	3	1	8	6	18	19	23	4	36	68	19	5	12	1					3		1	2	4	3	291

SECRET

Army Headquarters

WAR DIARY
INTELLIGENCE SUMMARY.

Army Form C. 2118.

Aug 39th Div

Page 1

Month: Mch 13

Place	Date	Hour	Summary of Events and Information	Remarks and references to Appendices
REMINGHELST E.34 d.3.0 Sheet 28.	1917 1/3		G.O.C. X Corps inspects 118 Infantry Brigade in Reserve	
"	2/3 3/3		Nothing to report.	
"	4/3		Completion of relief of 116 Infty Brigade in the Right Section by 118 Inf. Bde — 116 Inf. Bde now in Corps Reserve in camps in OUDERDOM Area. Very cold day.	
"	5/3		Snow fell during the night but disappeared very quickly during the day.	
"	6/3 7/3		Weather is still very cold.	
"	8/3		Major General C.J. Cuffe — C.B, C.M.G. proceeds on leave. Br. General G. Gillson D.S.O. CRA 39 Div, assumes Control as...	

H.Q. Branch

WAR DIARY

INTELLIGENCE SUMMARY

Army Form C. 2118.

Page 2

Place	Date	Hour	Summary of Events and Information	Remarks and references to Appendices
REINGHELST	1917 8/3	(Contin-ued)	Command of the Divn. Relief of Machine Gun Coy. & 1 T.M. Battery of 118 Inf Bde by 116 G.O.C Bde as in the Right Section	
	9/3		116 Inf. Bde relieves 118 Inf Bde in the Right Section. 118 " " " " " " Left Section 117 " " becomes Corps Reserve in OUDERDOM Area. Brigadier General G.A. Armitage D.S.O. assumed Command of 117 Inf. Bde vice Br. General R.J.F. Oldman DSO who proceeded to England to Command a Training Brigade	
			Weather very unsettled; nothing to report.	
	15/3		Completion of relief of the 118 Inf Bde by 117 Inf Bde in the Left Section	

Army Form C. 2118.

Page 3

A.Q. branch

WAR DIARY
or
INTELLIGENCE SUMMARY
(Erase heading not required.)

Instructions regarding War Diaries and Intelligence Summaries are contained in F. S. Regs., Part II. and the Staff Manual respectively. Title pages will be prepared in manuscript.

Place	Date	Hour	Summary of Events and Information	Remarks and references to Appendices
	1917			
REMICOURT	19/3 to 20/3		Slight improvement in weather.	
"	21/3		118 Infantry Brigade relieve 119. Infantry who it now become X Corps Reserve. Showers of rain during the day.	
"	22/3 23/3		Some firing the day	
"	24/3	11 PM	Introduction of summer time: 11PM become 12 midnight	
"	25/3		Nothing to return	
"	26/3 27/3	10.35 AM	The enemy's long l estimates at about 40 to 50 attacked in front of St PETER'S St Wr. attack was repulsed. Our casualties killed O.R. 4: Wounded 1 Officer and O.R. 20.	

Army Form C. 2118.

Page 4.

A.Q. March.
WAR DIARY
or
INTELLIGENCE SUMMARY.
(Erase heading not required.)

Instructions regarding War Diaries and Intelligence Summaries are contained in F. S. Regs., Part II. and the Staff Manual respectively. Title pages will be prepared in manuscript.

Place	Date	Hour	Summary of Events and Information	Remarks and references to Appendices
	1917			
REMICOURT	27/3		Two Battalions of 118 Inf Bde relieves in Right Front Sector by 2 Bns 116 Inf Bde in support of the Left Sector. Battalions of 117 Inf Bde	
"	28/3		Completion of Inf Bde Relief: 116 & 117 B. Left Right Sections, 118 Inf Bde in front Section and 117 Inf Bde in OUDERDOM Area in Corps Reserve.	
"	29/3		Major General E.G. Cuthbert C.B. CMG. returned from leave & resumed command of the 39th Division.	
"	30/3		Nothing to report.	
"	31/3		A list of casualties for March 1917 is attached.	

E.P. Newton Welwood
for Major General
Commdg 39 Division.

Casualties

March 1917.

Killed

Officers and Other Ranks.

===========

Officers.

Rank and Name.	Unit	Casualty	Date

Unit	1	2	3	4	5	6	7	8	9	10	11	12	13	14	15	16	17	18	19	20	21	22	23	24	25	26	27	28	29	30	31	Total to 31/3/34
11th Bn. R. Sussex Regt.	2	1												2							1											6
12th " " "	3	3												2																		8
13th " " "	2																					1										3
14th Bn. Hampshire Regt.																																
16th Bn. Notts & Derby Regt.															3																	4
14th " " "							1								1																	2
14th Bn. K.R.R.C.															1																	1
16th Bn. Rifle Brigade	1																															
1/6 Bn. Cheshire Regt.																									2							2
4/5 Bn. Black Watch																									4							4
1/1 Bn. Cambs. Regt.														2											2							4
1/1 Bn. Herts Regt.	3														4																	7
13th Bn. Gloucester Regt.	1																															1
Royal Artillery																		1														1
Royal Engineers																																1
A.S.C.	1						1																		1							
R.A.M.C.	1																															1
39th T.M. Battye (X,Y,Z)																																1
116 M.G. Coy.																																
117 M.G. Coy.																																
118 M.G. Coy.																																
Divisional Hdqrs.																																
118 T.M. Battery.																																
TOTAL	6	8	4			1								10		3		1			1	1			9		2					46

Casualties

March 1917.

Wounded

Officers and Other Ranks.

Officers :– Wounded and Missing

Rank and Name	Unit	Casualty	Date
T. 2/Lt. P.L. CLARK	11th Sussex	Wounded at duty	28.2.17
" J.C. WEBBER	"	"	"
Capt. A.H.B. CHAPLIN	1/1st Cambs.	"	14.3.17.
2nd/Lt. L. BULL	1/1 Herts att. 1/1 Cambs.	"	"
T. 2nd/Lt. G.W. TURNPENNEY	17 N & D.	" S.a.d.	16.3.17.
2nd/Lt. A. RANGDALE	"	"	"
T. 2nd/Lt. E.G. KEMPSON	17 KRRC	" acc.	17.3.17.
T. Capt. E. KROLIK	16 Rifle Bde.	" S.a.d.	23.3.17.
T. 2/Lt. H.C.R. BUTCHER	174 Bde R.F.A.	"	24.3.17.
2nd/Lt. HICKLEY. R.T.N.	1/1st Herts.	"	25.3.17.
" S.H. FREEMAN	186 Bde R.F.A.	"	27.3.17.

Unit	1	2	3	4	5	6	7	8	9	10	11	12	13	14	15	16	17	18	19	20	21	22	23	24	25	26	27	28	29	30	31	Total to 31.3.17
11th Bn. R. Sussex Regt.	14	1	5																												2	22
12th Bn " "	20	1												3											1				1			26
13th Bn " "										4	4					1	1	5	2	2	1									1	1	22
14th Bn Hampshire Regt.										1	1	1					5	1														9
16th Bn Notts & Derby Regt.	1																	1	1					1	1							5
17th " "	2	1	1	1										3											1		2		1		1	13
16th Bn Rifle Brigade																										1			1			2
17th Bn K.R.R.C.	1													4	1							1	1	1							1	10
1/6 Bn Cheshire Regt.									2	1														1		1						5
4/5 Bn Black Watch			2	1							1				1												2	2	1		1	14
1/1 Bn Cambs Regt.			1													2					1	1					7	2	1			15
1/1 Bn Herts Regt.				1						1								1	1				1			1	1		11	4	1	24
13th Bn Gloucester Regt.	17	1													2	1						3	1		1	2	2			3		30
Royal Artillery	1	7	1																				2				1	1	2	3		16
Royal Engineers	1	6																					1							1		10
A.S.C.																																
R.A.M.C.	1	1																														2
V/39 H.T.M. Battery																																
114 M.G. Coy.		1																					1		3							5
Divisional Hdqrs.																																
XY+Z/39 T.M. Battery																1																1
118 M.G. Coy.																																1
118 T.M. Battery	1																	1														2
116 M.G. Coy.																																
TOTAL	42	35	4	1	3	2	5		1	2	7	7	3	6	7	13	2	16	3	2	8	3	2	6	21	8	7	3	5	4		233

NO APO 39 P
Apr
Nov 14

On His Majesty's Service.

SECRET

A + Q Branches

Army Form C. 2118.

Page 1

WAR DIARY
~~INTELLIGENCE SUMMARY~~
(Erase heading not required.)

Place	Date	Hour	Summary of Events and Information	Remarks and references to Appendices
	1917			
REMINGHELST	1/4		39th Divisional School and Reinforcement Camp at VOLKERINCKHOVE are amalgamated.	
"	2/4		A.A. & Q.M.G. attends conference at X Corps Head quarters. Boundaries of new sector discovered in rear of 23rd Divn. (taking over East of first field by the 39th Divn.)	
"	3/4		39 Divn. Order No 101. received: 118 Inf. Bde to proceed in OUDERDOM area. 116 Inf. Bde on relief by 70 Inf. Bde (23rd Divn) to proceed in majority of 6/7th April to camp in BRAMS-HOEK area: one Bn of 117 Inf. Bde to take over Left subsection of Right Brigade. Relief of 118 Inf. Bde in the LEFT (HOOGE) Section by 117 Inf. Bde. 118 Inf. Bde proceeded to camps in OUDERDOM AREA and became Brigade in Corps Reserve.	
"	4/4		Nothing to report.	

A + Q Branches
WAR DIARY
INTELLIGENCE SUMMARY

Army Form C. 2118.

Page 2

Place	Date	Hour	Summary of Events and Information	Remarks and references to Appendices
	1917			
RENINGHELST	5/4		118. Infantry Brigade proceeded to HOUTKERQUE area. Personnel by train with transport by road: this Bde now comes into Corps Reserve. WINNIPEG, MONTREAL and TORONTO Camps evacuated and handed over to 2nd Divn who occupies them the same afternoon.	
" "	6/4		7th Inf. Bde relieved 116 Inf. Bde in the Right Subsection of Right Section. 116 Inf Bde to Reserve Divl. Reserve at BRANDHOEK.	
" "	7/4		39 Divn. Order No. 102 received ordering 118 Inf. Bde (which has now become Army Troops) to detrain working parties for Railway work in VIII Corps area.	
" "	8/4		39 Divn. order No. 102 cancelled and N.O. 103 received ordering 116 Inf Bde to relieve 117 Inf Bde on night of 11/12 of April: 39 D.O. No. 104 received ordering 118 Inf Bde to move to VIII Corps area: billeting arrangements modified.	
" "	9/4		Three Battalions 118 Inf Bde moved into Camps in VIII Corps area. Major E. GORE-BROWNE Rifle Bde, attached A & Q Staff as a Learner attended DAQMG XV Corps	

Army Form C. 2118.

Page 3

WAR DIARY
A + Q Branch
or
INTELLIGENCE SUMMARY.
(Erase heading not required.)

Instructions regarding War Diaries and Intelligence Summaries are contained in F. S. Regs., Part II. and the Staff Manual respectively. Title pages will be prepared in manuscript.

Place	Date	Hour	Summary of Events and Information	Remarks and references to Appendices
REKKCHELST	10/7		174 Bde RFA and C/186th RFA on relief by 23rd RA proceeded to WATOU, HER-ZEELE and HOUTKERQUE areas and became Corps Reserve. G.O.C. 39 Divn. inspected 134 R. Sussex Regt. at St LAWRENCE Camp. Snow.	
	11/7		116 Inf. Bde relieved 117 Inf. Bde in HOOGE Section; latter Bde to Divl Reserve at BRANDHOEK.	
	12/7		German Patrol attacked one of our listening posts.	
	13/7		117 Inf. Bde moved to BOLLEZEELE training area: 2 Battns and Hd Qrs by train with transport by road.	
	14/7		2 Battalions, TM Battery & Hd Q. 117 Inf. Bde moved by train to BOLLEZEELE area.	
	15/7		116 Inf. Bde relieved by night by 23rd Divn in HOOGE Sector and moved into Divisional Reserve at BRANDHOEK Camps.	

Army Form C. 2118.

A.Q. Branche
Page 4

WAR DIARY
INTELLIGENCE SUMMARY.
(Erase heading not required.)

Instructions regarding War Diaries and Intelligence Summaries are contained in F. S. Regs., Part II. and the Staff Manual respectively. Title pages will be prepared in manuscript.

Place	Date	Hour	Summary of Events and Information	Remarks and references to Appendices
	1917			
REMY AELST	16/4	8 am	39 Divn. transferred from X Corps to VIII Corps.	
"	17/4		116. Inf. Bde. relieved half of 38th & 55th Divns in HILL TOP Sector. Brigade Headquarters opened at CAMP BANK: 55 Divn on our Right. 38 Divn on our Left. Divn. HQ remained at REMY AELST.	
"	18/4		Nothing to report.	
"	19/4		Orders received for 174 Bde RFA to proceed to WISSANT area (near CALAIS) for 8 clear days training.	
"	20/4		174. Bde RFA moved by road from HOUTKERQUE area en route to WISSANT.	
"	21/4		174. Bde RFA moved to ALEMBON area.	
"	22/4		174 Bde RFA arrived in WISSANT training area.	

Army Form C. 2118.

Page 5

A.Q Branch
WAR DIARY
INTELLIGENCE SUMMARY.
(Erase heading not required.)

Instructions regarding War Diaries and Intelligence Summaries are contained in F. S. Regs., Part II. and the Staff Manual respectively. Title pages will be prepared in manuscript.

Place	Date	Hour	Summary of Events and Information	Remarks and references to Appendices
REMINGHELST	1917 23/4 24/4 25/4 26/4 27/4		Nothing to report.	
" "	28/4		118 Inf. Bde relieved 116 Inf Bde in HILLTOP Sector; 118 I.B moved to Divn Reserve in C Camp (A 30). 116 Inf Bde prepared to move back to training area.	
" "	29/4		REMINGHELST neighbourhood shelled during the day and night	
A 30 & 36 (Shot- 28) D Camp.	30/4	10 am	Divisional H.Q. closed at REMINGHELST and opened at D Camp. R.A 39 Divn. issued orders to 174 Bde RFA to return from WISSANT on May 1st, 2nd & 3rd, and 186 Bde RFA to move to POLINCOVE in Second Army Training Area on 3rd & 4th May from HERZEELE. A Return of casualties for April 1917 is attached.	

S.C. Owen Major-Gen
Major General
Commanding 39 Divn

Casualties

April 1917

Killed

Officers and Other Ranks.

Officers.

Rank and Name	Unit	Casualty	Date
2nd Lieut. H. C. Keogh	13th Bn. R. Sussex Regt.	Killed	4.4.17.
2nd Lieut. S. C. Boulting	118 T.M.B (recently 4th Suffolks att. 1st Cambs)	" accidentally	14.4.17.
T. 2nd Lieut. L. H. Rayner	13th Bn. R. Sussex Regt.	Killed	18.4.17.

Unit	1	2	3	4	5	6	7	8	9	10	11	12	13	14	15	16	17	18	19	20	21	22	23	24	25	26	27	28	29	30	TOTAL	Returnable
11th Bn. R. Sussex Regt.																														2	2	
12th " "																														2	2	
13th " "			1																				2								3	
14th Bn. Hampshire Regt.	2		1											2																	2	
16th Bn. Notts & Derby Regt.	2																														2	
17th " "																														1	1	
11th Bn. K.R.R.C.								1		2																						
16th Bn. Rifle Brigade																																
16th Bn. Cheshire Regt.																														1	1	
115th Bn. Black Watch	1																															
11th Bn. Cambs. Regt.																																
1st Bn. Herts Regt.									1																							
13th Bn. Gloucester Regt.																																
Royal Artillery									1																					1	1	
Royal Engineers																																
A.S.C.																																
R.A.M.C.									1																					1	1	
39st T.M. B'hys (R.Y.+2)																																
116 M. G. Coy.																																
117 M. G. Coy.																														1	1	
118 M. G. Coy.																																
Divisional Headqrs.													1																		1	
118 T.M. Battery																						2									1	
TOTAL	1	2	1	1				1	2	2			1	3								2								16	

Casualties

April 1917

Killed

Officers and Other Ranks

Officers.

Rank and Name	Unit	Casualty	Date
2nd Lieut. H. C. Keogh	13th Bn. R. Sussex Regt.	Killed	4.4.17.
2nd Lieut. S. C. Boulting	118 T.M.B (recently 4th Suffolks att. 1/1st Cambs)	" accidentally	14.4.17.
T. 2nd Lieut. L. H. Rayner	13th Bn. R. Sussex Regt.	Killed	18.4.17.

Unit	1	2	3	4	5	6	7	8	9	10	11	12	13	14	15	16	17	18	19	20	21	22	23	24	25	26	27	28	29	30	TOTAL	Remarks
11th Bn. R. Sussex Regt.																						2									2	
12th " " "																															2	
13th " " "		2	1	1																											3	
14th Bn. Hampshire Regt.													1	2																	2	
16th Bn. Notts & Derby Regt.									2																						2	
17th " " "								1																							1	
11th Bn. K.R.R.C.																																
16th Bn. Rifle Brigade																																
1/6th Cheshire Regt.																																
1/5th Bn. Black Watch	1																														1	
4th Bn. Cambo. Regt.																																
1/1st Bn. Herts Regt.																																
13th Bn. Gloucester Regt.																																
Royal Artillery									1																						1	
Royal Engineers																																
A.S.C.																																
R.A.M.C.									1																						1	
39th T.M. Btys (x.y.z)																																
116 M.G. Coy.																																
117 M.G. Coy.																																
118 M.G. Coy.																																
Divisional Headqrs.														1																	1	
118 T.M. Battery																						2										
TOTAL	1	2	1	1				1	2				1	3								2									16	

Casualties

April 1917

Wounded

Officers and Other Ranks.

Officers :- Wounded and Missing

Rank and Name	Unit	Casualty	Date
2nd. Lieut. F. Coutts.	4/5 Black Watch.	Wounded A.D.	4.4.17.
T/Major (a. Lt. Col.) Methuen. A.J.	17th. Bn. K.R.R.C.	"	5.4.17.
T/2nd. Lieut. Turnpenney G.W.	17th. Bn. Notts & Derby.	"	9.4.17.
Major Hon. B.J. Russell. D.S.O.	(Bde. Maj. R.A.) 39th. Div. Arty.	" s.a.d.	24.4.17.
T/2nd. Lieut. V.S. Cox.	13th Bn. R. Sussex (on probation)	" s.a.d.	24.4.17.

Unit	1	2	3	4	5	6	7	8	9	10	11	12	13	14	15	16	17	18	19	20	21	22	23	24	25	26	27	28	29	30	TOTAL	Remarks
11st Bn R. Sussex Regt	4					1								1				2		1	1	2	2								14	
12d "		1	1	1										4									1		3						11	
13d "	1	1	2	1	1									1	1										3						12	
14th Bn Hampshire Regt	4				1						1			3										2	4						15	
15th Bn Notts Derby Regt								1	5		1																				7	
17d "						1	1	2	1	2	2	1		1					1												12	
16th Bn Rifle Brigade									1	1	1	1		1																	5	
17th Bn K.R.R.C.												1																			2	
1st Bn Berkshire Regt																		2													2	
7/8d Bn Black Watch	7											1			1									1							9	
1st Bn Cambs Regt																															1	
1st Bn Worcs Regt																															3	
13d Bn Gloucester Regt	1									2		2																			5	
Royal Artillery							1		2	2		1	1									1									4	
Royal Engineers							1																								3	
A.S.C.																																
R.A.M.C.																																
1/39 H.T.M.Batty																																
117 M.G.Coy																																
Div.C.Headqrs							1							1																	1	
X.Y+Z/39 T.M.Bdgs																															1	
118 M.G.Coy																									1						2	
118 T.M.Bty																																
116 M.G.Coy																																
TOTAL	13	6	2	3	3	4	3	2	5	10	3	5	5	8	4			2	2	1	2	4	3	11						8	109	

Casualties

April 1917

Wounded

Officers and Other Ranks.

Officers - Wounded and Missing

Rank and Name	Unit	Casualty	Date
2nd Lieut. F. Coutts	7/5 Black Watch.	Wounded A.D.	4.4.17
T/Major (A/Lt.Col.) Methuen A.S.	17th Bn. K.R.R.C.	"	5.4.17
T/2nd Lieut. Turnpenney G.W.	17th Bn. Notts & Derby.	"	9.4.17
Major Hon. B.J. Russell D.S.O.	(Bde. Maj. R.A.) 39th Div. Arty.	" s.a.d.	24.4.17
T/2nd Lieut. V.S. Cox.	13th Bn. R. Sussex (on probation)	" s.a.d.	24.4.17

Unit	1	2	3	4	5	6	7	8	9	10	11	12	13	14	15	16	17	18	19	20	21	22	23	24	25	26	27	28	29	30	TOTAL	Remarks
11th Bn R Sussex Regt	4					1								4			2			2	1	2									14	
12th "		1	1	1																	1	1	1		3						11	
13th "		1	1	3	1	1						1	1												3						12	
14th Bn Hampshire Regt		4			1										3									2	4						15	
10th Bn Notts & Derby Regt								1	1	3	1		1																		7	
17th " "							1	2	1	2	2	1																			12	
16th Bn Rifle Brigade					1				1	1	1	1																			5	
17th Bn K.R.R.C.											1										1										2	
16th Bn Cheshire Regt	1																														2	2
15th Bn Black Watch											1	1											1								9	4
14th Bn Cambs Regt											1																				1	3
14th Bn Herts Regt								2			1																				3	
13th Bn Gloucester Regt	1								2		1	2																			5	
Royal Artillery																							1								4	
Royal Engineers							1	1																							3	
A.S.C.																																
R.A.M.C.																																
1/34 H.T.M.Batty																																
117 M. G. Coy														1																	1	1
Queen's. Headqrs							1																		1						1	
X.Y.Z/39 T.M.Bde																																
112 M. G. Coy																																
118 T.M. Bty																																
116 M. G. Coy																	2														2	
TOTAL	13	6	2	3	3	4	3	2	5	10	3	5	5	8	4		2			2	1	2	4	3	11						8,104	

Army Form C. 2118

WAR DIARY
or
INTELLIGENCE SUMMARY   A & Q 39th Divn.

Vol 5 Page 1

(Erase heading not required.)

Place	Date	Hour	Summary of Events and Information	Remarks and references to Appendices
A30 & A5 Sheet 28 N.W. D Camp.	1917 1st May		174 Brigade R.F.A moved from Training area at VISSAI & LICQUES and ALEMBON; 186 Bde R.F.A. left to Artillerie training at HERZEELE. Bright sunshine all day; enemy poor aerial activity.	
-"-	2/5.		174. Bde R.F.A. marched to MORDAUSQUES area enroute to WATOU. Weather very warm.	
-"-	3/5.		186. Bde R.F.A. marched to NOORDPEENE	
-"-	4/5.		186 Bde R.F.A. marched to POLINCOVE.	
-"-	5/5.		227 Field Coy R.E. relieved by 225 Field Coy in HILLTOP Sector. Bde areas shelled intermittently during day and night by the enemy. Bright sunshine and good visibility.	
-"-	6/5.		227 Field Coy moved to training area at HOLQUES.	
-"-	7/5.	8A5 P/L 11-45 1.15 PM	Bombardment of the enemy trenches, in retaliation for shelling of un art de areas, by all guns and howitzers in Second Army Front.	

Army Form C. 2118

Page 2

WAR DIARY
or
INTELLIGENCE SUMMARY
(Erase heading not required.)

Place	Date	Hour	Summary of Events and Information	Remarks and references to Appendices
A 30 b 4.5 Sect 28 N.W. A Cent.	7/5 8/5 9/5		Enemy artillery much quieter.	
—	10/5		Nothing to report.	
—	11/5		225 Field Coy. will a covering party from 116 Chesh. Regt blew up six German dugouts in Rue Marais & M.V.D	
—	12/5		Orders received for 117 Inf. Bde to relieve 118 Inf. Bde in HILL TOP SECTOR on nights 14/15 & 15/16 May, and for 116 Inf Bde to move by road and rail from BOUVELINGHEM on 14 & 15 to WORMHOUDT area on 15th & 16th May.	
—	13/5		Nothing to report.	
—	14/5	11.45 p.m.	Ramilly 11 Cambridgeshire Regt. the enemy trenches; front-line was located and two two wire taken. Our casualties one OR killed and three OR wounded.	
—	15/5		Relief of 118 Inf Bde in HILL TOP SECTOR by 117 Inf Bde located in A 30 centre. 118 Inf Bde on going into Divl Reserve in A 30 Cent.	

Army Form C. 2118

Page 3

WAR DIARY
or
INTELLIGENCE SUMMARY
(Erase heading not required.)

Instructions regarding War Diaries and Intelligence Summaries are contained in F. S. Regs., Part II. and the Staff Manual respectively. Title Pages will be prepared in manuscript.

Place	Date	Hour	Summary of Events and Information	Remarks and references to Appendices
A 30 d 4.5 Sheet 28	15/5 16/5		116 Inf. Bde moved from ARQUES area to NOORDPEENE area by road	
N.W. D Camp	17/5		116 Inf Bde moved from NOORDPEENE area to WORMHOUDT area by road	
"	18/5		Nothing to report	
"	19/5		227 Field Coy RE moved from HOLQUES training area to take over work of 234 Field Coy RE	
"	20/5		234 Field Coy RE moved to HOLQUES training area by road. Ammunition personnel conveyed by road. Strength 5 Officers & other ranks at STEENVOORDE	
"	21/5 22/5 23/5		Nothing to report	
"	24/5		234 Field Coy RE moved from training area HOLQUES to camp at A 28 & 1 A Sheet 28.	
"	25/5		Orders received for advance of 116 Inf Bde on night of 31st May/1 June and move of 118 Inf Bde to a training area.	

Army Form C. 2118

Page 4

WAR DIARY or INTELLIGENCE SUMMARY

(Erase heading not required.)

Instructions regarding War Diaries and Intelligence Summaries are contained in F.S. Regs., Part II. and the Staff Manual respectively. Title Pages will be prepared in manuscript.

Place	Date	Hour	Summary of Events and Information	Remarks and references to Appendices
A 30 & A 5. Sheet 28 N.W. D Centre	1917 26/5 27/5		Nothing to report	
— " —	28/5		Party of enemy (strength about 50) attempted a raid on trenches, retired, leaving one unwounded prisoner. Our casualties one O.R. wounded and one man missing.	
— " —	29/5		116 Inf. Bde relieved from WORM HOUDT by Centre in A 30. 11th Bde in — Centre in A 30. WORM HOUDT.	
— " —	30/5		Nothing to report.	
— " —	31/5		117 Inf. Bde relieving 116 Inf. Bde from A 30 Centre.	

Return of casualties for May 1917 is attached.

R. Owen Major for
GOC 39 DIVISION

Casualties.

May 1917.

Killed.

Officers and Other Ranks.

Officers.

Rank and Name	Unit	Casualty	Date.
T/Lt. A. Parry	17th K.R.R.C.	Killed	6.5.17

Unit	Total to 30.4.17	1	2	3	4	5	6	7	8	9	10	11	12	13	14	15	16	17	18	19	20	21	22	23	24	25	26	27	28	29	30	31	Total for month	Remarks
11th Gen. R. Sussex Bgd/2nd	166																																1	
12th " "	149																																1	
13th " "	127																																1	
14th " Hampshire "	90																	1															1	
No " Both Berks "	162																													1	1		2	
16 " " "	164																							1									1	
17 " K.R.R.C. "	142																											2	1	1			4	
16 " Rifle Bde "	95																			1													1	
16 " Cheshire "	120														1																		1	
15th Black Watch	93				2									1													1						3	
114 " Comber	80		2		5						2																1	4	2	1			13	
114 " Herts "	30																														3		3	
13 " Worcester	20													4																			1	
Royal Artillery	10																								1								1	
Royal Engineers	1																																1	
A.S.C.	10																								1								1	
R.A.M.C.	6																																1	
39th T.M. Battery (X&Z)	8																																4	
No M.G. Coy	5																																1	
114 T.M.G. Coy	5																																1	
115 M.G. Coy	1																																1	
Div. Headquarters	2																																	
115 T.M.Batty.																																		
TOTAL	1614	2			7						2		1	4		2				1				1	2		1	4	3	2			32	

Casualties.

May.   1917.

Killed.

Officers and Other Ranks.
_____

Officers.

Rank and Name.	Unit	Casualty	Date.
T. 2/Lt. H. Parry.	17th K.R.R.C.	Killed	6.5.17.

Unit	Total to 30.4.17	1	2	3	4	5	6	7	8	9	10	11	12	13	14	15	16	17	18	19	20	21	22	23	24	25	26	27	28	29	30	31	Total to 31.5.17	Remarks
11th Bn. R. Sussex Regt	124																																1	
12th " "	166																																1	
13th " "	149																																1	
14th " Hampshire	128																											1					1	
16th " Notts Derby	90																											1	1				2	
2nd " "	162																		1														1	
17th " K.R.R.C.	164																											2	1			1	4	
17th " Rifle Bde	142																																1	
16th " Cheshire	75																1																1	
4/5 Black Watch	120															1	1																3	
11th " Cameron	93									2																1	4					13	
4/11 Leeds	80		2									1																					3	
13th " Worcester	50																																	
Royal Artillery	20													4									1									1		
Royal Engineers	10																									1						1		
D.L.C.	1																															1		
R.A.M.C.	10																											4					4	
301 M. Bally (nr.Z)	6																															1	1	
116th M.G. Coy.	8																															1	1	
117th M.G. Coy.	5																											1					1	
118th M.G. Coy.	5																															1	1	
Div. Headquarters	1																																	
115th T.M. Battery	3																															1	1	
TOTAL	**1614**	2	2		7					2		2	1	4	2					1			1	2		1	4	3	2				32	

Casualties.

May. 1917.

Wounded.

Officers and Other Ranks.

Officers:- Wounded and Missing.

Rank and Name.	Unit	Casualty	Date.
T.Lt. P.J. Davis	234 Fd. Coy. R.E.	Wounded A.D.	7·5·17.
2/Lt. B.H. Johnson.	1/1st Herts.	"	13·5·17.
T.7/Lt. L.S. Edmonds.	A/174 Bde. R.F.A.	"	13·5·17.
2/Lt. H.V. Raven	5th Suffolks att. 1/1st Cambs.	" at duty	14·5·17.
T.Lt. D.H. Holley	225 Fd. Coy. R.E.	"	19·5·17.
Lt. N.S. Temple	17th Notts & Derby.	" at duty	23·5·17.
T. Maj. C.J. Garland	227 Fd. Coy. R.E.	"	24·5·17.
7/Lt. (A/Capt.) A.L. Armstrong	1/1st Cambs.	acc. S.I. wounded	27·5·17.
7/Lt. (T/Lt.) A. Brown	1/6th Cheshires.	acc. wounded	27·5·17.
T. Maj. H.A. Leggett.	16th Notts & Derby.	Wounded	31·5·17.
2/Lt. (T Capt) A. Stevenson (M.C).	16th Notts & Derby	"	31·5·17.

Unit	Total to 30.4.17	1	2	3	4	5	6	7	8	9	10	11	12	13	14	15	16	17	18	19	20	21	22	23	24	25	26	27	28	29	30	31	Total for month	Remarks
11th Bn R. Sussex Regt	751																	1															1	
12th "	703																													1			1	
13th "	693																																-	
14th Hampshire	655																									3				1			4	
16th R. Warwickry	590								1																	1	6		2				12	
17th "	751																				1			1	3	1				1			8	
16th Rifle Bde	820													1	1							1		1	4	1			2	3	1		14	
17th R.K.R.C.	636													1	2										1					2			6	
11th Cheshire	527				1	2		1				1	1			1																		5	
12th Black Watch	734				2	1		3				1	2	1	1																1			12	
11th Bamks	636		1			5		3	2	2		1	5													2	2	9		1				23	
11th Herts	447			1					2																									13	
13th Gloucester	282			1										1		1										1								1	
Royal Artillery	117																									3				2				6	
Royal Engineers	124																										2							4	
A.S.C.	3															2			1															1	
R.A.M.C.	124																																	3	
V/39 H.T.M.Btty	6																																	1	
114 M.G. Coy	63							1																										1	
Brig Headquarters																4																		1	
X.Y.+Z.39 T.M.Btty	17																																	4	
115 M.G. Coy	44							1															1											2	
118 T.M.Btty	9																																	1	
116 M.G. Coy	72																													1				1	
TOTAL	5860	1	1	3	7	8		8	2	3		3	6	6	4	7		4	2	1	1	1	2	4	8	5	3	17	11	6	3		119	

Casualties.

May   1917.

Wounded.

Officers and Other Ranks.

=====

Officers:- Wounded and Missing.

Rank and Name	Unit	Casualty	Date
T/Lt. P.L. Davis	234 Fd. Coy. R.E.	Wounded A.B.	7.5.17.
2/Lt. B.H. Johnson	1/1st Herts	"	13.5.17.
T/2/Lt. L.S. Edmonds	A/1/74 Bde. R.F.A.	"	13.5.17.
2/Lt. H.V. Raven	5th Suffolks attd. 1/1st Cambs.	" at duty	14.5.17.
T/Lt. D.H. Holley	225 Fd. Coy. R.E.	"	19.5.17.
Lt. N.S. Temple	1/7th Notts & Derby	" at duty	23.5.17.
T. Maj. E.J. Garland	227 Fd. Coy. R.E.	"	24.5.17.
2/Lt. (T/Capt). A.S. Armstrong	1/1st Cambs.	acc. S.I. wounded	27.5.17.
2/Lt. (T/Lt.) A. Brown	1/6th Cheshires	acc. wounded	27.5.17.
T. Maj. H.A. Leggett	6th Notts & Derby	Wounded	31.5.17
2/Lt. (T/Capt) A. Stevenson (M.C.)	6th Notts & Derby	"	31.5.17.

Unit	Total to 30-4-17	1	2	3	4	5	6	7	8	9	10	11	12	13	14	15	16	17	18	19	20	21	22	23	24	25	26	27	28	29	30	31	Total for month	Remarks
1/1 Bn. R. Sussex Regt.	751																														1		1	
1/12 "	703																	1															1	
1/13 "	693																													3	1		4	
1/14 " Hampshire	658																										1	6	2	3	1		12	
1/10 " Mddx Rgt	590									1								1					1						1	1			8	
1/7 " "	751																									3	4	3	3	3			14	
1/8 " Rifle Bde	326													1									1				1						6	
1/9 " K.R.R.C.	656												1																2				5	
1/6 " Cheshire	527													2											1						1		12	
1/4 " Black Watch	734			2	1			3					1	2	1	1										2	2	7		1			23	
1/7 " Gordon	630			5				3	2						1																		13	
1/4 " Herts	447		1										5													1							1	
13 " Worcester	252		1																						3				2				6	
Royal Artillery	117																		1											2	2		4	
Royal Engineers	24																									1							1	
A.V.C.	3														3																		3	
R.A.M.C.	121															4																	1	
139 H.T.M. Batty	6																																1	
117 M.G. Coy	63																																1	
Div Headquarters	17																																	
KN. 184 T.M. Batty	44				1			1																									4	
118 M.G. Coy	44																												1				2	
118 T.M. Batty	9																																1	
116 M.G. Coy	72																																1	
Total	8860	1	1	3	7			8	2	3			3	6	6	4	7		4	2	1	1	2	4	6	5	3	17	11	6	3		119	

SECRET

Instructions regarding War Diaries and Intelligence Summaries are contained in F. S. Regs., Part II. and the Staff Manual respectively. Title pages will be prepared in manuscript.

WAR DIARY
or
INTELLIGENCE SUMMARY.
(Erase heading not required.)

Aug 39 Bn

Army Form C. 2118.

Vol ~~III~~ 6

Page I

Place	Date	Hour	Summary of Events and Information	Remarks and references to Appendices
	1917			
BORDER CAMP (A 30 b 3 5) Sheet 28	1st June		Army Commander of 5th Army visited the front held by the Division. Enemy's artillery active on back areas especially at night.	
— " —	2nd to 5th June		Increased activity on part of enemy's artillery against our back areas, transport lines and routes.	
— " —	6th June		4/5 Bn the Royal Highlanders moved from Reserve Bde area at WORMHOUDT to D camp near DIV HQ for work. Hostile artillery very active against our back areas and enemy aeroplanes frequently flew over our lines at a very low altitude.	

(A7092). Wt. W12839/M1293. 750,000. 1/17. D. D. & L., Ltd. Forms/C.2118/14.

Army Form C. 2118.

Page 2

WAR DIARY
or
INTELLIGENCE SUMMARY.
(Erase heading not required.)

Instructions regarding War Diaries and Intelligence Summaries are contained in F. S. Regs., Part II. and the Staff Manual respectively. Title pages will be prepared in manuscript.

Place	Date	Hour	Summary of Events and Information	Remarks and references to Appendices
BORDER HILL CAMP			Attack by Second Army with two Corps on PLOEGSTREET WOOD and OBSERVATORY RIDGE successful.	
	8th		Reorganisation of Brigade Camp Band 204 & 205 Cos R.E. to RESTIMBERT.	
	9th		1st Army Intelligence Reports. 5th Divn.	
	10th		Fifth Army took over areas of II rd and VIII th Corps from the Second Army, with Headquarters at LA LOVIE CHATEAU. 4/5 Black Watch returned to WORMHOUDT	

WAR DIARY or INTELLIGENCE SUMMARY

Army Form C. 2118.
Page 3

Place	Date	Hour	Summary of Events and Information	Remarks and references to Appendices
BORDER CAMP	10th June	9.45	Second Army Commander visited Divl HQ. Fifth Army Commander visited Divl HQ.	
"	11th June		118 Inf Bde marched from NORTHOUDT Area to NOORDPEENE Area. Divl Hqrs moved to LUMBRES.	
"	12th June		118 Inf Bde marched from NOORDPEENE Area to QUELMES.	
"	13th June		118 Inf Bde on a short from QUELMES to BAYENGHEM-LES-SENINGHEM area with Headquarters at LUMBRES.	
		Noon	XVIII Corps take over from XIII Corps the front formerly of 39 Divn with Corps HQ on Concurrent.	
			VOGELTJE (F.22 Central).	
			39 Divn relieves 38th (Welsh) Divn. on the LANCASHIRE FARM Sector etc.	

Army Form C. 2118.

Page 4

WAR DIARY
or
INTELLIGENCE SUMMARY.
(Erase heading not required.)

Place	Date	Hour	Summary of Events and Information	Remarks and references to Appendices
BORDER IGH CAMP.	19th to 20th June		117 Infantry Bde relieves 116 Infantry Bde in the HILL TOP SECTOR. Nothing to report.	
		21st	116 & Int. Bde moved by motor lorries to the Training Areas at MOULLE and HOULLE (West of ST OMER). A 30 group of Hauling Bde marched from BAYENGHEM LES SEMINGHEM to MOULLE training area.	
	23rd		39th Divisional School at VOLKERINCKHOVE closed and taken over by XVIII Corps School. Field Coy RE relieving the 225th Field Coy RE which marched to Camp at 30. 227th Field Coy RE (Gran Dinf) relieved part of 117 Int. 153rd Inf. Bde (Gran Dinf) relieved part of 117 Inf Brigade	

Army Form C. 2118.

Page 5

WAR DIARY
or
INTELLIGENCE SUMMARY.

Place	Date	Hour	Summary of Events and Information	Remarks and references to Appendices
BORDER CAMP	1917 25th 26th 27th 28th		Nothing to report	
	29th		118 Infts Bde moved from TILQUES Training area to A 30 gmt sf Camp near Div. HQ. 133 Field Ambulance moved from ST. CLOISTER'S TO PERNYHE to GWENT FARM. No 4 Coy. Div. Train moved from SALPERWICK to camp at F 28 a. Reliefs of 117 Infts Bde in the HILL TOP Section by 118 Infts Bde	
	30th		List of Casualties for June 1917 attached.	

J.C. Duke Major for
G.O.C. 39 t Div.

Army Form C. 2118

"A" Branch.
WAR DIARY
or
INTELLIGENCE SUMMARY
(Erase heading not required.)

HQ AFR 392 Page 1
Vol 17

Place	Date	Hour	Summary of Events and Information	Remarks and references to Appendices
BORDER CAMP (A.30.d.4.5) Sheet 28	1st 1917		117 Infantry Brigade proceeded to training area N of TILQUES from camps in A.30. morning of DEBROQUES. Fotering the HQ detachment at DEBROQUES. 116 Inf. Bde. training also in training area N of TILQUES with the exception of HQ and 11th [illegible] at [illegible] [illegible] the enemy artillery fire known with A General of [illegible] the enemy batteries from border.	
	2nd AM		Our division at [illegible] miles more fire from border [illegible] in sector 18 Nothing to report.	
	4th			
	5th	2 AM	Our division [illegible] 11:30 am 16 enemy [illegible] bombarment and [illegible] line seven prisoners [illegible] our casualties only [illegible]	
	6th to 10th	2 PM	3rd Division HQ at ENU ASHRE FARM Sh.51 [illegible] Nothing to report.	

1875 Wt. W593/826 1,000,000 4/15 J.B.C. & A. A.D.S.S./Forms/C. 2118.

SECRET

F. "Q" Branches.

WAR DIARY or INTELLIGENCE SUMMARY

Army Form C. 2118

Page 2

Place	Date	Hour	Summary of Events and Information	Remarks and references to Appendices
Camp (96 & 19) (Sheet 28)	1917 July 12th		39 Divn Order No. 126 received ordering relief of 118 Inf Bde on HILL TOP Sector by 33rd Inf Bde (less 1 Bn) on night of 15/16th July. Night quiet – nothing to report.	
"	13th		Fifth Army arrangements received for concentration of trains log trains & no soft vehicles & motors drawn on Section.	
"			Additional arrangements issued to Brigades for concentration of trains by Bde. P Sticker Ord E in 8cL Reg. & 456 Fd Amms Coln.	
"	14th		39 Divn Order No. 128 received ordering move of 116 Infantry Brigade from MOULLE to ST JAN-TETE-GIEZEN area, 118 Inf Bde and RHQ from A 30 coords to PERINGHE and inner of 118 Inf Bde from A 30 coords to MOULLE on night of 16th.	
"	15th		Received 234 Fd Coy RE. in HILL TOP Sector in A 22 S. Nicol Coy RE. Relief of 118 Inf Bde by 33rd Inf Bde (11th Divn). 118 Inf Bde returned to camps in A 30.	

WAR DIARY or INTELLIGENCE SUMMARY

Army Form C. 2118

"17" 'Q' Branches.

Page 3

Place	Date	Hour	Summary of Events and Information	Remarks and references to Appendices
C. Camp	16/9/17		Makes of 18 Brigade by train from A.30 area to training area HOUTLE and R.G. ordered from HOUTLE training area to Camp at ST JAN. TEN BIEZEN W. of POPERINGHE	
		9 am	G.S.C. Staff. A Divn. left for command of HILL TOP sector from G.O.C. 39 Divn.	
	17th	11 am	G.O.C. 39 A Divn. held a conference of all staffs of Divn. at Divl. H.Q. to discuss details of forthcoming operations.	
	18th		Hostile shelling of back areas	
	19th		22.8 Lt. Machine Gun Coy formed 3rd A Divn. as M.G. Ainsworth. Machine gun Coy	
	20th		39 Divl. order No. 130 received — Warning order of relief by 26 th (39 nth) 3rd Divn. in HILL TOP Sector to take place on night 26/27 (Lil Inf Bde & EGK 2 Inf. Bde Linger and 116 and 117 Inf. Bde take over 118 Bde front on 26/27 Bde HQ taking over Divisional HQ Bde on 27/28 HQ A Bde to return to C. Camp	
	21st		Moves of 117 Inf Bde on Buglers SETRQUES area to A Brigade group at Camp at A.30 or AGI	

SECRET

"A" + "Q" Branches.
WAR DIARY or INTELLIGENCE SUMMARY

Army Form C. 2118

(Erase heading not required.)

Place	Date 1917	Hour	Summary of Events and Information	Remarks and references to Appendices
Camp	23rd July		118 Infantry Brigade Group (in MY GR Bus from SERQUES) accommodated at Biague. Front of Camps at ST. JAN-TER-BIEZEN. Move of Bde. rule from ST JAN. TER-BIEZEN to MONT ST. ELOI dist-Rule- A. 30 Gentm.	
"	24th		Orders received from XVIII Corps that Fifth Army will attack in conjunction with First- French Army in its left on a date later than the 30th and 31st. Divisions will be notified later. The 30th and 31st Divisions of XVIII Corps will be the attacking Divisions at Div. HQ attended Divisional commander held a conference at Div HQ. attended by all Staff Officers and Heads of Departments to discuss arrangements for the future operations	
"	25th			
"	26th		30 Div. Order No 132 received conveying 30, 3, 0 No 130; instructions to the Division for attack (Appendix No 2)	
"	27th		MONT ST ELOI to BRANDHOEK	
"	28th		116th Infantry Brigade Group Infantry Battalions with (batt) Infantry Brigade brigades relieved 32nd Inf Brigade in the 39th Division in firing line.	

SECRET

"A" & "Q" Branches

WAR DIARY or INTELLIGENCE SUMMARY

Army Form C. 2118

Page 5

Place	Date 1917	Hour	Summary of Events and Information	Remarks and references to Appendices
C. Camp	July 29th		118. Infantry Brigade moved by Motor Bus from ST. JAN TER BIEZEN. B A 30g. grnts of camp in Div. reserve.	
		9 PM	117. Inf. Bde. moved from A 33 grnt of camp to CANAL BANK: also 2 Battalions of this Brigade. 2nd B. Bde. crosses to R. side of River. 225, 227 and 234 Field Coys and 138th Ghoorkas (Pioneers) withdrawn from line. G.O.C. Brigade issued his order.	
	30th		116. and 117. Infantry Brigades move to assembly positions. 118. Brigade in reserve near RYTER.	
	31st		THE THIRD BATTLE OF YPRES.	

A list of casualties for July 1917 is attached.

J.E. Orton Major for
Major & A.Q.M.G.
39 Division

Casualties. Officers.
Killed.   July. 1917

Rank and Name	Unit	Casualty	Date
T/2/Lt. J. R. Frampton.	13 Glosters	Killed	3.7.17
T/2/Lt. G. L. Stokes	D/174 Bde R.F.A.	"	5.7.17
2/Lt. R. C. Brierley	1/6 Cheshires	"	14.7.17
2/Lt. W. J. Horner	R.G.A. (V/39. T.M.B)	Wd. Since died of W.	15.7.17
Capt. W. A. S. Buchanan	50. M.Y.S.	Killed	24.7.17
T/2/Lt. J. R. Carne	12" Sussex	Wd. Since died of W.	25.7.17
T/2/Lt. F. Eaton.	13" Glosters	Killed	31.7.17
2/Lt. C. J. Gandy.	234 Fd. Coy. R.E.	"	"
T/Capt. S. M. Hunter.	R.A.M.C. attd. 1/1 Cambs.	"	"
T/2/Lt. F. P. Waterson	17" Notts & Derbys	"	"
T/2/Lt. J. A. Barrell	16" R.B.	"	"
2/Lt. A. B. Taylor. (T.F. London. Regt.)	" "	"	"
2/Lt. B. Hollis	4/5" Black Watch	"	"
Capt. F. C. Jonas	1/1 Cambs	"	"
2/Lt. (T/Lt.) A. J. Gray.	" "	"	"
2/Lt. A. H. Muirhead	" "	"	"
2/Lt. W. L. Ritchie	" "	Wd. Since died of W.	"
2/Lt. F. E. Spicer	" "	Wd. Since died of W.	"
2/Lt. R. W. Till	" "	Wd. Since died of W.	"
Maj. (T/Lt. Col.) F. Page. D.S.O.	1/1 Herts.	Killed	"
2/Lt. (T/Capt.) A. R. Milne	" "	"	"
Capt. S. H. Lowry. M.C.	" "	"	"
2/Lt. (T/Lt.) B. W. Head	" "	"	"
2/Lt. C. Scott. (Essex Regt. attd.)	" "	"	"
2/Lt. (T/Capt.) J. Lee. M.C.	1/6 Cheshires.	"	"
2/Lt. G. B. Cowpe.	" "	"	"
2/Lt. S. King	" "	"	"
T/2/Lt. W. J. Collyer	11" Sussex	"	"
2/Lt. Symington	12" Sussex	"	"
T/2/Lt. L. J. W. Andrews.	13" Sussex	Wd. Since died of W.	"
2/Lt. D. G. W. Kewill	14" Hants.	Killed	"
2/Lt. J. N. Falconer (Hants. Cambs. attd.)	" "	"	"
2/Lt. P. W. Collis	" "	Wd. Since died of W.	"
T/2/Lt. J. W. Bells	17" Notts & Derby.	Killed	"
2/Lt. A. K. Gatto. M.C. (5" Beds. attd.)	1/1 Herts.	"	"
2/Lt. W. F. Francis	" "	"	"
2/Lt. R. H. Scarelan	" "	"	"
2/Lt. (T/Lt.) E. Macintosh	" "	"	"
2/Lt. A. W. Rash	1/1 Cambs	Wd. Since died of W.	"
T/Lt. J. C. Hobson.	1/6 M.G. Coy.	Killed	"

OR (NS)

Unit	1	2	3	4	5	6	7	8	9	10	11	12	13	14	15	16	17	18	19	20	21	22	23	24	25	26	27	28	29	30	31	TOTAL for MONTH	Remarks
11th Br R Sussex Regt																							1	1		3			2		31	39	
12th " " "																													1		24	29	
13th " " "																							2								24	26	
14th " Hampshire "														1																	30	31	
15th " Hants+Berby "	2																									1			3		32	38	
16th " " "																														1	48	49	
17th " K.R.R.C.	1								1																		1				30	32	
18th " Rifle Brigade																															30	30	
19th " Cheshire "					4																					1					5	11	
19th " Blackwatch					2				5	2																			2		37	46	
19th " Cambridgeshire "	2							4	3		1	1		4																	32	39	
19th " Herts "					1			1			1																				31	35	
19th " Gloucestershire "				2		1						1	1	2											1						4	11	
" Royal Artillery					2		1																								1	6	
" Royal Engineers					1																	1				2			1		3	6	
" A.S.C					1																												
" R.A.M.C															4											1	1		1			7	
1st M. Battery (x,y,z)																																1	
116 M.G. Coy																															4	4	
117 M. G. Coy																															9	9	
118 M. G. Coy																															5	5	
Divisional Headquarters																																	
118 I.M. Brhy																							1		1	1	2			1	2	7	
228 M. L. Bry																															6	6	
116 I.M.B																															2	2	
TOTAL.	3	-	2	11	-	1	5	9	2	1	1	5	4	-	-	-	-	-	-	1	4	1	1	10	3	1	14	2	384	466	

Casualties. Officers.
Wounded and Missing.   July. 1917.

Rank and Name.	Unit.	Casualty.	Date.
Capt. G. M. Brown. M.C.	1/1 Herts S.C. 118 Bde.	wounded	1. 7. 17.
T/Maj. F. R. Leith.	39th D.H.Q. (Gen. List.)	"	3. 7. 17.
2/Lt. F. L. Spicer	1/1 Cambs.	" at duty	4. 7. 17.
2/Lt. R. W. Hill	"	"	"
2/Lt. H. Symons.	1/1 Herts	wounded	"
Lt. S. M. Crew.	1/7 attd. 1/6 Cheshires	missing, believed killed	5. 7. 17.
2/Lt. A. J. Marriott.	39th D. A. C.	Wd. slightly. at Duty	"
2/Lt. (A/Capt) M. B. Heath.	B/174 Bde. R.F.A.	" "	"
2/Lt. A. A. Cuthbertson.	4/5 Black Watch	wounded	11. 7. 17.
2/Lt. S. Bell.	"	"	"
2/Lt. D. C. Wilson.	"	"	12. 7. 17.
Capt. V. H. Palmer.	1/6 Cheshires	Wd. (Gas) Shell	6. 7. 17.
T/2/Lt. J. D. Lewis.	11th Sussex	wounded	17. 7. 17.
2/Lt. J. F. C. Fogerty.	227 Field Coy. R.E.	"	18. 7. 17.
Lt. J. L. R. Haycroft.	" " "	" at Duty	"
2/Lt. (A/Capt) W. Jones.	D/174 Bde. R.F.A.	" S.a.d	16. 7. 17.
T/Capt. E. Mansfield.	133 Field Amb.	Wd. (Gas) Shell (Lach)	18. 7. 17.
2/Lt. (T/Lt.) G. R. Simms.	39th D. A. C.	wounded S.a.d.	20. 7. 17.
2/Lt. G. L. G. Harrison.	11th Sussex.	"	22. 7. 17.
T/2/Lt. C. H. Conway.	"	Missing	"
2/Lt. W. F. Fisher.	12th Sussex.	"	24. 7. 17.
2/Lt. (T/Lt.) S. J. Powers.	16th Rifle Brigade	Wounded	27. 7. 17.
T/2/Lt. J. S. Simpson.	12th Sussex.	"	29. 7. 17.
Capt. (A/Maj.) W. B. Telling M.C.	A/174 Bde. R.F.A.	"	31. 7. 17.
2/Lt. A. M. Diamant	39th D. A. C	" at duty	"
2/Lt. J. A. Passerly.	C/174 Bde. R.F.A.	" "	"
2/Lt. J. A. W. Griffith	186 Bde. R.F.A.	" Gas (S.T.L)	13. 7. 17.
T/2/Lt. J. M. Hussey.	14th Herts.	" S. a. d.	31. 8. 17.
T/Capt. J. P. Charles.	R.A.M.C. attd. 1/1 Herts.	wounded.	31. 7. 17.
T/2/Lt. J. E. Neal.	17th Bn. Notts & Derby Regt.	"	"
T/2/Lt. W. G. Lilley.	" " " "	"	"
2/Lt. W. S. Call.	16th Bn. Rifle Brigade	"	"
2/Lt. G. H. Ridley	" " " "	"	"
T/2/Lt. J. B. Camp.	" " " "	" at Duty	"
T/Lt. K. G. Sutherland.	117th M. G. Coy.	"	"
Lt. J. M. Bruce-Gardyne. M.C.	4/5 Black Watch	"	"
Lt. (A/Capt) J. R. Phillip	"	"	"

Casualties. Officers.
Wounded and Missing. July. 1917.

Rank and Name.	Unit.	Casualty.	Date.
2/Lt. D. P. Ramsay	4/5 Black Watch	Wounded	31. 7. 17.
2/Lt. S. Cameron.	" " "	"	"
2/Lt. R. Lyell.	" " "	"	"
2/Lt. J. J. Milne.	" " "	"	"
2/Lt. R. Inch.	" " "	"	"
2/Lt. B. Hunter.	" " "	"	"
2/Lt. J. Puckett.	" " "	"	"
2/Lt. J. O. Adams (on pas) attd. 118. T.M.B.	" " "	"	"
2/Lt. P. T. Watson	" " "	"	"
2/Lt. (A/Capt.) A. B. H. Dunlop M.C.	1/1 Cambs. Regt	"	"
2/Lt. (A/Lt.) C. L. Tebbutt.	" " "	"	"
2/Lt. G. S. Smith	" " "	"	"
2/Lt. (T/Lt.) G. Blackburn	" " "	"	"
2/Lt. H. V. Raven (5' Suffolk, attd.)	" " "	"	"
2/Lt. B. W. Silk	" " "	"	"
2/Lt. E. S. Twelvetrees	" " "	"	"
2/Lt. (T/Lt.) A. M. Ivson	" " "	"	"
2/Lt. (A/Capt.) L. R. du Fisher M.C.	1/1 Herts Regt	"	"
2/Lt. E. W. Marchington	" " "	"	"
2/Lt. G. H. y Gilbert M.C.	" " "	"	"
2/Lt. H. J. Ritchie	" " "	"	"
2/Lt. H. J. Edwards	" " "	"	"
2/Lt. (T/Lt.) S. King	" " "	" & missing	"
Capt. (T/Lt. Col.) W. H. Stanway D.S.O., M.C., (S.W.B)	1/6 Cheshire Regt	" at Duty	"
2/Lt. (A/Capt.) L. G. Ruddin	" " "	"	"
2/Lt. G. W. Ideson.	" " "	"	"
2/Lt. G. T. Chorlton	" " "	"	"
2/Lt. H. R. Spicer.	" " "	"	"
2/Lt. W. G. T. Lever.	" " "	"	"
2/Lt. G. Rowley. M.C.	" " "	"	"
2/Lt. (A/Capt.) C. G. Keston	" " "	"	"
T/2/Lt. W. G. TL Cutts	118th M. G. Coy	"	"
T/2/Lt. G. M. Inglis	" " "	"	"
Capt. C. L. Awbery M.C. (4t Essex. attd.)	1/1 Cambs. Regt	Missing	"

Casualties. Officers.
Wounded and Missing — July 1917.

Rank and Name.	Unit.	Casualty	Date.
2/Lt. R. L. Hardy	1/1 Herts Regt	Missing	31. 7. 17.
2/Lt. F. G. Lake	" " "	"	"
2/Lt. W. Thompson	" " "	"	"
2/Lt. F. S. Walthew	" " "	"	"
2/Lt. W. E. Rogers (attd. 118. T.M.B.)	1/6 Cheshire Regt	"	"
T/2/Lt. W. E. Thomas	118 M.G. Coy.	"	"
2/Lt. T. M. Sparkes	1/6 Cheshire Regt	Wounded	"
T/Lt. T. W. A. Jones	" " "	" & missing	"
2/Lt. H. O. W. Moynan (Brecknock Bn. attd.)	" " "	" & missing	"
2/Lt. S. Torston	" " "	Wounded	"
Maj (T/Lt. Col) G. A. McL. Scales D.S.O. (a. T.C.H.)	4/5 Black Watch	Wounded at Duty	"
T/Capt. C. H. L. Rixon	R.A.M.C. attd. 16th Notts & Derby	Wounded	"
T/Capt. J. H. C. Gatchell	R.A.M.C. attd. 11th Sussex	Wounded, at Duty	"
T/Capt. Dr J. McDougall	" " 13th "	Wounded	"
T/2/Lt. (a/Capt) C. A. Allen. M.C.	11th R. Sussex	"	"
T/2/Lt. E. W. Tice	" "	"	"
2/Lt. J. S. Collins	12th R. Sussex	"	"
T/Lt. (a/Capt.) N. de P. MacRoberts M.C.	13th R. Sussex Regt	"	"
T/2/Lt. (a/Capt) L. J. Dobbie	" " "	"	"
T/2/Lt. S. Taylor	" " "	"	"
T/2/Lt. J. H. Robinson	" " "	"	"
T/2/Lt. J. O. Cristin	" " "	"	"
T/2/Lt. A. Wheeler	" " "	"	"
T/2/Lt. R. W. Evans	" " "	"	"
T/2/Lt. F. E. Turney	" " "	"	"
T/2/Lt. F. H. Lake	" " "	"	"
T/Capt. A. C. Gammon. M.C.	14th Bn. Hants	"	"
T/2/Lt. N. F. Tyler	" " "	"	"
T/2/Lt. C. Chevallier	" " "	"	"
2/Lt. G. A. Pest (Berks Yeo. attd.)	" " "	"	"
T/2/Lt. P. S. Turner	" " "	"	"

Casualties. Officers.
Wounded and Missing.   July 1917.

Rank and Name.	Unit.	Casualty.	Date.
T/Capt. & Adj. T. Thornton M.C. (Yorks & Lancs)	17th Bn. Notts & Derby	Wounded	31.7.17
2/Lt. (A/Capt.) J.W.J. Millar	" " "	"	"
2/Lt. A.S. Beck (T.F.)	" " "	"	"
2/Lt. A.S. Mellor	16th Bn. Notts & Derby	"	"
T/2/Lt. R.J. Whitley	11 Sussex	"	"
T/Lt. S.J. Brown	116 M.G. Coy.	"	"
T/2/Lt. R.C. Mann	17 K.R.R.C.	missing believed killed	"
T " V.F. Turner	"	wounded	"
T/Lt. L.M. Hasler	117 M.G. Coy.	wounded, at Duty	"
T/2/Lt. F.F. Lewis	117 T.M.B. (K.R.R.C. attd.)	" "	"
T/ " J.A. Pinneger	16 R. Bde.	" "	"
2/Lt. F.S. Spicer	1/1 Cambs.	wounded since died	"
Capt. (T.Maj) A/Lt.Col. Hon. E. Coke	16 R. Bde.	wounded, at Duty	"
2/Lt. (T/Lt) R.W. Head	1/1 Herts	wounded & missing	"
T/Capt. H.J. De Brest	R.A.M.C. attd. 1/6 Cheshires	wounded, at Duty	"
T/2/Lt. L.A. Dabdin	225 Fd. Coy. R.E.	" Gas	26.7.17
2/Lt. R-n Farwell	1/1 Herts	" Gas shell	16.7.17
" J.R. Warner	A/186 Bde R.F.A.	" at duty	22.7.17

(105 wounded / 14 missing)

119
14

105

R. Wounded & missing

Unit	1	2	3	4	5	6	7	8	9	10	11	12	13	14	15	16	17	18	19	20	21	22	23	24	25	26	27	28	29	30	31	MONTH TOTAL
11th Bn R. Sussex Regt														3					6	4		4	4		1	1		4	6	4	168	168+10
12" "											2							1		1						8			3	2	101	126
13" "																		1				2	2					3			163	170
2/4" Hampshire																	1	1	2									3			195	202
16" " Midd× Regt	2			2														3											3	2	182	191
17" " "	2		1	1									1	1			3						1				6			5	227	234
16" Rifle Brigade	1	2		2																											273	280
7" " K.R.R.C.	2			2			1			4					8												6		5	4	190	200
10th " Cheshire	2	4			19		9		4		1	3		3	4		2		1												214	214
14/5" " Black Watch		4	2		15					2		5	1	2	2	2	1		2				1					3			158	222
11/12 " Cambridgeshire	3	1		3			8		3		3	6	3		1			2								3					195	240
11" " Herts	1	2	2	2			4		2			2	11	1	6			1								2				4	223	266
13" " Gloucestershire	3	3	3	5	3		3		8		3	3	3	1			1							2					3		23	56
Royal Artillery	6	2		7	3		2	1			1	4															3			1	87	87
Royal Engineers	2	1		1			1				2	2		1	2		9	1	3				3				3				11	58
A.S.C.																											1	5	1	1	1	1
R.A.M.C.				9															1				3									17
H.T.M. Batty															8												3				3	3
117 M.G.Coy						1									2																19
A.V.Coy																															19	19
Division C Headquarters																																1
N.Z.Z./39 J.M.Bngs	2		3						1		1		1		1		3		1			1				2						4
118 M.G.Coy									1				1																		25	33
118 T.M.Batty																	1														17	18
116 M.G.Coy									1													1					5				22	27
236 Employed Coy																			3												3	3
116 T.M.Batty																						2	1							1	10	13
228 M.G.Coy																															9	9
117 T.M.Batty																										3					3	3
TOTAL	26	17	7	55	45	9		28	16	17	15	35	36	36		5	7	19	12	8	-	8	16	11	3	27	12	18	24	26	246	447

	15.7.17	23.7.17	25.7.17	29.7.17	31.7.17	Total
Infantry O.R.						
1/2 R. Sussex Regt				17		17
2/2 " "				16		16
13" "				43		43
14" Hampshire				44		44
15" N.D. Rifles		3		3		6
16" "				4		4
17" K.R.R.C.				13		13
18" Rifle Brigade				19		19
19" "				251		251
20" Middlesex Regt				74		74
21" Black Watch				41		41
22" Lancs				265		265
23" Yorks Regt						
114 M.G.C.				4		4
115 "				3		3
116 "				11		11
117 "						
118 "	1					1
Royal Art						
Royal Eng						
A.S.C.						
R.A.M.C.				1		1
X.Y.Z. M.B.						
V. T.M.B.		1		1		2
228 T.M.B.				1		1
116 T.M.C.						
116						
TOTAL	1	4	1	3	964	441

Casualties. Officers.
Killed.   July. 1917

Rank and Name	Unit	Casualty	Date
1/2/Lt. J. R. Frampton	13 Glosters	Killed	3.7.17
1/2/Lt. G. L. Stokes	D/174 Bde R.F.A.	"	5.7.17
2/Lt. R. C. Brierley	1/6 Cheshires	"	14.7.17
2/Lt. W. J. Horner	R.G.A. (V/39 T.M.B.)	W. Since died of W.	15.7.17
Capt. W. G. S. Buchanan	50. M.V.S.	Killed	24.7.17
2/7/Lt. J. R. Carne	12" Sussex	W. Since died of w.	25.7.17
1/2/Lt. A. Eaton	13" Glosters	Killed	31.7.17
2/Lt. C. J. Gandy	234 Fd. Coy. R.E.	"	"
T/Capt. B. M. Hunter	R.A.M.C. attd. 1/1 Cambs.	"	"
1/2/Lt. F. P. Waterson	17" Notts + Derbys	"	"
1/2/Lt. J. A. Barrett	16" R.B.	"	"
2/Lt. A. B. Taylor (T.F. London Regt.)	" "	"	"
2/Lt. B. Hollis	1/5" Black Watch	"	"
Capt. F. C. Jonas	1/1 Cambs	"	"
2/Lt. (T/Lt.) A. J. Gray	" "	"	"
2/Lt. A.H. Muirhead	" "	"	"
2/Lt. W. L. Ritchie	" "	Wd. Since died of w	"
2/Lt. F. E. Spicer	" "	Wd. Since died of w	"
2/Lt. R. W. Hill	" "	Wd. Since died of w	"
Maj. (T/Lt. Col.) F. Page. D.S.O	1/1 Herts	Killed	"
2/Lt. (T/Capt.) A. R. Milne	" "	"	"
Capt. S. H. Lowry. M.C.	" "	"	"
2/Lt. (T/Lt.) B. W. Head	" "	"	"
2/Lt. C. Scott (Essex Regt. attd.)	" "	"	"
2/Lt. (A/Capt.) J. Lee. M.C.	1/6 Cheshires	"	"
2/Lt. G. B. Cowpe	" "	"	"
2/Lt. S. King	" "	"	"
1/2/Lt. W. J. Collyer	11" Sussex	"	"
2/Lt. Syminton	12" Sussex	"	"
1/2/Lt. B. J. W. Andrews	13" Sussex	Wd. Since died of w.	"
2/Lt. D. G. W. Kewill	14" Hants	Killed	"
2/Lt. J. K. Falconer (Hants. Carbs. attd.)	" "	"	"
2/Lt. P. W. Collis	" "	Wd. Since died of w.	"
1/2/Lt. T. W. Bells	17" Notts + Derby	Killed	"
2/Lt. A. N. Gallo. M.C. (5" Beds. attd.)	1/1 Herts	"	"
2/Lt. W. F. Francis	" "	"	"
2/Lt. R. H. Secretan	" "	"	"
2/Lt. (T/Lt.) E. Macintosh	" "	"	"
2/Lt. A. W. Rash	1/1 Cambs	Wd. Since died of w	"
1/Lt. J. C. Hobson	1/6 M.G. Coy	Killed	"

O.R. Killed

Unit	1	2	3	4	5	6	7	8	9	10	11	12	13	14	15	16	17	18	19	20	21	22	23	24	25	26	27	28	29	30	31	Total
11" R.B. Sussex Regt																							1			3			7		31	39
12" " "																													1		24	29
13" " "																															24	24
14" Hampshire "														1																	30	31
" Hert & Berks "			2																				2			1			3		32	38
" " " "	2																													1	46	49
17 " K.R.R.C.	1																														30	30 + 39
" " Rifle Brigade																											1				30	30
16 " Cheshire					4				1																						5	11
14/5" Blackwatch					2		4	1	5	2	1															1					37	46
1/2 " Cambridgeshire									3																				2		32	37
1/4 " Herts			2									1	1									1									31	36
1/7 " Worcestershire					2								1	4																	4	11
Royal Artillery					1																					2					3	6
Royal Engineers								1														1									3	6
A.S.C.																																
R.A.M.C.															4																	7
3" " M Bn.y (X, Y, Z)																																1
16" M.G.Corp																															4	4
17 " M.G.Corp																															9	9
18 " M.G.Corp																					1				1	1					5	5
Divisional Headquarters																																
18 I.W. Baty.																											2			1	2	7
228 M.G.Coy.																															2	2
TOTAL	3	-	2	11	-	1	5	9	2	1	1	5	4	-	-	-	-	1	4	1	10	3	1	14	2	384	466

Casualties Officers
Wounded and Missing.
July. 1917.

Rank and Name	Unit	Casualty	Date
Capt. G. M. Brown. M.C.	1/1 Herts. S.C. 118 Bde.	Wounded	1. 7. 17.
T/Maj. F. R. Leith.	39th. D.A.Q. (Gen. List)	"	3. 7. 17.
2/Lt. F. E. Spicer	1/1 Cambs.	" at duty	4. 7. 17.
2/Lt. R. W. Hill	"	"	"
2/Lt. H. Symons.	1/1 Herts	Wounded	"
Lt. D. M. Crew.	1/1 attd. 1/6 Cheshires	Missing, believed killed	5. 7. 17.
2/Lt. A. J. Marriott.	39th. D.A.C.	Wd. Slightly at duty	"
2/Lt. (A/Capt) M. B. Heall.	B/174 Bde. R.F.A.	" "	"
2/Lt. A. A. Cuthbertson.	4/5 Black watch	Wounded	11. 7. 17.
2/Lt. D. Bell.	"	"	"
2/Lt. D. L. Wilson.	"	"	12. 7. 17.
Capt. V. H. Palmer.	1/6 Cheshires	Wd. (Gas) Shell	6. 7. 17.
T/2/Lt. J. B. Lewis.	11th Sussex	Wounded	17. 7. 17.
2/Lt. J. F. C. Fogarty.	227 Field Coy. R.E.	"	18. 7. 17.
Lt. J. L. R. Maycroft.	" " "	" at duty	"
2/Lt. (A/Capt) W. Jones.	D/174 Bde. R.F.A.	" S.A.d.	16. 7. 17.
T/Capt. E. Mansfield.	133 Field Amb.	Wd. (Gas) Shell (Lachry)	18. 7. 17.
2/Lt. (T/Lt.) G. R. Simms.	39th. D.A.C.	Wounded S.A.d.	20. 7. 17.
2/Lt. G. L. G. Harrison.	11th Sussex.	"	22. 7. 17.
T/2/Lt. C. H. Conway.	"	Missing	"
2/Lt. W. F. Fisher.	12th Sussex	"	24. 7. 17.
2/Lt. (T/Lt.) S. J. Powers.	16th Rifle Brigade	Wounded	27. 7. 17.
T/2/Lt. J. S. Simpson.	12th Sussex.	"	29. 7. 17.
Capt. (A/Maj.) W. B. Telling. M.C.	A/174 Bde. R.F.A.	"	31. 7. 17.
2/Lt. A. M. Beament	39th. D.A.C.	" at duty	"
2/Lt. J. A. Casserly	C/174 Bde. R.F.A.	" "	"
2/Lt. J. A. W. Griffith	186 Bde. R.F.A.	" Gas (S.—L)	17. 7. 17.
T/2/Lt. J. M. Hussey	1/1 Herts	" S.A.d.	31. 7. 17.
T/Capt. J. P. Charles	R.A.M.C. attd. 1/1 Herts.	Wounded	31. 7. 17.
T/Lt. J. E. Neal.	17th Bn. Notts & Derby Regt.	"	"
T/2/Lt. W. G. Lilley.	"	"	"
2/Lt. W. S. Cull.	16th Bn. Rifle Brigade	"	"
2/Lt. G. H. Ridley	"	"	"
T/2/Lt. J. B. Camp.	"	" at duty	"
T/Lt. K. G. Sutherland.	117th M.G. Coy	"	"
Lt. J. M. Bruce-Gardyne M.C.	4/5 Black watch	"	"
Lt. (A/Capt) J. R. Phillip.	"	"	"

Casualties Officers
Wounded and Missing
July 1917.

Rank and Name	Unit	Casualty	Date
2/Lt. D.P. Ramsay	4/5 Black Watch	Wounded	31. 7. 17
2/Lt. S. Cameron	" "	"	"
2/Lt. R. Lyell	" "	"	"
2/Lt. J.J. Milne	" "	"	"
2/Lt. R. Inch	" "	"	"
2/Lt. B. Hunter	" "	"	"
2/Lt. J. Quckett	" "	"	"
2/Lt. J.O. Adams (on pro) attd. 118 T.M.B.	" "	"	"
2/Lt. P.T. Watson	" "	"	"
2/Lt. (a/Capt.) A.B.H. Dunlop M.C.	1/1 Cambs Regt	"	"
2/Lt. (a/Ct.) C.L. Tebbutt	"	"	"
2/Lt. G.S. Smith	"	"	"
2/Lt. (T/Lt.) G. Blackburn	"	"	"
2/Lt. H.V. Raven (5' Suffolk, attd.)	"	"	"
2/Lt. B.W. Sill	"	"	"
2/Lt. E.S. Twelvetrees	"	"	"
2/Lt. (T/Lt.) A.M. Fison	"	"	"
2/Lt. (a/Capt.) L.R. da Fonte M.C.	1/1 Herts Regt	"	"
2/Lt. E.W. Marchington	"	"	"
2/Lt. G.H.Y. Gilbert M.C.	"	"	"
2/Lt. H.J. Ritchie	"	"	"
2/Lt. H.J. Edwards	"	"	"
2/Lt. (T/Lt.) S. King	"	" + missing	"
Capt. (T/Lt. Col.) W.H. Stanway D.S.O., M.C. (S.W.B)	1/6 Cheshire Regt	" at duty	"
2/Lt. (a/Capt.) L.G. Ruddin	"	"	"
2/Lt. G.W. Ideson	"	"	"
2/Lt. G.T. Phorlton	"	"	"
2/Lt. H.R. Spicer	"	"	"
2/Lt. W.G.T. Leven	"	"	"
2/Lt. G. Rowley M.C.	"	"	"
2/Lt. (A/Capt.) C.G. Kirton	"	"	"
T/2/Lt. W.E.N. Cutts	118th M.G. Coy	"	"
T/2/Lt. G.M. Inglis	"	"	"
Capt. C.L. Awbery M.C. (4' Essex attd.)	1/1 Cambs Regt	Missing	"

Casualties Officers
Wounded and Missing — July 1917

Rank and Name	Unit	Casualty	Date
2/Lt R. L. Hardy	1/1 Herts Regt	Missing	31.7.17
2/Lt F. G. Lett	" "	"	"
2/Lt W. Thompson	" "	"	"
2/Lt F. S. Walthew	" "	"	"
2/Lt W. E. Rogers (attd. 118. T.M.B)	1/6 Cheshire Regt	"	"
T/2/Lt W. E. Thomas	118 M.G. Coy	"	"
2/Lt T. M. Sparkes	1/6 Cheshire Regt	Wounded	"
2/Lt T.W.A. Jones	" "	" + missing	"
2/Lt H. O. W. Moynan (Brecknock Bn. attd.)	" "	" & missing	"
2/Lt S. Yorston	" "	Wounded	"
Maj (T/Lt-Col) G.U. McL. Seales D.S.O. (a.T.S.H.)	4/5 Black Watch	Wounded at Duty	"
T/Capt C. H. L. Rixon	R.A.M.C. attd. 16th Notts & Derby	Wounded	"
T/Capt J. H. C. Gatchell	R.A.M.C. attd. 11th Sussex	Wounded at Duty	"
T/Capt D. J. McDougall	" " 13th "	Wounded	"
T/2/Lt (a/Capt) C. A. Allen M.C.	11th R. Sussex	"	"
T/2/Lt E. W. Tice	" "	"	"
2/Lt J. S. Collins	12th R. Sussex	"	"
T/Lt (a/Capt) N. de P. MacRoberts M.C.	13th R. Sussex Regt	"	"
T/2/Lt (a/Capt) L. J. Dobbie	" "	"	"
T/2/Lt S. Taylor	" "	"	"
T/2/Lt J. H. Robinson	" "	"	"
T/2/Lt J. O. Cristin	" "	"	"
T/2/Lt A. Wheeler	" "	"	"
T/2/Lt R. W. Evans	" "	"	"
T/2/Lt F. E. Turney	" "	"	"
T/2/Lt F. H. Lett	" "	"	"
T/Capt A. O. Gammon M.C.	14th Bn. Hants	"	"
T/2/Lt N. F. Tyler	" "	"	"
T/2/Lt C. Chevallier	" "	"	"
T/Lt G. H. Pert (Berks Yeo. attd.)	" "	"	"
T/2/Lt P. S. Turner	" "	"	"

Casualties Officers
Wounded and Missing   July 1917

Rank and Name	Unit	Casualty	Date
T/Capt & Adjt T Thornton M.C (Yorks & Lancs)	7· Bn. Notts & Derby	Wounded	31. 7. '17
2/Lt. (A/Capt.) J. W. J. Millar	" " "	"	"
2/Lt. A. S. Beck (T.F.)	" " "	"	"
2/Lt. A. S. Mellor	16· Bn. Notts & Derby	"	"
T/2/Lt. R. J. Whitley	11 Sussex	"	"
T/Lt. S. J. Brown	116 M.G. Coy.	"	"
T/2Lt. P. C. Mann	17 K.R.R.C.	Missing, believed killed	"
T/ " V. F. Turner	"	Wounded	"
T/Lt. L. M. Hasler	117 M.G. Coy.	Wounded; at duty	"
T/2/Lt. J. F. Lewis	117 T.M.B.(K.R.R.C. attd)	" "	"
T/ " J. A. Pinneger	16 R. Bde.	"	"
2/Lt. F. E. Spicer	1/1 Cambs.	Wounded Since died	"
Capt. (T.Maj) A/Lt.Col. Hon. S. Coke	16 R. Bde.	Wounded, at duty	"
2/Lt. (T/Lt.) R. W. Head	1/1 Herts	Wounded & missing	"
T/Capt. H. J. De Brett	R.A.M.C. attd 1/6 Cheshires	Wounded, at duty	"
T/2/Lt. L. A. Dubdin	225 Fd. Coy. R.E.	" Gas	26. 7. 17
2/Lt. R. n Farwell	1/1 Herts	" Gas shell	16. 7. 17
" J. C. Warner	A/186 Bde R.F.A	" at duty	22. 7. 17

Missing O.R.	16.1.17	23.1.17	25.1.17	29.1.17	1.2.17	Total
11th B. Fusilier Regt.		2			15	17
12th "					16	16
13th "					43	43
14th " Hampshire "					44	44
16th " Notts & Derby "				3	3	6
17th " "					14	14
17th " K.R.R.C.					13	13
16th " Rifle Brigade					19	19
12th " Lancashire Regt					251	251
4/5 " Black Watch					74	74
11th " Cambs					41	41
11th " Herts					205	205
13th Bn. Yorks Regt.					4	4
116 Tr. M.B.					3	3
117 " "					11	11
118 " "						
Royal Art.						
Royal Eng.						
A.S.C.	1					1
R.A.M.C.						
SS/SZ. T.M.B.			1			1
V. T.M.B.				1		1
228 M.G.C.				7	7	7
116 T M B.						
118 "						
TOTAL	1	2	1	3	764	771

Of Wounded & missing

Unit	1	2	3	4	5	6	7	8	9	10	11	12	13	14	15	16	17	18	19	20	21	22	23	24	25	26	27	28	29	30	31	Total for Month
11th Rn R. Sussex Regt																		6		4	4	4	4	2	1	1	4		6	3	166	170
11th " "		2																		1				8		8	3		3	2	101	156
12th " "					3														2				2				3				163	170
13th " "																														3	195	202
14th " " Hampshire														1			1	2											3	2	192	191
16th " " Post & Ready	2	2												1			1	2							1				3	5	222	234
17th " "		1	2									1		3										1		1	1			1	273	280
16th Rifle Brigade	1	2	1						1														1						5	5	180	200
17th K.R.R.C.	2	2	2								5									1						6					214	244
16th Cheshire	2				19	15	4	9	4	4		1	1	8	2	1								8						1	158	225
17th Black Watch	4		27			2			2	4	5	3	3	4	2		2									3				4	195	226
11st Cambridgeshire	3	2	3	3	3	3	2	8	3	3	1	8		6			3		2												223	246
11st " Herts	1	7		3	3	2	1	3	1	4	2	11	1	2		1		1													53	56
13th " Gloucestershire	3	3	5		7	9	1	3	1	6	1	3	1	1			1						3	2						4	23	57
Royal Artillery	6	1		3	4		2		1		1	10	3	1	2	3	9	1	3				3	3					5	1	11	55
Royal Engineers	2						1	1			1	2											1				5					35
A.V.C.																										1					1	
R.Q.M.C.							1							8									3	3	1				1		3	27
1/39 H.T.M.Baty.														2																	3	3
117 M.G. Coy.																													1		19	19
A.V.C.																															1	1
Divisional H.d. Qr.	2														1									1				2			4	4
××2/39 H.M.Baty.				3								1				1															25	33
115 M.G. Baty.										1																					17	18
115 J.M.Baty.																												5			22	27
116 M.B. Coy.																								1								
226 Employ. Coy																	3														10	13
116 T.M.Baty.J																							3	1		1						9
226 M.B. Coy.																													3		3	3
TOTAL	26	17	7	55	45	28	15	28	16	16	17	15	35	6	36	5	4	19	12	8	—	8	16	147	3	27	12	18	24	26	2016	2997

TOP SECRET

WAR DIARY or **INTELLIGENCE SUMMARY**
Army Form C. 2118

HQ Anzac 39 R.D. II

Place	Date	Hour	Summary of Events and Information	Remarks and references to Appendices
C Corps	August 1917 1st and 2nd		THE THIRD BATTLE OF YPRES. is continued	
—	2nd	8PM	39 Div. Order No. 137 received giving instructions for the relief of the Division by the 48th Division and subsequent withdrawal to rest — details were two Battns. 117 Inf Bde. to be relieved by two Battns. of 118 Inf Bde.	
—	4th		118 Inf Bde were relieved in the Canal Bank by a Bde of 48 Div. and moved by train to camps at St Jan ter Biezen WEST of POPERINGHE	
—	5th		During the night of 5/6th 117 and 118 Infantry Brigades relieved the 4 & 8 Divn. and took over the C.NAN BANK Front and rear defences and new REIGERSBURG CHATEAU.	
—	6th	4PM	39 Div Order No. 138 received ordering the Division G.O.C. Command of x Corps Area & the details and arrangement to 5 Corps and details of line activity was forthcoming Army area.	

Army Form C. 2118

Page 2

WAR DIARY
or
INTELLIGENCE SUMMARY
(Erase heading not required.)

Place	Date	Hour	Summary of Events and Information	Remarks and references to Appendices
METEREN	August 7/1917	10 AM	39 Div. Headquarters opened at 6 camp and closed at METEREN. Communication established with X Corps. 118th Brigade Headquarters moved to RIE on CANAL BANK dugouts and RIEGERSBURG & HATTEAU camp siding N. of FLETRE and METEREN (West of BAILLEUL).	
	8 PM		Three of enemy's 39 Divisions in Artillery Gr Area contemplated the Division will remain for a week resting, drilling and reorganizing prior to offensive. After front of the 4th — DIVN. Note: Total number of prisoners captured by Division exclusive of unwounded wounded prisoners sent to OFFICERS: 15. OTHER RANKS: 918. Artillery captured: six 77 mm guns, one Howitzer, five 5.9" Howitzers. Trench Mortars one heavy & one medium; one Anti-tank gun, one unknown gun & other six-mounted machine guns. Our casualties were 114 officers and 3564 killed, wounded and missing.	

Army Form C. 2118

Page 3

WAR DIARY
or
INTELLIGENCE SUMMARY
(Erase heading not required.)

Place	Date	Hour	Summary of Events and Information	Remarks and references to Appendices
METEREN	Aug 9th & 10th 17		Nothing to report.	
"	11th		39 Div order No 139 received for the relief of 41st Divn on nights of 13/14th and 14/15th August — 116 Inf Bde to relieve 122nd Inf Bde in the Right (HOLLEBEKE) Section on night of 13/14th Aug. and the 117 Inf Bde to relieve 124th Inf Bde in the Left (KLEIN ZILLEBEKE) Section on night of 14/15th Aug. 118. Inf Bde to be in Divl. Reserve in RIDGEWOOD.	
"	12th		H.Q. 116 Inf Bde moved from BERTHEN area to RIDGEWOOD.	
"	13th		the 117 Inf. Bde moved from BERTHEN area to RIDGEWOOD	
"	13/14		The 116 Inf Bde proceeded to the HOLLEBEKE Section relieving 122nd Inf Bde (41st Divn) establishing H.Q. at Shrl. bank.	
"	14th		H.Q. 118 Inf Bde moved from BERTHEN area to RIDGEWOOD.	

WAR DIARY
or
INTELLIGENCE SUMMARY
(Erase heading not required.)

Army Form C. 2118

Page 4

Place	Date 1917	Hour	Summary of Events and Information	Remarks and references to Appendices
METEREN	Aug 14/15		Relief of 124 Inf Bde (41st Div) in the KLEIN-ZILLEBEEK Section by the 117 Inf Bde	
WESTOUTRE	15th		39 Div H.Q. moved from METEREN to WESTOUTRE	
	16th 17th 18th		Nothing to report.	
	19th		Relief of 117 Inf Bde in the left KLEIN-ZILLEBEEK Section by 118 Inf Bde. — More of 117 Inf Bde to DIVL Reserve in RIDGE WOOD	
	20th		MAJOR-GENERAL E. FEETHAM C.B. C.M.G assumed command of the 39 th Division vice MAJOR-GENERAL C.T. CUTHBERT C.B. C.M.G. Motored to return. 39 Divl Artillery arrived in WESTOUTRE area from XVIII. Corps.	
	21st 22nd			
	23rd		Relief of 116 Inf Bde by 117 Inf Bde in the Right (HOLLEBEEK) Section on relief 116 Inf Bde moved to Camps in RIDGE WOOD and Arcanne Bde in Divl. Reserve.	

WAR DIARY or INTELLIGENCE SUMMARY

Army Form C. 2118

Page 5

Place	Date 1917	Hour	Summary of Events and Information	Remarks and references to Appendices
WESTOUTRE	Aug 24th		Capture of 2 men of 19th I.R.I.R. Regt. 9th Reserve Division by 118th Brigade. These two were carrying the mail to 59th front-line and lost their way.	
"	25th/26th		Nothing to report.	
"	27th		39 Divn. over I.D. 149 relieved for the relief of 117 Infanterie Brigade (39 Divn.) on the night of 24/25th August.	
"	27th/28th		116 Brigade relieved the 118 Brigade in the left KLEIN-ZILLEBEKE Sector. 118 Brigade on relief moved to camps in RIDGE WOOD and became Divl. Reserve.	
"	29th/30th		Relief of 117 Infanterie Brigade in the right HOLLEBEKE Sector by the 63rd Brigade (37th Divn.) and move to camps between L.A. CLYTTE and RENINGHELST.	
			A relation of Casualties for August 1917 is attached.	

J.E. Owen, Major for G.O.C. 39 Divn.

Casualties

August. 1917.

Wounded.

Officers and Other Ranks.

Officers :- Wounded and Missing.

Rank and Name	Unit	Casualty	Date.
2/Lt. S.H. Maasted	B/186 Bde. R.F.A.	Wounded	2.8.17
Lt.(A/Maj) W. Strachan	D/174 Bde. R.F.A.	"	"
T. 2/Lt. E.V. Johnson	B/174 Bde. R.F.A.	" at duty	"
T. 2/Lt. J.P. Thomas	16 Rifle Brigade	"	1.8.17
2/Lt. A.B. McCrae	16 Rifle Bde (Scot. Rifles. attd.)	"	2.8.17
T. 2/Lt. C. Marriott	16 Rifle Bde.	"	"
T. 2/Lt. W.B. Arnold	16 Rifle Bde.	"	"
T. 2/Lt. D.P. Playfair	117 M.G. Coy.	"	1.8.17
Maj. J.Y. Rogers	R.A.M.C. attd. 4/5. Bl. Watch	" At duty	2.8.17
Lt. W.A. Pecher	4/5 Black Watch	"	"
2/Lt. J.C. Ross	4/5 Black Watch	"	"
T. Capt. J. Anderson	R.A.M.C. attd 16 Notts & Derby	"	5.8.17
T. Capt. B.O.W. Robinson	12 Sussex	"	1.8.17
Capt. C.C. Trevor Roper	14 Hants	"	2.8.17
T. Capt. P.H. Coleridge. M.C.	16 Notts & Derby	"	5.8.17
2/Lt. A. Dain	16 Rifle Bde.	"	2.8.17
T. 2/Lt. C. Bartlett	13 Sussex	" At duty	2.8.17
T. 2/Lt. J.C. Branson	13 Sussex	"	"
T. 2/Lt. L.E. Cox	13 Sussex	"	"
T. 2/Lt. A.E. Lawrence	13 Sussex	"	"
2/Lt. B.V. Hughes	17 Notts & Derby	"	1.8.17
Lt. & Qr. Mr. L.G. Johnston	134 Fld. Amb.	" S. at duty	5.8.17
Lt. J.H. Askwith	16 Notts & Derby	"	3.8.17
2/Lt. H.W. Bell	16 Rifle Bde. attd. 117 T.M.B.	"	"
Maj.(T.Lt.Col.) E.P.A. Riddell. D.S.O.	Rifle Bde. attd. 11 Cambs.	" At duty	5.8.17
Wes. Chaplain P.J. HUTCHISON	A.C.D. attd 117 Inf. Bde.	"	1.8.17
T. 2/Lt. W.P. Donovan	117 M.G. Coy.	"	5.8.17
2/Lt. J.E. James	17 K.R.R.C.	"	13.8.17
2/Lt. A.S. Mellor	16 Notts & Derby	"	15.8.17
T.Lt. J.C. Thompson	A/186 Bde. R.F.A.	"	16.8.17
Capt.(T.Lt.Col.) C.C. Herbert Stepney. D.S.O.	16 Notts & Derby	"	15.8.17
T. 2/Lt. R. Summerscale	225 Fld. Coy. R.E.	"	17.8.17
T. 2/Lt. A.J. Williams	118 M.G. Coy.	"	18.8.17
T. Capt. C.J. Harris	134 Fld. Amb.	"	17.8.17
2/Lt. H.D. Harks (14 Gordons attd.)	118 M.G. Coy.	"	19.8.17
T. 2/Lt. E.W. Parkin	39. Signal Coy. R.E.	"	18.8.17

Units	1	2	3	4	5	6	7	8	9	10	11	12	13	14	15	16	17	18	19	20	21	22	23	24	25	26	27	28	29	30	31	Total for Month	Remarks
11th Bn. R. Sussex Regt.		2												9	4	1	3	1	2	2	1	4	2	1	1			3				36	
12 "		3												1	1	1	1	2	1	1		1	1									10	
13 "		2		1														2	2		1											11	
14 " Hampshire															1	6	2	2	11													20	
15 " Royal Irish Rifles																25	2	3										3				17	
16 " "																1	4	7	4	1						9						10	
17 K.R.R.C.																1	22	6	1	2	1		1	2	2	1						35	
No. Division		2	1														6	4	2	1				1	5							12	
11/5 Black Watch	1	10	5	6														6		2		1			4	1		1				24	
11 " Cameronians					2															4				2	1							11	
11 " Lewis																		1						1	3		1	3				10	
13 " Gloucestershire	4	5	1	2							1		5	6	8		2			5			1		7							20	
Royal Artillery	4	1	5	6	1		8						6	6	8	18	3	10	4	4					1							100	
Royal Engineers	28	5	4														2			3					1			1				33	
A.S.C.	6	1	2	4		1																										14	
L.T.M. Batty.															1		19	1	1						1							23	
V/34 T.M. Batty.																			2													2	
117 M.G. Coy.																																2	
Divisional Headquarters																			2			1										9	
X142/34 T.M. Battys														2				1														3	
118 M.G. Coy														5	2				5													8	
118 T.M. Batty	1	2														2																3	
116 M.G. Coy																																1	
236 Employed Coy.																																1	
116 T.M. Batty																																	
225 M.G. Coy																																	
A.V.C.																																	
117 T.M.B.																																	
" M.G.																																	
TOTAL	52	19	20	19	11	3	8	—	5	—	1	5	6	24	19	61	39	49	51	23	22	7	4	5	19	10	10	8	—	1		480	

Rank and Name	Unit	Casualty	Date
T. 2/Lt. W. E. Boswell	17" Notts & Derby	Wounded. At duty	18-8-17
2/Lt. F. Wild	D/186 Bde. R.F.A.	"	21-8-17
T. 2/Lt. R. F. Sawyer	17 K.R.R.C.	Missing, believed wounded	25-8-17
2/Lt. J.H. Keating	1/1" Cambs	Wounded. At duty	27-8-17
Lt. W. J. Hastings	16 Notts & Derby	Wounded	27-8-17
Lt. E. Masters (4 Seaforths attd)	118 M.G. Coy	Wounded (Gas, Shell)	20-8-17
T./Lt. L Stephenson	A.G/186 Bde. R.F.A.	" " "	18-8-17
T. Capt. C.H.J. Rixon	R.A.M.C. attd 16 Notts & Derby	" Shell Shock	2-8-17
T. Capt. (A/Maj) E. Wright	B/186 Bde. R.F.A.	" At duty	20-8-17
T. 2/Lt. C.B. Dallas	17 K.R.R.C.	" Shell Shock	2-8-17
2/Lt. W. Thompson	C/152 Bde. A.F.A.	" (Gas)	6-8-17

Rank and Name	Unit	Casualty	Date
T. Capt. R. J. Harris	134 Fd. Amb.	Wounded	17.8.17
2/Lt. H.D. Hanks (24/Londons att'd)	118 M.G. Coy.	"	19.8.17
T. 2/Lt. E.W. Parkin	39. Sig. Coy. R.E.	"	18.8.17
T. 2/Lt. W.E. Boswell	17. Notts & Derby	" at duty	18.8.17
2/Lt. F. Wild	D/186 Bde. R.F.A.	"	21.8.17
T. 2/Lt. R.J. Sawyer	17 K.R.R.C.	Missing believed wounded	25.8.17
2/Lt. J.H. Keating	1/1 Cambs	Wounded. At duty	27.8.17
Lt. E. Masters (4 Seaforths att'd)	118 M.G. Coy.	Wounded (Gas, Shell)	20.8.17
T./Lt. J. Stephenson	H.Q./186 Bde. R.F.A.	" " "	18.8.17
T. Capt. C.H.J. Rixon	R.A.M.C. att'd 16 N'd'n	" (Shell Shock)	2.8.17
T. 2/Lt. C.B. Dallas	17 K.R.R.C.	" " "	2.8.17
T. Capt (A/Maj.) E. Wright	B/186 Bde R.F.A.	" At duty	20.8.17
2/Lt. W. Thompson	C/52 Bde A.F.A.	" (gas)	6.8.17

MISSING.

O.R.	1	2	3	4	5	6	7	8	9	10	11	12	13	14	15	16	17	18	19	20	21	22	23	24	25	26	27	28	29	30	31	Total for Month	Remarks
11 R. Sussex Regt		1																														1	
12 " " "		1																														1	
13 " " "																																	
14 " Hants																																1	
16 " Notts & Derby "																																1	
17 " " "																																	
16 " Rifle Bde															1																	1	
17 K.R.R.C.																																	
116 " Cheshire "																																	
14/5 Black Watch	1		2																													3	
1/1 Cambs "																					1	1									3	
1/1 Herts "		1																															
13 Glosters "																						1											
116 M.G. Coy																						1											
117 " " "							1									1																3	* 39th Sigs atta 17th Bde
118 " " "															1																		
Royal Artillery	2	1*																														3	R.F.A. Bde Hd. Qrs.
Royal Engineers																	1															1	
A.S.C.																																	
R.A.M.C.																1																1	
X.Y.Z/T.M. Batty																																	
V/T.M. Batty																																	
22S M.G. Coy																																	
116 T.M. Batty																						1										1	
Total	3	3	2	-	-	-	1	-	-	-	-	-	-	-	3	2	1	-	-	-	-	1	-	-	-	-	-	-	-	-	-	18	

Casualties.

August. 1917

Killed.

Officers and Other Ranks.

Officers :- Killed

Rank and Name	Unit	Casualty	Date
2/Lt. (T/Lt.) G.A. Scrallon. M.C.	4/5 Bl. Watch (A.&S.H. attd)	Killed.	1.8.17
T. 2/Lt. A.W.G. Head	117 M.G. Coy.	"	1.8.17
T. 2/Lt. (A/Capt.) R.E. Lupton	12 Sussex	Wd. Since died of wounds.	1.8.17
2/Lt. E. Denney	17 K.R.R.C.	Wd. 3/8/17. Since died of wounds.	4.8.17
Capt. & Adjt. J.S. Beck. M.C.	17 K.R.R.C.	Killed	16.8.17
2/Lt. A.S. Ball	A/186 Bde. R.F.A.	"	16.8.17
Capt. W.M.V. Banbury	16 Rifle Brigade (R. of O.)	"	17.8.17
Lt. (A/Maj.) S.A. Joseph	227 Fd. Coy. R.E.	Wd. Since died of wounds	18.8.17
T. 2/Lt. R.W. Clark	17 Notts & Derby	Killed	18.8.17
T. 2/Lt. J.E.G. Chaise	13 Sussex	Wd. 2/8/17. Died of wounds	18.8.17
2/Lt. A.M. Pratt	A/186 Bde. R.F.A.	Killed	21.8.17

Unit	1	2	3	4	5	6	7	8	9	10	11	12	13	14	15	16	17	18	19	20	21	22	23	24	25	26	27	28	29	30	31	Total	Remarks
11 Bn R. Sussex Regt		1													3	1	1															6	
12 " " "															3																	5	
13 " " "														1		5	2															7	
14 " Hampshire "																1	1															2	
16 " M₇s₇ Rosty																1		+														5	
17 " " "																													1			1	
17 " K.R.R.C.																	5		1													7	
16 " Rifle Brigade	1																															1	
1/6 " Cheshire																											1	1				7	
1/5 " Black Watch			3	3																												1	
1/1 " Cambridgeshire																						1										1	
1/1 " Herts																																1	
13 " Worcestershire						2	3					2	1		5	5	5	5	1		1											24	
Royal Artillery	7	1																1	6						1							15	
Royal Engineers		1																	1													1	
A.S.C.																			1													1	
R.A.M.C.																																	
29 T.M. Battys (X,Y&Z)																	1															1	
116 M.G. Coy																																	
117 " "																																	
118 " "																																	
Divisional Headquarters													2		1																	3	
115 T.M. Batty																																	
22 M.G. Coy																																	
116 T.M. Batty																																	
TOTAL	9	4	3	2	-	3	-	-	-	-	-	2	7	4	14	6	9	12	1	6	1	-	-	-	1	-	2	-	1	-		88	

Casualties.

August. 1917.

Killed.

Officers and Other Ranks.

Officers :- Killed.

Rank and Name	Unit	Casualty	Date
2/Lt. (T/Lt.) G. A. Scratton. M.C.	4/5 Black Watch. (A&S.H. attd.)	Killed	1.8.17.
T. 2/Lt. A.W.G. Head.	117 M.G. Coy.	"	1.8.17.
T. 2/Lt. (A/Capt) R.B. Lupton	12 Sussex	Wounded. Since died	1.8.17.
2/Lt. E. Denny.	17 K.R.R.C.	" 3/8/17 " "	4.8.17.
Capt. & Adjt. J.A. Deck. M.C.	17 K.R.R.C.	Killed	16.8.17.
2/Lt. A.G. Ball.	A/186 Bde. R.F.A.	"	16.8.17
Capt. W.M.V. Banbury	16 Rifle Brigade (R. of O.)	"	17.8.17
Lt. (A/Maj.) S.A. Joseph.	227 Fld. Coy. R.E.	Wounded. Since died	18.8.17
T. 2/Lt. R.W. Clark.	17 Notts & Derby	Killed	19.8.17.
T. 2/Lt. J.E.G. Chaize	13 Sussex	Wounded 2/8/17. Died of wounds	18.8.17
2/Lt. A.M. Pratt	A/186 Bde. R.F.A.	Killed	21.8.17.

Unit.	1	2	3	4	5	6	7	8	9	10	11	12	13	14	15	16	17	18	19	20	21	22	23	24	25	26	27	28	29	30	31	TOTAL for MONTH	Remarks
11 Bn R. Sussex Regt	1												3	3	1		1															8	
12 " " "													1																			2	
13 " " "																															1	1	
14 " Hampshire															5		2															7	
11c " Notts & Derby														1	1		1	4														2	
17 " " "																																5	
17 " K.R.R.C																1			1													1	
16 " Kelts Engine.	1													1	1		5															7	
16 " Cheshire	3	3																					1					1				7	
45 " Black Watch																																1	
11 " Cambridgeshire																					1											1	
111 " Herts																																1	
15 " Worcestershire																																2 "	
Royal Artillery	7	1		2		3					2	1		5	5					6												15	
Royal Engineers															1					1												1	
A.S.C.																				1												1	
R.A.M.C																		1														1	
29 T.M.Bs. (X.Y&Z.)															1																	1	
116 " " Coy.																																1	
117 " " "																																	
118 " " "																																	
Divisional Headquarters													2			1																3	
148 T.M.B																																	
222 M.B. Coy.																																	
116 T.M.B																																	
TOTAL.	9	4	3	2	–	3	–	–	–	–	–	2	7	4	14	6	9	12	1	6	1	–	–	–	1	–	–	2	–	–	1	86	

Casualties.

August 1917.

Killed.

Officers and Other Ranks.

Officers.

Rank and Name	Unit	Casualty	Date
2/Lt. (T/Lt.) G. H. Scratton. M.C.	4/5 Black Watch (A.&S.H. attd)	Killed	1.8.17
T.2/Lt. A.W.G. Head	117. M. G. Coy.	"	"
T.2/Lt. (A/Capt) R. R. Jupton	12 Sussex	Wd. Since died of wounds	"
2/Lt. E. Denny	17 K.R.R.C.	Wd. 7/8/17. Since died of wounds	4.8.17.
Capt. & Adjt. J. S. Beck. M.C	17 K.R.R.C.	Killed	16.8.17
2/Lt. A. L. Ball	A/186 Bde. R.F.A.	"	"
Capt. W.M. V. Banbury	16 Rifle Bde. (R. of O)	"	17.8.17.
Lt. (A/Maj) P.H. Joseph	227 Fd. Coy. R.E.	Wd. Since died of wounds	18.8.17.
T.2/Lt. R.W. Clark	17 Notts & Derby.	Killed	"
T.2/Lt. E.G. Chaize	13 Sussex	Wd. 16/8/17. Died of Wounds	"
2/Lt. A.M. Pratt	A/186 Bde. R.F.A.	Killed	21.8.17.

Unit	1	2	3	4	5	6	7	8	9	10	11	12	13	14	15	16	17	18	19	20	21	22	23	24	25	26	27	28	29	30	31	Total for Month	Remarks
1st Bn E. Surrey Regt.													3	3	1			1														8	
2nd "	1												1																			2	
3rd "															5																	7	
4th Hampshire																																2	
K.O. A. & S. + Rents																		2														5	
17 "			3	3											1	1	1	1	+											1		7	
17 " K.R.R.C.																	8															7	
4 " R.M. Rifles	1													1	1																	7	
1/6 " Blackheath																1																1	
1/5 " Blackheath														1	1																	1	
4 " Cambridgeshire																	1			1												7	
15 " A.& S.																																1	
B" Gloucestershire				2									2	1	5	5	5											1				24	
Royal Artillery		1			2			3											6													15	
Royal Engineers	7			1													1															7	
A.S.C.																																1	
R.A.M.C.																																1	
Sqdn M.B. (xxxx)															1					1												1	
16 M.G. Coy														2	1				1													1	
17 "																																1	
18 "																																	
Brigade of Rifle Corps																																3	
111 T.M. Batty																																	
2nd T.M. Batty																																	
11 T.M. Batty																																	
TOTAL	1	4	3	2	3			3					3	7	4	14	6	9	12	1	6	1		1	2		1	2		1		89	

Officers:- Wounded and Missing.

Name.	Unit.	Casualty.	Date.
2/Lt. S.E. Housed	C/056 Bde. R.F.A.	Wounded	2.8.17.
Lt.(A/Maj.) W. Strachan	D/174 Bde. R.F.A.	"	"
2/Lt. E.J. Johnson	B/154 Bde. R.F.A.	" at duty	"
2/Lt. L.J.P. Thomas	16 Rifle Brigade	"	1.8.17.
2/Lt. A.B. McCrae	16 Rifle Bde. (Cert. R.fin. alld.)	"	2.8.17.
T. Lt. C. Marriott	16 Rifle Bde.	"	"
T. 2/Lt. W.D. Arnold	16 Rifle Bde.	"	"
T. 2/Lt. D.P. Playfair	117 M.G. Coy.	"	1.8.17.
Maj. J.A.Y. Rogers	R.A.M.C. att 1/5 B. Watch	" at duty	2.8.17.
Lt. W.H. Decker	1/5 Black Watch	"	"
2/Lt. J.C. Ross	1/5 Black Watch	"	"
T. Capt. J. Anderson	C.A.V.C. att. to Notts & Derby	"	5.8.17.
T. Capt. B.C.W. Atkinson	12 Sussex	"	1.8.17.
Lieut. C.C. Trevor Roper	14 Hants	"	2.8.17.
T. Capt. P.H. Clevedon, M.C.	16 Notts & Derby	"	5.8.17.
Lt. A. Rain	16 Rifle Bde.	"	3.8.17.
T. 2/Lt. C. Bartlett	13 Sussex	" at duty	2.8.17.
T. 2/Lt. V.C. Branson	13 Sussex	"	"
T. 2/Lt. C.E. Cox	13 Sussex	"	"
T. 2/Lt. A.C. Lawrence	13 Sussex	"	"
2/Lt. C.V. Hughes	17 Notts & Derby	"	1.8.17.
Lt. & Q.M. R.G. Johnston	13th Fd. Amb.	" S. at duty	5.8.17.
Lt. J.H. Askwith	16 Notts & Derby	"	3.8.17.
2/Lt. A.W. Bell	16 Rifle Bde. attd. 117 T.M.B.	"	"
Maj.(T. Lt. Col.) E.P.A. Riddell, DSO	Rifle Bde. attd 1st Cambs	" at duty	5.8.17.
Wes. Chaplain. P.T. HUTCHISON	A.C.D. attd 117 Inf. Bde.	"	1.8.17.
T. 2/Lt. W.P. Donovan	117 M.G. Coy.	"	5.8.17.
2/Lt. J.E. James	17 K.R.R.C.	"	13.8.17.
2/Lt. A.L. Mellor	16 Notts & Derby	"	15.8.17.
T. Lt. T.B. Thompson	A/186 Bde R.F.A.	"	16.8.17.
Capt.(T. Lt. Col.) C.C. Herbert-Stepney, DSO	16 Notts & Derby	"	15.8.17.
T. 2/Lt. L. Summerscale	225 Fld. Coy. R.E.	"	17.8.17.
T. 2/Lt. A.J. Williams	118 M.G. Coy	Casualty	18.8.17.

Casualties
August 1917.
Wounded.
Officers and Other Ranks.

MISSING. O.R.

	1	2	3	4	5	6	7	8	9	10	11	12	13	14	15	16	17	18	19	20	21	22	23	24	25	26	27	28	29	30	31	Total Month	Remarks
11th A.R. Horse Regt.	1																															1	
12th " "		1																														1	
13th " "																																	
14th " Hampshire "				1														1														1	
16th " Middx. Regt. "																																	
17th " "																																	
7th " Rifle Bde				1													1															1	
7th " K.R.R.C.																																	
1/4th " Cheshire "			2																	1												3	
1/4/5 " Black Watch	1																																
1/6 " Camb																																3	
1/7 " A+SH		1																					1										
1/8 " Clester																																	
116 M.G. Corps						1																											
117 " "																1			1													3	x S+B 115
118 " "	2			1 ×															1													3	and 171+182 R.F.A. Waggr.
Royal Artillery																	1															1	
R.A.M.C.																																	
x, Y+Z F.M. bodys																1																1	
V/1 M. body																																	
225 th C. Coy																																	
116 T. M. Baty																																	
TOTAL	3	3	1	2	–	–	1	–	–	–	–	–	–	–	–	3	1	2	1	–	–	–	1	–	–	–	–	–	–	–	–	18	

Unit	1	2	3	4	5	6	7	8	9	10	11	12	13	14	15	16	17	18	19	20	21	22	23	24	25	26	27	28	29	30	31	Total known	Remarks
11th Br. R. Surrey Regt.	2													9	4	1	3	1		2	1	4	2			1						29	
12th " " "	3													1	1	1	1	2	1	2		1			1							10	
13th " " "	2																1	1		2	1		1	1								11	
14th " Hampshire "													1		6	25	3	3	11		1						3					50	
16th " Middx+Berky "														1			1	4	3								9					16	
17th " "																4	11	4														19	
16th " Rifle Brigade																1		22		4		1	2	2	1							35	
17th " K.R.R.C.		5														1		6	6				5		5	1						25	
16th " Cheshire "	2	1													4		1	1		2			4									12	
H/Sussex Rgl. Fus.	1	10					2								1			1		4		1			1							16	
14th " Northumberland		5		1																		1		2	3							11	
14th " Leeds				6																			1	1	1							10	
15th " Warwickshire	4	5		2													2		10	4			2		3							20	
Royal Artillery	4	1	5	6		1	2			5		1	5	6	8	13	3	2	10	4	5	4										100	
Royal Engineers	2		5	4													2		2	3				1								43	
A.S.C.																	2															35	
R.A.M.C.	2		2			1											19	1														25	
V/29 H.T.M. Bo. Hy.																																2	
107 A.A. Coy.																			2													2	
Divisional Hd. Qrs.																					1											1	
X.Y.Z./29 T.M.Battys																																	
118 A.A. Coy																					1											1	
119 T.M. Bu. Hy.																			1													1	
116 H.R. Coy														2		2			2				5									9	
236 Sieg. b.ty. Coy														3																		3	
116 T.M. B.Coy																2		1														3	
228 F.A. Coy	1	2														2																3	
A.V.C.																																2	
117 I.W.B.																																2	
A.W.B.																																1	
TOTAL	52	19	20	19	4	3	2		5		1	5	6	24	19	61	38	49	31	23	22	7	4	5	19	6	10	10	8		1	450	

Casualties

August   1917

Wounded.

Officers and Other Ranks.

Officers:- Wounded and Missing

Rank and Name	Unit	Casualty	Date
2/Lt. S.H. MacLeod	B/186 Bde. R.F.A.	Wounded	2.8.17.
Lt. (A/Maj.) W. Strachan	A/174 Bde. R.F.A.	"	"
T. 2/Lt. E.V. Johnson	B/174 Bde. R.F.A.	" At duty	"
T. 2/Lt. L.J.P. Thomas	16 Rifle Brigade	"	1.8.17
2/Lt. A.D. McCrae	16 Rifle Bde. (Scot. Rifles, attd)	"	2.8.17.
T. 2/Lt. E. Morriett	16 Rifle Bde.	"	"
T. 2/Lt. W.B. Arnold	16 Rifle Bde.	"	"
T. 2/Lt. D.P. Playfair	117 M.G. Coy.	"	1.8.17.
Maj. J.S.Y. Rogers	R.A.M.C. attd 4/5 Bl. Watch	" At duty.	2.8.17.
Lt. W.H. Pecher	4/5 Black Watch.	"	"
2/Lt. J.C. Ross	4/5 Black Watch.	"	"
T. Capt. J. Anderson	R.A.M.C. attd 16 Notts & Derby.	"	5.8.17.
T. Capt. B.O.W. Robinson	12 Sussex	"	1.8.17.
Capt. C.C. Trevor Roper	14 Hants.	"	2.8.17.
T. Capt. D.H. Coleridge M.C.	16 Notts & Derby.	"	5.8.17.
2/Lt. A. Bain	16 Rifle Bde.	"	3.8.17.
T. 2/Lt. C. Bartlett	13 Sussex	" At duty.	2.8.17.
T. 2/Lt. V.C. Branson	13 Sussex	"	"
T. 2/Lt. L.C. Cox	13 Sussex	"	"
T. 2/Lt. A.E. Lawrence	13 Sussex	"	"
2/Lt. G.V. Hughes	17 Notts & Derby.	"	1.8.17.
Lt. & Q.M. R.G. Johnston	134 Fld. Amb.	" S. at duty.	5.8.17.
Lt. L.H. Askwith	16 Notts & Derby	"	3.8.17.
2/Lt. H.W. Bell	16 Rifle Bde. attd. 117 T.M.B.	"	"
Maj.(T/Lt.Col.) E.P.A. Riddell D.S.O.	Rifle Bde. attd. 1/1 Cambs.	" At duty	5.8.17.
Wes. Chaplain. P.J. HUTCHISON	A.C.D. attd. 117 Inf. Bde.	"	1.8.17.
T. 2/Lt. W.P. Donovan	117 M.G. Coy.	"	5.8.17.
2/Lt. L.E. James	17 K.R.R.C.	"	13.8.17.
2/Lt. A.S. Mellor	16 Notts & Derby.	"	15.8.17.
T. Lt. Y.B. Thompson	A/186 Bde. R.F.A.	"	16.8.17.
Capt.(T/Lt.Col.) C.C. Herbert Stepney. D.S.O.	16 Notts & Derby	"	15.8.17.
T. 2/Lt. R. Summerscale	225 Fld. Coy. R.E.	"	17.8.17.
T. 2/Lt. A.J. Williams	118 M.G. Coy.	"	18.8.17.
T. Capt. R. Harris	134 Fld. Amb.	"	17.8.17.
2/Lt. H.D. Hanks (2 Londons, attd.)	118 M.G. Coy.	"	19.8.17.
T. 2/Lt. E.W. Gaskin	39 Signal Coy. R.E.	"	18.8.17.

Unit	1	2	3	4	5	6	7	8	9	10	11	12	13	14	15	16	17	18	19	20	21	22	23	24	25	26	27	28	29	30	31	TOTAL for MONTH	Remarks
11ᴮ R. Essex Regt.		2	4											9	4		1	3		2	1	4	2			1						28	
12ᵗʰ "		3													1		1	2		1		1	1		1							10	
13ᵗʰ "		2	1														1	1	2	2	1			1			3					11	
14ᵗʰ Hampshire													1	6	25	2	4	2	11			1										50	
16ᵗʰ Notts-Derby				1											1			3									9					18	
17ᵗʰ "																4	1	1	4	1												16	
16ᵗʰ Rifle Brigade			5	1												1		22				2		1	2	1						35	
17ᵗʰ K.R.R.C.			1	5	6										6	4	6	6		1	2	1		1	5							25	
16ᵗʰ Cheshire		2																							1							12	
14/5 Black Watch		1	10	5	4												4			2	4			1	4	1		1				29	
11ᵗʰ Cambridgeshire				6	2										1			3	1							3						11	
11ᵗʰ Herts																			1							1	7	1				10	
13ᵗʰ Gloucestershire		4	5	1	2			5		1		5	6	8	18	3		2			5	1										20	
Royal Artillery		4	1	5	6	8												10		4	4					1						100	
Royal Engineers		28		5	4											2				2	3											48	
M.L.C.					2	1																											
R.A.M.C.		6	1	2	4												19	1	1							1						35	
V/39 H.T.M. Batty																1			2													3	
117 M.G. Coy.																																	
Divisional H.Qrs.																																	
X.Y.Z./39 T.M. Batty														2					2	5												9	
118 M.G. Coy																																	
118 T.M. Batty															1		1														1	2	
No. M.G. Coy														2		2																9	
236 Employed Coy														5	2																	8	
116 T.M. Batty			2												2							1										3	
22 F.M. L. Coy																																2	
A.V.C.																																1	
117 T.M. Batty																																	
M.M.P.																																	
TOTAL.		52	19	20	19	11	3	8		5		1	5	6	24	19	61	38	47	31	23	22	7	4	5	19	10	10	8	—	1	480	

Rank and Name	Unit	Casualty	Date
T. 2/Lt. W. E. Boswell	17" Notts & Derby	Wounded. At duty	18.8.17
2/Lt. F. Wild	D/186 Bde. R.F.A.	"	21.8.17
T. 2/Lt. R. F. Sawyer	17" K.R.R.C.	Missing, believed wounded	25.8.17
2/Lt. J. H. Keating	1/1" Cambs.	Wounded. At duty.	27.8.17
Lt. W. J. Hastings	16 Notts & Derby	Wounded	27.8.17
Lt. E. Masters (4" Seaforths attd.)	118 M.G. Coy.	Wounded. (Gas, Shell)	20.8.17
T. Lt. J. Stephenson	H.Q./186 Bde. R.F.A.	" " "	18.8.17
T. Capt. C. H. J. Rixon	R.A.M.C. attd. 16 Notts & Derby	" Shell Shock	2.8.17
T. 2/Lt. C. B. Dallas	17" K.R.R.C.	" " "	2.8.17
T. Capt.(A/Maj) E. Wright	B/186 Bde. R.F.A.	" At duty.	20.8.17
2/Lt. W. Thompson	C/52 Bde. R.F.A.	" (Gas).	6.8.17

WAR DIARY

INTELLIGENCE SUMMARY

HQ A&Q 39.

Army Form C. 2118

Place	Date	Hour	Summary of Events and Information	Remarks and references to Appendices
WESTOUTRE	1917 1st		39 Div order received. Front line from 28.J.31.s.7.5.0 to 30.D.M.P. Lo.75.6 to be taken over by 39 Div from 24 Div on night of 1st/2nd Sept. 118 Inf Bde to take over and hold the new front.	
"	2nd		39 Div order 153 received (warning order) giving forward scheme of attack in future operations to be carried out on X Corps front. Relief of 116 Inf Bde in KLEIN ZILLEBEKE by 118 Inf Bde of 39 Div. 118 Inf Bde relieved 17th Inf Bde 24 Div in SHREWSBURY FOREST Sector.	
"	3rd	10 AM	GOC 39 Div assumed command of SHREWSBURY FOREST Sector (Right sector) X Corps front.	
"	4th		39 Div order 154 received ordering 117 Inf Bde to move to STEENVOORDE Training area on 6th & 8th inst.	
"	5th		39 Div order 155 received ordering 116 Inf Bde to relieve 118 Inf Bde on night of 8th/9th Sept. 118 Inf Bde moving into Div Reserve.	

A H Q Manual
WAR DIARY
INTELLIGENCE SUMMARY
(Erase heading not required.)

Army Form C. 2118

Page 2

Place	Date 1917	Hour	Summary of Events and Information	Remarks and references to Appendices
WESTOUTRE	8th Sept		Relief of 118 Infce Bde by 116 in the SHREWSBURY FOREST Sector by 116 Infce Bde	
— " —	9th		39 Divn Order 157 received. Divnl H.Q. to move to Div 2 Div Centre near LA CLYTTE on 12th Septr	
— " —	11th		39 Divn order 158 received. Objectives and Boundaries of 39 Divn in 1st Army front covering Offal attacks.	
— " —	12th	10am	39 Divl. H.Q. moved to Div 2 Divl Camp near LA CLYTTE	
		2pm	Move of 118 Inf Bde by Light Railway from STEENVOORDE to RIDGEWOOD and 117 Div — Relieve H.Q. at N4d 118 Inf Bde moved from RIDGEWOOD to WESTOUTRE Area. 117 and 18 Thursday. Relief of 116 Infce Bde on SHREWSBURY Forest Sector by 117 Inf Bde. 116 Infce Bde moved to Div Reserve in MILLEKRUISSE Area.	
DERBY CAMP	13th		39 Divl order 159 received. Army days & of attack.	
— " —	14th		39 Divl order 160 received orders to 116 Infce Bde relieve 117 Battalion in the line on the night of 15/16 & Sept	

A Q Branch

WAR DIARY
or
INTELLIGENCE SUMMARY

Army Form C. 2118

Page 3

(Erase heading not required.)

Place	Date 1917	Hour	Summary of Events and Information	Remarks and references to Appendices
DE ZDM Camp	Sept. 15th		39 Div. order 161 received giving out-line of moves and reliefs. 116 Inf. Bde relieved 117 Inf. Bde in MIC-KRUISSE area & provide for actions of the next 5 days.	
"	16th A DAY		39 Div. order 162 received (39 D.O 163 flg cancelled) giving new details arrangements for everything but necessary for offensive operations.	
"	17th B DAY			
"	18th C DAY		39 Div. order 163 received ordering 39 Div. to attack the Q (Reserve) Regime A Divn. attack on the Front on 20th Sept (E DAY) relief of 116 Inf Bde by 117 Inf Bde dur. 19th Inst. 116 Inf Bde to remain in WEST OUTRE area in Div. Reserve.	
"	19th D DAY		arrangements complete for relief on mid. night 19th/20th Sept. 116 Inf Bde in Div. Reserve.	
"	20th E DAY		39 Divn attack their Z.E.R's from 5.30 am.	
"	21st		Battle continues 39 Div. Casualties 47 Offcers 929 O.R killed wounded & missing	

Army Form C. 2118

Page 4

APO France
WAR DIARY
or
INTELLIGENCE SUMMARY
(Erase heading not required.)

Place	Date 1917	Hour	Summary of Events and Information	Remarks and references to Appendices
DE ZON CAMP.	Sept 22nd		39 Divn Order No 167 received ordering relief of 37/119 Infantry Bde by 39 Divn Bde Shrewsbury Forest Sector on night of 24/25 Sept and 118 Infantry Bde to take over TOWER HAMLETS Sector. Other arrangements include an attack on the enemy lines at a later date.	
"	23rd	7am	39 Divn took over TOWER HAMLETS Sector with a view to attack on 27 Sept	
"	24th		39 Divn order 168 received giving details of an attack on Divn Front in conjunction with other Divisions on the front of Ft Armee	
"	26th		39 Divn order 169 issued ZERO Hour 5.50 am 27th Kn 10.20 OR filled numbers & amount of 37 & 34 Divns	
"	27th		39 Divn order 170 (written immediately receipt of enemy counterattack) relieving 37 Divn for a winter of accompaniment and withdraw of 34 Divn on night of 27/28 Sept — 39 Divn order 171 received relieving guns of 31st & 3 Div by 39 Divn on the left of 31 Div to be ready for support. (Order to Brigade)	

HQ Troops

WAR DIARY
INTELLIGENCE SUMMARY
(Erase heading not required.)

Army Form C. 2118

Page 5

Place	Date	Hour	Summary of Events and Information	Remarks and references to Appendices
ST JANS CAPPEL	Sept 28th 1915	10 am	39 A.D.Q. Arrived at REVECOTEN and stood at CHATEAU ST JANS CAPPEL. Brigade moved to 1x Cyclists Reserve Order. Field Coys R.E. and Pioneer Battn. Reference later 39 DA remaining in Corps.	
	29th		Re-anything and disarming of 9 th Div	
	30th		Instructions of 13 +(S) Battalion the Gloucesters Regt. by G.O.C. 39 Div	

J.E. Owen Major for
G.O.C. 39 Divn

Officers

Rank and Name	Unit	Casualty	Date
T/Lt S. C. Firth	13. Rifles	Killed	1.9.17
T/Maj (A/Lt Col) J. A. Houghton	11 Notts & Derby		13.9.17
T/Lt (A/Capt) C. F. Bowes		accidentally	
T/Lt Cpt F. Hopkins	11 Rifle Bde		20.9.17
" S. G. Gordon			
T. A. F. Lewis	17. K.R.R.C. atta 117 T.M.B.		
T. S. F. Siebert	11 R.B.	W. shipping trench & cards	21.9.17
T/Capt P. V. Laws M.C.	11 Notts & Derby	Killed	20.9.17
T/Lt H. Seed	17 "		9.17
" E. A. Rice	17. K.R.R.C.	Killed	20.9.17
" C. A. Hooker	(1 London Rgt)		
T/Lt E. S. Palmer	117 M.G. Coy		
T/Lt J. La. Thurston		W. 20.9.17 Died Wds.	21.9.17
T/Capt R. N. Riesley	16 R.B.	W.	20.9.17
Lt F. G. Graves	11 Notts & Derbys	Killed	20.9.17
T/Lt F. N. Bewsley	"		"
2/Lt J. E. J. Marsh	1/1 Cambs		24.9.17
Lt J. F. L. Fogarty	227 Fd Coy R.E.		25.9.17
T/Lt L. H. Mulkern	122 M.G. Coy (atta)	Wounds 26th Died	26.9.17
2/Lt W. R. Evans	B/95 Bde R.F.A. (atta)	Killed	24.9.17
T/Lt J. G. Morris	16. Notts & Derby	W. 12.9.17 Died	23.9.17
T/2/Lt H. R. Richinson	118 M.G. Coy	Killed	26.9.17
Lt R. Hardie	Sfsq Bde R.F.A. atta		27.9.17
2/Lt L. E. Williams	17 Notts & Derbys		20.9.17
T/2/Lt H. Bracewell	17 "	W. 20.9.17 Since died	21.9.17
T/Capt H. T. Finsbury	133. Fd Amb.	Killed	21.9.17
2/Lt (A/Capt) F. W. Ford	1/1 Cam by		26.9.17
Capt R. A. Champton	4/5 R.B.		27.9.17
2/Lt W. B. Holmes	1/1 Cheshires		20.9.17
2/Lt C. T. Scott			
2/Lt E. Cockerell			
2/Lt E. Kenneson	11 R Sussex		24.9.17
2/Lt W. R. Bettany			25.9.17
Maj J. H. C. Fetchell	R.A.M.C. att " "		27.9.17

Casualties

September 1917

Killed

Officers

Officers. Wounded and Missing.

Rank and Name	Unit	Casualty	Date
2/Lt. A. B. Watson	4/5 Black Watch	wounded	3. 9. 17
Capt. N. B. Riseley	16 Rifle Bde.	wounded at duty	3. 8. 17
2/Lt. L. G. Llewellyn	39. D. A.C.	"	11. 9. 17
T/2/Lt. A. Robinson	15 Notts & Derbys	"	12. 9. 17
2/Lt. (A/Capt.) J. Lamb	B/174 Bde. R.F.A	wounded at duty	15. 9. 17
2/Lt. S. M. Bennett	A/52 Bde. R.F.A attd.	"	16. 9. 17
T/Lt. F. A. Linsell	39° Signal Coy. R.E.	"	"
T/2/Lt. W. L. Wright	13 Sussex	"	"
T/2/Lt. G. D. Shaw	B/174 Bde	"	18. 9. 17
2/Lt. S. R. Butler	1/6 Cheshires	"	20. 9. 17
2/Lt. W. D. Riley	"	"	"
2/Lt. W. R. Clayton	"	"	"
2/Lt. P. R. L. Cherrington	16° Rifle Bde	"	20. 9. 17
T/2/Lt. R. B. Smith	"	"	"
2/Lt. R. S. G. Epps	"	"	"
T/2/Lt. H. J. Ingram	"	"	"
T/2/Lt. D. L. T. Dally	"	"	"
T/2/Lt. O. F. Whitacker	"	"	"
T/Capt. E. Krolik	"	" at duty	"
T/2/Lt. W. A. Medcalf	15° Notts & Derbys	"	"
T/Lt. (A/Capt.) W. P. Stubbs	17° " "	"	"
T/2/Lt. C. W. S. Cree	" "	"	"
T/2/Lt. G. Ross	" "	"	21. 9. 17.
T/2/Lt. H. B. Marriott	17° K.R.R. Corps	"	20. 9. 17
T/Lt. M. S. Wollmoth	"	"	"
T/2/Lt. G. A. Parfitt	"	"	"
T/2/Lt. R. E. Burgon	"	"	"
Lt. W. P. Sproul	7° Scots Rifles attd.		"
Lt. J. H. Rutledge	117 M.G. Coy.		"

Casualties

September 1917.

Wounded

Officers.

Officers

Rank and Name	Unit	Casualty	Date
T/Lt. G.C. Langdale	13. R. Sussex	missing believed killed	26 9 17
T/Maj. F. Goldsmith	16. Hants	killed	27 9 17
Capt. T.K. Nicholls	"	"	26 9 17
T/Lt. J.S. Bainbridge	"	"	26 9 17
T/2/Lt. B.A.W. Wilson	"	"	26 9 17

39

Officers Wounded and Missing.

Rank and Name	Unit	Casualty	Date
Lt. E. Hais	1/1 Cambs.	Wounded	26. 9. 17
2/Lt. M.P. Betts	6. E. Surrey attd. 1/1 Cambs	"	"
Lt. L.S. Graham	1/1 Cambs	Missing	"
2/Lt. C.R. Robinson	"	"	"
2/Lt. L.O. Nicholl	4/5 Black Watch	"	"
2/Lt. R.J.A. Johnstone	"	"	"
Lt. (A/Capt) J.R. Murray	"	Wounded	"
2/Lt. J. Renny	"	Missing	"
T/Lt. (A/Capt) E. Walker	1/1 Cambs.	Wounded at duty	26. 9. 17
Maj. J.S.Y. Rogers D.S.O.	R.A.M.C. attd. 4/5 B.W.	"	27. 9. 17
2/Lt. C.M. Chaplin	1/1 Cambs	Missing	26. 9. 17
2/Lt. R. Lyell	4/5 Black Watch	Wounded (Gas)	25. 9. 17
2/Lt. D.C. Wilson	" "	"	27. 9. 17
2/Lt. F.G. Proctor	1/6 Cheshires	"	26. 9. 17
T/Lt. P.M.N. Boustead M.C.	14 Hants	" (Gas)	25. 9. 17
T/2/Lt. R.T.H. Hall	118 M.G. Coy.	Wounded	21. 9. 17
2/Lt. N.V. Marshall	16 Rifle Bde.	"	20. 9. 17
T/2/Lt. J.C. Fisher	225 Fd. Coy. R.E.	"	23. 9. 17
2/Lt. R.H.T. Rowley	1/1 Herts	"	22. 9. 17
Capt. Wm. Fort	1/6 Cheshires	Wounded	22. 9. 17
T/Lt. (A/Capt) F. Naden M.C.	"	"	"
2/Lt. C.H.P.C. Penney	4/5 Bk Watch	"	"
2/Lt. V.N. Lansdowne	1/1 Cambs.	"	23. 9. 17
T/Lt. W.R. Harvey	95 Bde. R.F.A. attd.	"	23. 9. 17
Lt. W. Bee	D/94 Bde R.F.A.	"	24. 9. 17
2/Lt. D.F. Eaton	C/95 " "	" at duty	23. 9. 17
T/Lt. C. Murray Lyon	B/190 "	"	24. 9. 17
Lt. A.J. McFarlen	1st Can. T. Coy.	"	23. 9. 17
T/2/Lt. R.H. Membrey	16 Rifle Brigade	" at duty	21. 9. 17
Capt. A. Stevenson M.C.	16 Notts & Derby	"	22. 9. 17
T/2/Lt. S.C. Steele	12 R. Sussex	"	24. 9. 17
T/2/Lt. F.W. Chestney	14 Hants	"	"
T/2/Lt. H. Naylor	12 Sussex	"	"

Officers - Wounded and "Missing".

Rank and Name	Unit	Casualty	Date
2/Lt F. Mc. N. Drury	1/1 Herts	wounded	24. 9. 17
T/Lt T. S. Beach	227 Fd. Coy. R.E.	"	25. 9. 17
2/Lt D. Macpherson	B/174 Bde. R.F.A.	"	26. 9. 17
Capt (A/Maj) Bt.Maj. D. Paige	A/94 Bde. R.F.A. attd.	"	"
Lt (A/Maj) E. Brandish	A/90 " " "	" at duty	"
T. Capt. W. D. Field	134 Fd. Amb.	wounded	"
T. Capt. F. W. Stone	" " "	"	"
1/Lt E. R. Haines (Med. Off.)	United States attd. 13 Sussex	"	23. 9. 17
T/Lt A. J. R. Clark	14 Herts	"	"
2/Lt D. T. Shaw	1/6 Cheshires	"	26. 9. 17
2/Lt T. A. Beeching	"	wounded Acc.	"
Lt (A/Capt) E. J. R. Kemplen	1/1 Cambs.	" at duty	23. 9. 17
T. Capt. A. F. Warwick	133rd Fd. Amb.	" "	26. 9. 17
T/2/Lt H. E. Dupré	16. Rifle Bde.	" at duty	27. 9. 17

Casualties November 1916
Wounded
Officers and Other Ranks

Officers Wounded to 31.X.16 = 314
" Missing to 31.X.16 = 54

Officers (Wounded & Missing)

Rank	Name	Unit	Casualty	Date
2/Lieut	Jones F.W.	1/6 Cheshires	Wounded	2.11.16
T "	Brenshaw F.L.	14th Notts & Derby	"	4.11.16
T "	Gassham N.O.	16th Rifle Bde	"	6.11.16
T "	Cartwright S	5th E Surrey att 16 R.B	"	"
T Lieut	Wayte J.W.	R.A.M.C. attd 14 Hants	"	"
T 2/Lieut	Barber G.B.	14th K.R.R.C	"	14.11.16
T Capt	✳ Stevenson J	4/5 Bk Watch	"	9.11.16
2/Lieut	McIntyre J.C.	"	"	10.11.16
2/Lieut	Constant E.D.	12 Sussex	"	12.11.16
Capt	Dodge W.D.	1/6 Cheshires	"	13.11.16
2/Lieut	Jenkins J.W.	" (3/1 S.W.B)	"	"
Lieut	Alexander S.A	"	"	"
2/Lieut	Mackersey J.J	4/5 Bk Watch	"	"
T/Capt	✳ Stevenson T	"	"	"
2/Lieut	McCririck C.S.	"	"	"
T/Lieut	Hart F.L.	1/1 Herts	"	"
2/Lieut	Frith W.	"	"	"
"	MacMellan J	"	"	"
"	Kemble J.P.	" (1/8 Middx)	"	"
"	Jones K.F.	" (4/10 ")	"	"
2/Lieut	Bayne W.C.	1/6 Cheshires	Shell Shock	14.11.16
T/Capt	Andrew W.C.	118 MG Coy	Wounded	"
2/Lieut	Cramb F.R.	"	"	"
T/Lieut	Brockbank C.L.	"	"	15.11.16

Total Wounded to 30.11.16   338
" Missing to 30.11.16   54

Unit	Detail 31/3/10	1	2	3	4	5	6	7	8	9	10	11	12	13	14	15	16-29	30	Total to 30/4/10	Remarks
111th Bn Rl Sussex	652	12										6	4	5					699	
112th — do —	609	5	4			8		1				1	3	4					641	
113th — do —	621					3	2							3					629	
114 H. Bn Hants R.	5335		2			22	13			2	1								5375	
16th Bn Middx Derby	461													49	1				511	
117th — do —	663				4	5	1	5						5	2				685	
16th Bn Rifle Bde	712		3	2	20			1											740	
111th Bn K2RR	620				1	12	1	5					1						640	
116th Bn Cheshire	3112	2	16	5	2							1	122	5					4495	
4/5 L. Bn Rl Mdx	538	1	2	1				5	1			99	9						656	
110th Gordon H.	504		1	4								42	19						599	
111 st Bn Herts R	234	2	4	9								100	14						383	
13th Bn Glos R	216	4										1		3	1				225	
R.I.A.	58												1						61	
Rl Engineers	101	1	1	1										1	2				105	
Q.L.C.	3																		3	
RQ MC	104													1					105	
V/29 K1 M G	2				2	5	2			1									5	
114 MG Coy	43																		57	
Band San Sec	1																		1	
X.Y-Z TMBys	12							1					4		2				14	
115 MG Coy	30	2																	39	
118 JMG By	7				1														8	
116 MG Coy	620	2																	655	
TOTALS	4443	26	36	10	19	7	67	30	1	36	8	12	10	438	56	5	—	2	4436	

Grand Total 4443 26 36 10 19 7 67 30 1 36 8 12 10 436 56 5 — 2 4936

Re Missing to 31.X.16 1408   Missing November 1916   Total Missing to 30.XI.1916 = 1477

	1st	6th	4th	13th	14th	TOTALS
11th Bn Royal Sussex	5					5
14th Bn Hamps. Regt		3	3			6
14th Bn Notts & Derbys			+		1	1
16th Bn Rifle Bde		1	x	1		1
11th M.G.C.					15	15
13th Royal Sussex				15		11
16th Bn Notts & Derbys				10	1	20
11th Cheshires				20		5
4/5th Suffolk				5		4
1/1 Cambs				4		
1/1 Kent						
	5	4	4	55	1	69

WAR DIARY
—OF—
INTELLIGENCE SUMMARY

Army Form C. 2118

Place	Date	Hour	Summary of Events and Information	Remarks and references to Appendices
ST. JANS CAPPEL.	1917 OCT 1st.		Inspection of 117. Inf. Bde, billeted in and around LOCRE, by G.O.C. 39 DIV. One field Coy R.E. moved to OUTERSTEENE for work on the field Cas. Clearing Station.	
"	2nd		One field Coy. R.E. moved to camp near VOORMEZEELE for work on dugouts under the C.E. IX Corps. One field Coy R.E. and one company 13th Gloucesters (Pnr Bn.) moved to camps near KEMMEL for winter training work.	
"	3rd		Inspection of 116 and 118. Inf. Bdes by G.O.C. 39 DIV. Nothing to report.	
"	4th		117. T.M. Battery moved to STEEN-DEGHEM for training. 2 Batteries 118 Siege de moved to camps W. of VOOR-MEZEELE for work on light railways under I Anzac Corps.	
"	5th		Inspection of 228 Machine Gun Coy (Div. M.G. Coy) and 39 Div. Signal Coy. at BERTHEN by G.O.C. 39 DIV.	

Army Form C. 2118

A.D.S. / Anaesth

WAR DIARY
or
INTELLIGENCE SUMMARY
(Erase heading not required.)

Page 2

Instructions regarding War Diaries and Intelligence Summaries are contained in F.S. Regs., Part II. and the Staff Manual respectively. Title Pages will be prepared in manuscript.

Place	Date 1917	Hour	Summary of Events and Information	Remarks and references to Appendices
ST. JAMS CAPPEL.	OCT. 6th		186. Brigade R.F.A. relieved in action on night of 6/7th Oct and marched back to STRAZEELE area to rest.	
—"—	7th		2 Battalions 118 Inf. Bde moved to camps near POTIJZE for work on roads in the forward area under II d ANZAC Corps. 39 Div. Musketry Camp started at LUMBRES.	
—"—	8th 9th 10th		Nothing to report.	
—"—	11th		39 Divn Warning order No 173 received attaching the 39 Divn (less Artillery) to 37 Divn in the TOWER HAMLETS sector on the night of 14/15th Oct.	
—"—	12th		39 Divn Order No 174 received instructing relief of 31st Divn on night of 15/16th Oct. Instructions received from IX Corps for 174 Bde R.F.A. to come into action on the night of 13/14th in relief of 37 Divn. Arty and move to billets at STRAZEELE for rest.	
—"—	13th		39 Divn Order No 175 received cancelling 39 Divn order 174 & giving details of relief of 37 Divn in TOWER HAMLETS Sector by 39 Divn on the night of 15/16th Oct.	

1875 Wt. W593/826 1,000,000 4/15 J.B.C. & A. A.D.S.S./Forms/C. 2118.

AQ (branch)
WAR DIARY
INTELLIGENCE SUMMARY
(Erase heading not required.)

Army Form C. 2118
Page 3

Place	Date 1917	Hour	Summary of Events and Information	Remarks and references to Appendices
ST. JANS. CAPPEL	OCT 15th		Start of relief of 37th Divn. by 39 Divn. Two Battalions 118 Inf. Bde. went in under II Anzac Corps. relieved 5 118 Sperres near KEMMEL and WESTOUTRE from.	
-"-	16th		116 Inf Bde took over the whole Divt. Front.	
-"-		10 AM	Divn. H.Q. moved to DE ZON. CAMP (Sheet 28 M 12c 7·4) 39 Divn. over No 1 & No 2 receiving areas from K of 39 Divn. 5 x Cdn. and reinforced by 116 Inf Bde & by 117 Inf Bde. on night of 19/20th OCT. 263 Bde joining 118 Inf Bde in reserve in the II Anzac Corps reserve at VIERSTRAAT No 1 & No 2 centres.	
DE ZON Hd CAMP 18th			Nothing to report.	
-"-	19th		116 Inf Bde in forward HAMLETS. Sector relieved by 117 Inf Bde 39 Divn over No 1. 77. received orders of its relief of 39 Divn in the line on night of 24/25th Oct. by 7th Divn. it & 39 Divn with 5 Cdn attached, to go into reserve on a later date.	
-"-	20th 21st 22nd		Preparations for the above to continue despite threats which appeared.	

Army Form C. 2118

Page 4

A.D.G. (illegible)
WAR DIARY
or
INTELLIGENCE SUMMARY
(Erase heading not required.)

Place	Date 1917	Hour	Summary of Events and Information	Remarks and references to Appendices
DE ZON CAMP	OCT 23RD		118 Inf Bde in Divl Reserve relieved by 91st Inf Bde (7th Divn). 118 Inf Bde moved to camps between L.A.CLYTTE and RENINGHELST – 116 Inf Bde relieved instantly by 20th Inf Bde and moved to reserve area near WESTOUTRE.	
-"-	24th		117 Inf Bde in the line relieved by 91st and 22nd Inf Bdes of 7th Divn. and moved to camps near NIERSTRAAT.	
-"-	25th	10AM	Command of TOWER HAMLETS Sector handed over from G.O.C. 39 Divn to G.O.C. 7th Divn. – 39th DHQ remains at DE ZON CAMP.	
-"-	26th		39 Divn Arty moved from STRAZEELE to camps near VEST– OUTRE and RENINGHELST.	
-"-	27th		39 Divn order 179 received with instructions for relief of 17 & Divn by the 39 Divn on night of 28/29 Oct.	
-"-	28th		Nothing to report.	
-"-	29th		118 Inf Bde relieves 22nd Inf Bde.	
-"-	30th		Nothing to report.	
-"-	31st			

J.C. Owen Major for
G.O.C. 39 Divn

Return of Casualties for October 1917 attached.

October   1917

Officers:- Killed.

Rank and Name	Unit	Casualty	Date
T/2/Lt. D. St. G. Pettigrew	17 Notts & Derby's	Wd. 22/10/17 D of Wds. 23/10/17.	23.10.17.
T/Lt. G. Montgomery	116 M.G. Coy.	Wd. 14/10/17 D. of Wds. 14/10/17	14.10.17.

OCTOBER. 1917.

Officers :- Wounded and Missing.

Rank and Name	Unit	Casualty	Date.
T/Capt. J. A. Young	17th Notts & Derbys	Missing	4.10.17.
2/Lt. R. M. Carse.	HQ. 174/Bde R.F.A.	Wounded (Gas).	19.9.17.
Major A.E. Earl of Dunmore V.C., M.V.O., D.S.O.	R. of O. GSO2 39 Divn.	Wounded	15.10.17.
Capt. J. Morris	R.A.M.C. (T.F.) 132 Fld. Amb.	Wounded. Gassed [at duty to Hosp 26/10]	16.10.17.
T.2/Lt. H. M. Geary	11 Sussex	Wounded	18.10.17.
T. Capt. R.D. Nasmyth	R.A.M.C. 134 Fld. Amb.	Wounded (Gas).	20.10.17.
T/Lt. R.E. Currey	A+S.H. (39 Sig Coy. R.E.)	Wounded	22.10.17.
2/Lt. C. L. Ringer	1/1 Herts	Wounded.	24.10.17.
2/Lt. T. E. Penney	1/1 Herts.	Wounded	28.10.17.
2/Lt. E. F. M. Brown	1/1 Herts	Wounded	28.10.17.
T/Lt. A.D. Parkin	16 Notts & Derbys	Wounded	22.10.17.
T. Capt. H.K. Stokes	R.A.M.C. attd 4/5 Bl. Watch	Wounded (Gas).	28.10.17.
2/Lt. S.J. Davie	4/5 Black Watch	Wounded.	29.10.17.
2/Lt. E.W. Watkins	1/6 Cheshires	Wounded.	29.10.17.
2/Lt. G.D. Marsden	1/6 Cheshires	Wounded	31.10.17.
2/Lt. C.F. Nicholls	1/1 Herts.	Wounded (Shell Shock).	27.10.17.
2/Lt. J.R.S.L Eighy	1/1 Cambs.	Wounded.	31.10.17.
T.2/Lt. A.E. Lawrence.	13 Sussex	Wounded	17.10.17.
2/Lt. S.H. Nasted.	B/156 Bde. R.F.A.	Wounded (Gas)	10.10.17.

- A'Q Branches • 39' Division.

WAR DIARY
INTELLIGENCE SUMMARY
(Erase heading not required.)

Army Form C. 2118

Page I.

Place	Date	Hour	Summary of Events and Information	Remarks and references to Appendices
DEZON CAMP LA CLYTTE	1917 1st Nov		39th Divn. Order No 182 received ordering relief of 118 Inf Bde in the line by 117 Inf Bde on night of 3/4 Nov.	
"	2nd 1917		39th Divn. Order No 183 received cancelling No 182 of 1st Nov. and ordering 116 Inf Bde to relieve 118 Inf Bde on night of 3/4 of Nov. 117 Inf Bde to remain in Divl. Reserve.	
"	3rd	A.M.	39 Divn. Order No 184 received with reference to continuation of operations by the Second Army. 114 Bde RFA relieved 162 Bde RFA. Relief of 118 Inf Bde in the TOWER HAMLETS Sector by 116 Inf Bde C.O.L. 118 Inf Bde rest in camps near LA CLYTTE.	
"	4th A.M.		39 Divn. Order No 185 received. 39 Divn to assist 5th Divn in the attack on 2 day.	
"	5th		Wire from IX Corps received. Hd-front held by 39 Divn to be taken over by 9th Divn. G.O.C. the REUTEL BECELAERE Sector and 34 Divn to take (?) the front from X & IX Corps on 12th Nov. 118 Inf Bde to be relieved 2nd by 117 Inf Bde. encamped in area around WERSTRAAT. 117 Bde to be area camps to-include LA CLYTTE and RENINGHELST. 116 Bde preceded 118 Inf Bde	

HQ Branches • 39' Division

WAR DIARY
or
INTELLIGENCE SUMMARY
(Erase heading not required.)

Army Form C. 2118

Page 2

Place	Date	Hour	Summary of Events and Information	Remarks and references to Appendices
DEZ ON CAMP	6th Nov.		Second Army resumed the attack on PASCHENDAELE RIDGE. X Corps attacked POLDER HOEK CHATEAU. II & 5th DIV. 39 DIV (warning) orders received regarding extension of front and relief of 5th Div on firm M. on the REVELSBERG on 7/11 & 8/11 Nov. and transfer of Div. to IX Corps.	
"	7th Nov.		Relief of 116 Inf. Bde in the TOWER HAMLETS Sect. by 117 Inf. Bde. 116 Inf. Bde moved to camps between LA CLYTTE and REMIGHELST and 3 Coy Bns. 16 NEERSTRAAT Camps.	
"	8th Nov.		3 Bns. 116 Inf. Bde. moved into rest in camps between LA CLYTTE and REMIGHELST and 2 Bns. 118 Inf. Bde moved into DIV. Reserve in camps around NEERSTRAAT. Relief of 227 Fld. Coy R.E. in CAMRAI STREET Tunnels by 225 Fld. Coy R.E. 39 Div. Order No 189 received re relief of 5th Div by 39 Div. on night of 9/11/12 Nov. Nil to report.	
"	10th Nov.		Second Army resumed the attack on PASCHENDAELE Ridge.	

WAR DIARY

INTELLIGENCE SUMMARY

AA Q Branch 39'D.

Page 4

Army Form C. 2118

Place	Date 1917	Hour	Summary of Events and Information	Remarks and references to Appendices
WESTOUTRE	18th Nov		16 General Q.A.S. CAFÉ. CRA 39 Divn assumed temporary command of 39th Divn. vice Major General E. FEETHAM C.B. C.M.G. to the united Kingdom on leave.	
	19th Nov		39 Divn. H.Q.s to 40 Divn. H.Q.s taking over that area of relief of 7 in 9 (Rest) by 118 INF. Bde. on relief of 39th Inf. Bde. 39 Divn. Arty No. 143 received instructions to relieve artillery of 39 Div. AC	
	20th Nov		39 DA ate to relieve 30 D.D.A.	
	21st Nov		Relief of 39 DA by 30 DA Completed 116 Ini Bde relieved by 117 Inf. Bde NS to report.	
	22nd Nov		Relief of the troops 39th R.I.R. (1st R Divn) IX Corps other received instructions relief of 39 Divn. by 36th Divn and transfer to IXth Corps.	
	23rd Nov		39 Divn Bde H.Q. 145 received gunny orders for relief of 89th Divn 39th Divn. NS to report. 119 I'nfn. (in Reserve) relieved by 10th Inf R. B.a (36th Divn) in 9.10 3a Peeseternley to Rhen to WATSU AREA	
	24th Nov			
	25th Nov		One armoured grew over 86 R.I.R. 36th Divn collected by Right Bde.	

Army Form C. 2118

Page 5

A.P.Q. Branch 39'D.

WAR DIARY
INTELLIGENCE SUMMARY
(Erase heading not required.)

Place	Date 1917	Hour	Summary of Events and Information	Remarks and references to Appendices
WESTOUTRE	25th Nov. (continued)		Two machine gun teams 116 Infantry proceeded by train to WIMIE-EELE Area on relief by 1st Battn. 21st Inf. Bde. (30th Divn.) 90th Infantry (30th Divn.) from Reserve relieved 118 Inf. Bde. by Bn. Co. Bn. 117 Inf. Bde. moved to VLAMERTINGHE AREA for work. 118 Inf. Bde. proceeded to ECKE AREA by train.	
"	26th Nov.		2 Bns. 116 Inf. Bde. in billets on relief by 2 Bns. 2/01 Inf. Bde. 30th Divn. proceeded to camps in present area. 2nd Bn. of 117 Inf. Bde. moved to VLAMERTINGHE area for work.	
STEEN-VOORDE	27th Nov.		G.O.C. 39th Divn. hands over command to G.O.C. 30th Divn. 39th Divnl. Art. WESTOUTRE and re. of 2 Batteries of 116 Inf. Bde. are moved by train to WINNEZEELE Area. Brigades rested and refitted.	
"	28th Nov.			
"	29th Nov.		Remainder of 10 Brs. of Bdes moved to POPERINGHE-VLAMERTINGHE-YPRES area for Bivouacs or tents, Railways gun positions in the VIII Corps. Inf. 15 Divn. Pioneer Bn and R.E. Coys relieved in work in forward area.	
"	30th		A return of Casualties for Nov. 1917 is attached.	

J.C. Owen, Major for
Major General
Cmdg 39 Division.

November. 1917.

Officers :- Killed.

Rank and Name	Unit	Casualty	Date
2/Lt. (A/Capt) J.S. Paterson	4/5 Black Watch	Killed	1.11.17.
Captain W.D. Aston	1/1 Cambs.	Wd. Since died of wds.	2.11.17.
2/Lt. C.L.S. Harrison	11 Sussex	Killed	7.11.17.
Lt. (A/Capt & Adjt) J. Stevenson M.C	4/5 Black Watch	"	14.11.17.
2/Lt. J. Smith	4/5 Black Watch	Wd. Since died of wds.	14.11.17.
T.2/Lt. V.F. Allen	16 Rifle Bde.	Killed	17.11.17.
T.2/Lt. J.A. Trask	14 Hants	Wd. Since died of wds.	20.11.17.
2/Lt. P. Brookes	1/6 Cheshires	Killed	22.11.17.

NOVEMBER. 1917.

Officers: Wounded and Missing.

Rank and Name	Unit	Casualty	Date.
T 2/Lt. C. Gordon Cleather	13 Sussex	Wounded	5.11.17.
T Capt. M. Hermans	RAMC. attd 1/6 Cheshires	Wounded (Gas)	3.11.17.
Capt. (T/Lt. Col) W.A. Stanway	1/6 Cheshires	Wounded (Gas)	5.11.17.
T 2/Lt. A.P. Sayers	13 Sussex	Wounded. At duty.	6.11.17.
2/Lt. N. Walker	174/Bde R.F.A.	Wounded.	6.11.17.
T Major C. Bartlett	13 Sussex	Wounded	12.11.17.
T Capt. H.R. Cairkness	132 Fld. Amb.	Wounded. (Gas)	13.11.17.
T 2/Lt. S.I. Davies	11 Sussex	Wounded	15.11.17.
T 2/Lt. P.H. Hill	12 Sussex	Wounded	15.11.17.
T 2/Lt. (A/Capt) S.A. Andrews	12 Sussex	Wounded	15.11.17.
Lt. W. Whyte	4/5 Black Watch	Wounded.	15.11.17.
T 2/Lt. F.L. Sweet	234 Fld. Coy. R.E.	Wounded	16.11.17.
2/Lt. R.L. Wootton	16 Rifle Bde.	Wounded	17.11.17.
T 2/Lt. J. McD. Burke	16 Sherwood Foresters	Wounded	19.11.17.
2/Lt. W.H. Davidson	1/6 Cheshires	Wounded	20.11.17.
2/Lt. (A/Capt) C.W. Mawby	1/1 Cambs	Wounded.	20.11.17.
2/Lt. A.A. Geater	1/1 Cambs	Wounded	20.11.17.
Lt. (A/Maj) M.B. Heath	A/174 Bde R.F.A.	Wounded (Gas)	18.11.17.
Lt. E.A. Field	A/174 Bde R.F.A.	Wounded (Gas)	18.11.17.
2/Lt. G.C.C. Walker	A/174 Bde R.F.A.	Wounded (Gas)	18.11.17.
T Capt (A/Maj) S.I. Quin	B/186 Bde R.F.A.	Wounded (Gas)	19.11.17.
T 2/Lt. J.E. Warner	B/186 Bde R.F.A.	Wounded (Gas)	20.11.17.
2/Lt. A. MacNab	B/186 Bde R.F.A.	Wounded (Gas)	20.11.17.
T Capt (A/Maj) P. Wright	B/186 Bde R.F.A.	Wounded (Gas)	20.11.17.
2/Lt. E.V. Mason	B/186 Bde R.F.A.	Wounded (Gas)	20.11.17.
T 2/Lt. A.C. Brannon	14 Hants	Wounded (Gas)	20.11.17.
2/Lt. E.L. Bird	14 Hants	Wounded. At duty.	22.11.17.
2/Lt. W.S. Walker	A/174 Bde R.F.A.	Wounded.	26.11.17.
T Capt. F. Newhouse	225 Fld. Coy. R.E.	Wounded. (Gas)	16.11.17.
2/Lt. L.G. Llewellyn	A/174 Bde R.F.A.	Wounded.	20.11.17.
T Lt (A/Capt) J.S. Ogden	1/6 Cheshires	" (Gas)	8.11.17.
T Lt. G. Rowley MC	"	" "	23.11.17

T.2/Lt J. Hatton	} 1/6 Cheshires	Wounded (Gas)	23.11.17
T2/Lt S Green			
T2/Lt G Brewer			
2/Lt (T/Lt) A/Capt C. Walker M.C.	1/1 Cambs	" (Gas)	10.11.17
2/Lt A. McG. McKenzie	4/5 Bk Watch	" (Gas)	7.11.17
Capt R.S. McIntyre M.C.		" (Gas)	14.11.17
T.2/Lt C.A. Dingle	11 Sussex	"	21.11.17
T2/Lt C.L. Jarvis	14 Hants	" at duty	23.11.17
Lt. R.A. Young	B/186 Bde R.F.A.	" (gas)	20.11.17

41

Army Form C. 2118.

"A" "Q" Branches

WAR DIARY
or
INTELLIGENCE SUMMARY.
(Erase heading not required.)

Page 1.   Vol 22

Place	Date	Hour	Summary of Events and Information	Remarks and references to Appendices
STEENVOORDE	1917 Dec 1st		116, 117 & 118 Inf Bdes, 225, 227 & 234 Field Coys RE, and 13th Gloucester shire Regt (Pioneers) engaged on work in forward area East of VLAMER-TINGHE under VIII A Corps.	
"	3rd		Major-General E. FEETHAM. C.B. C.M.G. returned from leave to the United Kingdom and re-assumed command of the 39th Divn. vice Br-General E.A.S. Cope R.A.	
"	4th		VIII Corps order received re relief and transfer of 39th Divn. to X Corps. To STEENVOORDE area	
"	5th		39 D.A.O. No. 199. received re relation of Inf Bdes to STEENVOORDE area and later move to LUMBRES Area.	
"	6th		After order to STEENVOORDE, D.O. No. 199. received giving details of move to LUMBRES area Relation of 118 Inf Bde to BECKE area by train	

"A" "Q" Branches

WAR DIARY
or
INTELLIGENCE SUMMARY.
(Erase heading not required.)

Army Form C. 2118.

Page 2

Place	Date 1917	Hour	Summary of Events and Information	Remarks and references to Appendices
STEENVOORDE	Dec 7.		Transport of 118 Inf Bde gnd marched to LUMBRES area staging night of 7/8 Dec. in RÉTRESCURE area. 117 Inf Bde moved by train to WATOU area.	
"	8.	8 A.M.	116 Inf Bde moved by train from POPERINGHE to WINNIZEELE area.	
"	"		118 Inf Bde gnd moved by train from ECKE area to LUMBRES area.	
"	"		Transport of 117 Inf Bde gnd marched to LUMBRES area staging night 8/9 Dec. in 39 Div. area nights LUMBRES area staging night 8/9 Dec. in RÉTRESCURE area.	
"	9.		117 Inf Bde detrained entrained at GODEWAERSVELDE and proceeded to LUMBRES area. Transport of 116 Inf Bde gnd marched to LUMBRES area staging night 9/10 Dec. at RÉTRESCURE area. 118 Inf Bde proceeded by march route from 15 T.C. area.	
"	10.	2.0 a.m.	39 Div. HQ closed at STEENVOORDE and reopened at MIELLES-LEZ-BLEQUIN. 39 Div. HQ Curro march orders x Cmpo. 116 Inf Bde gnd entrained at GODEWAERSVELDE and proceeded to area LUMBRES.	
MIELLES-LEZ-BLEQUIN				

"A" HQ Branch

WAR DIARY
or
INTELLIGENCE SUMMARY.
(Erase heading not required.)

Army Form C. 2118.

Page 3.

Place	Date 1917	Hour	Summary of Events and Information	Remarks and references to Appendices
MEEES-LEZ BLEQUIN	DEC		Brigade refitted and rested.	
"	12th 16th 17th		Training carried out by Brigades. Conference at DHQ. 39 Div. D.O. received re move of 1 Field Coy RE's under orders at INGHAM II RD Corps Comd.	
"	18th		39 Div. Name Canteen & 35 MD Canteen & Coffee Canteen to administer canteen supplies during very cold weather.	
"	19th 20th 21st		39 A.D.O. received re transfer of 39 Div. R.A. and move to MONDREME.	
"	22nd		Orders received from II Corps re move of 39 Divn. to forward area and relief in the line of 32nd Divn.	
"	25th		39 D.O. MDS. 20b and 20c received re move of 39 Div to forward area	
"	28th		117 IFB de Egypt. Transports moved from LUMBRES area to ST MOMELIN. Part of 117 IFBde. moved from LUMBRES to BA area. Snow drifts blocked many of the roads.	
"	29th		117 IFBde Cyclists moved by train from WIZERNES to CAPPA. Bank near. " " " Transport in march from ST MOMELIN to ST JAMSTER BIEZEN	

"A" "Q" Branch
WAR DIARY
or
INTELLIGENCE SUMMARY.
(Erase heading not required.)

Army Form C. 2118.

Page 4

Place	Date 1917	Hour	Summary of Events and Information	Remarks and references to Appendices
MERLES-LES-BÉQUIN	DEC 29th		116 Inf. Bde. guns transport from LUMBRES area to ST MOMELIN by road.	
	30th		118 Inf. Bde. guns from C area to B area: owing to state of roads only partly completed.	
"	30th	8 PM	More of 118 Inf. Bde. guns to 5 forward area positions 24 hours	
			117 Inf. Bde. guns handed from ST OMER to BÉQUIN to forward area	
			- ST MOMELIN to ST JMRSTER BILLETS	
			116 " " " "	
			116 " " " moved by train from WATERINGS to Renew BH area SIEGE CAMP	
			118 " " " completed move to B area	
			39 Div HQ closed at MERLES-LES-BÉQUIN. 12 NOON and reopened at BORDER CAMP. 28 A.2.4. B) 117 Inf Bde received all Infantry in line	
BORDER CAMP	31st		Transport 116 Inf Bde guns moved from ST JMRSTER BILLETS to SIEGE CAMP	
			118 " " " LUMBRES area & reopened at 4 mm BATT & ST MOMELIN	
		10 AM	39 Div HQ closed at BORDER CAMP and reopened at 4 mm BATT	
			& ST 39 DIVN took over command of the section from G.O.C. 32ND DIVN.	

Lt. Owen Magin
Major General
Comdg. 39 Divn.

31/12/1917.

Army Form C. 2118.

DUPLICATE Page 1.

WAR DIARY
A 70 Bngdr
or
INTELLIGENCE SUMMARY.
(Erase heading not required.)

Instructions regarding War Diaries and Intelligence Summaries are contained in F. S. Regs., Part II. and the Staff Manual respectively. Title pages will be prepared in manuscript.

Place	Date 1917	Hour	Summary of Events and Information	Remarks and references to Appendices
STEEYVOORDE	Dec 1st		116, 117 & 118 Inf Bdes, 2 & 5, 227 & 234 Field Coys R.E., and 13th Gloucester (Pioneer Regt) Pioneers engaged in work in forward area East of VLAMER-TINGHE under VIII Corps.	
" -	3rd		Major-General E. FEETHAM. C.B. CMG returned from leave to the United Kingdom and re-assumed command of the 39th Divn vice Br-General G A S Cape R.A.	
" -	4th		VIII Corps orders received re relief and relief of 39th Divn working in forward area and transfer of 39th Divn to II Corps to STEEVORDE area	
" -	5th		39 D.O. No 199 received in relation of IF[?]Bs ovr to LUMBARTS Area and later move to LUMBARTS Area	
" -	6th		After noted to D.O. No 199, received giving details of move to LUMBARKs area. Return of 118 InfBde to EECKE area by train.	

T2134. Wt. W708—776. 500090. 4/15. Sir J. C. & S.

Army Form C. 2118.

A/Q Branch

WAR DIARY
or
INTELLIGENCE SUMMARY.
(Erase heading not required.)

Page 2

Instructions regarding War Diaries and Intelligence Summaries are contained in F.S. Regs., Part II. and the Staff Manual respectively. Title pages will be prepared in manuscript.

Place	Date 1917	Hour	Summary of Events and Information	Remarks and references to Appendices
STEENVOORDE	Dec 7		Transport of 118 Inf Bde marched to LUMBRES area & 117 & 118 to Bde in RENESCURE area. 117 Inf Bde moved by train to WATOU area.	
" "	8th		116 Inf Bde moved by train from POPERINGHE to WINNEZEELE area. 118 Inf Bde group moved by train from ESQUES area to LUMBRES area staying night 8/9 Inf Bde & "B" area moved to LUMBRES area. Transport of 117 Inf Bde group moved to LUMBRES area staying night 8/9 at RENESCURE area.	
" "	9th		117 Inf Bde group entrained at GODEWAERSVELDE and proceeded to LUMBRES area. — Transport of 116 Inf Bde group marched to LUMBRES area — also remaining by 8th of 9th Inf Bde at RENESCURE & marched from B.G.C. area and 118 Inf Bde (less transport) entrained by train & returned air.	
MELLIS-LEZ- BLEQUIN	10 & 10 am		39 Div: HQ closed at STEENVOORDE. NIEURLET-LEZ-BLEQUIN. 39 & Div. rear Group north of West & Coys 116 Inf Bde group entrained at GODEWAERSVELDE and proceeded to "A" area in LUMBRES.	

Army Form C. 2118.

Page 3

"A" Branch

WAR DIARY
or
INTELLIGENCE SUMMARY.
(Erase heading not required.)

Place	Date 1917	Hour	Summary of Events and Information	Remarks and references to Appendices
MERRIS-LEZ BLEQUIN	DEC		(Brigade refitted and rested)	
"	12th to 17th		Training carried out by Brigades	
"	17th		Conference at BHQ. 39 Div. D.O. received re move of 1 Field Coy. R.E. with 41st MILLAM Ind. Corps. Conf.	
"	18th		39 Div. Hinge Seued re 11 Ind Corps div & Corps Continue to administer. Training continues, few but very cold weather.	
"	19th 20th 21st		39 D.O. received re transfer of 39 Div HQ and move to MORBECQUE	
"	22nd		Orders received from II Corps re move of 39 Div to 2nd area and relief in the line of 32nd Div.	
"	25th		35 D.O. Nos 20 & 233 received re move of 39 Div to forward area	
"	26th		117 Inf Bde Group Transport moved from LUMBRES area to ST MOMELIN. Paid 28/17 Infantry Bde moved from LUMBRES to BSA area. Snow lifts. Billeted in camp of the accom.	
"	29th		117 Inf Bde Gp moved by train from MOMELIN to CAMP. Back road. " " " " Transport moved from ST MOMELIN to ST JANS TER BIEZEN	

Army Form C. 2118.

"A" Branch

WAR DIARY
or
INTELLIGENCE SUMMARY.
(Erase heading not required.)

Page 4

Place	Date 1917	Hour	Summary of Events and Information	Remarks and references to Appendices
MEILLES-LES-BLEQUIN	DEC 29th		116 Inf Bde Group Transfer from LUMBRES area to ST MARTIN by road	
			118 Inf Bde Group from C area to B area. Owing to state of roads only partly completed	
		8 PM	More of 118 Inf Bde Group to forward area (further 24 hrs)	
	30th		117 Inf Bde Group transfer from ST OMER area to forward area	
			116 " " " ST MARTIN to ST JANVIER Bilets	
			116 " " " Moved by train from MOLINGHEM to RENIVRE Bde area. SIEGE CAMP	
			118 " " " Completed move to B area	
			39 Div HQ Opened at MEILLES-LES-BLEQUIN. (ARGUIR LANOUR and renfort at BORDER CAMP (28A.2.a.d) 117 Inf Bde relieved 148 Inf Bde in Line	
BORDER CAMP	31st.		transfer 116 Inf Bde Group moved from ST JANVIER Billets to SIEGE CAMP	
			118 " " " LUMBRES Area	
		10 AM	39 Div HQ Closed at BORDER CAMP and rendered at 6 AM as BORK of 57 39 Divn. Takes over command of the Section from G.O.C. 32nd Divn.	

Lt. Owen Mayin for
Major General
Comdg. 39 Divn.

31/12/1917

SECRET AND CONFIDENTIAL.

D. A. G.,
   3rd Echelon,
     G. H. Q.

     Reference this office No.39/113/A dated 15th May, 1918.

     It is requested that the Orders, etc., forwarded herewith may be attached to the "A & Q" Staff War Diary for December, please.

17th May, 1918.

                         Brigadier-General,
                Commanding 39th Division.

SECRET.   39/1658/AQ6/4.

Reference Adendum No.2 to 39th Division Order No.199

1. Para.1 (a & b).

   Personnel will proceed by train with 116th Brigade Group but will detrain at LUMBRES and march to destinations.
   Rations for 10th instant will be carried on the man.
   Rations for consumption 11th instant will be drawn at destination.
   Transport of these two sections will be detached from the 116th Brigade Group Column on morning of the 10th instant under orders to be issued by G.O.C. 118th Brigade, and will march direct to destination.

2. Para.3 (a).

   This Transport will leave 116th Brigade Group at SAMETTE.

   SUPPLIES.

   Rations for troops and transport proceeding to 'C' Area for consumption 11th instant will be dumped at MAISON BLANCHE on 9th instant. The rations for the transport will be placed on the Supply Wagons before moving on the 10th. The rations for units concerned will be reloaded and conveyed by lorry direct to "C" Area on 10th instant. One man should accompany each units rations from MAISON BLANCHE to guide and take over at destination.

                                                H.F. Dawes. Capt.

                                                for
                                                Lieut.-Colonel.
7th December, 1917.   A.A.& Q.M.G., 39th Division.

   COPIES ISSUED TO :- Recipients of Adendum No.2 to 39th Div.
                        Order No.199.

S E C R E T.   39/1858/AQ6/2.

A

ADMINISTRATIVE INSTRUCTIONS No.2 ISSUED WITH REFERENCE
TO 39th DIVISION ORDER No.199 dated 5.12.17.

Ref. Maps - Belgium & France Sheet 27. 1/40,000
            Hazebrouck   5a 1/100,000.
            Calais   13 1/100,000

1. TRAIN ARRANGEMENTS.

   All moves by train from the STEENVOORDE Area to the LUMBRES Area will be carried out in accordance with instructions to be issued later.

2. ADVANCE PARTIES.

   (a) Two lorries per Brigade have been ordered to be at each Brigade Headquarters at 7.0 a.m., 7th December to convey personnel, blankets and rations of Advance Parties for billeting to the LUMBRES Area.
   Strength of Billeting Parties will be :-

Bde. Headquarters	-	1 Officer, 1 N.C.O. & 1 French Interpreter.
Each Inf. Bn.	-	1 Officer, 5 N.C.O's. (1 N.C.O. per Bn.H.Q. plus 1 per Coy.).
Machine Gun Coy.	-	1 Officer & 1 N.C.O.
T.M. Battery.	-	1 Officer & 1 N.C.O.
Coy. of Divl. Train	-	1 Officer & 1 N.C.O.
Field Ambulance	-	1 Officer & 1 N.C.O.

   Brigades will arrange that the above parties are fully rationed up to and inclusive of the date on which they rejoin their respective units.
   One bicycle per unit may be taken on these lorries.

   (b) The C.R.E. will arrange to send Advance Billeting Parties by train to DESVRES on 8th December to take over billets which will be allotted by Area Commandant "C" Area. (see para. 3 B below).

3. BILLETING.

   (a) Transport of Brigade Groups.

   Brigades will send their Brigade Transport Officer or a representative as under to report to Area Commandant, RENESCURE who will allot billets for personnel, and point out the fields hired by W.D. in which animals will be picketed and vehicles parked.
   This Area is near MAISON BLANCHE in O.31 (Sheet 27).
   No field, which has not been previously used by transport, will be taken without the authority of the Area Commandant.
   B.T.O., or representative, 118th Infantry Bde. will report to Area Commandant, RENESCURE by 11.0 a.m. 6th December, and those of 116th and 117th Inf. Bdes. by 11.0 a.m. 7th December.
   Brigades are responsible for billeting their Brigade Groups.

P.T.O.

(2).

3. **BILLETING** (contd.).

    (a) <u>Transport of Brigade Groups (contd.).</u>

B.T.O's. will report actual numbers of Officers and O.R. billeted to the Area Commandant before leaving the Area.

Area Commandant, RENESCURE is on the telephone

    (b) <u>LUMBRES Training Area.</u>

The area is divided as follows:-

Divl. H.Q. Area	-	NIELLES-LEZ BLEQUIN.
'A' Area (116th Inf.Bde.)	-	LUMBRES) SAMETTE)
'B' Area (117th Inf.Bde.)	-	LOTTINGHEM.
'C' Area (118th Inf.Bde.)	-	HENNEVEUX.
Area Commandant 'A' Area	-	Coln. COUCHMAN, LUMBRES, (on telephone).
" " 'B' "	-	Coln. STRACEY, LOTTINGHEM.
" " 'C' "	-	Major ISACKE, HENNEVEUX.
116th Inf. Bde. H.Q. will be at	-	SAMETTE.
117th " " " " "	-	VELINGHEM.
118th " " " " "	-	ALINCTHUM.

Area Commandants 'A','B' and 'C' Areas will allot billets for their respective areas.
Billeting parties will on arrival report at once to Area Commandant concerned.

    (c) The C.R.E., Field Coys, & Pioneer Battalion will be billeted as follows in 'C' Area:-

C. R. E.	-	COLEMBERT.
234 — 1 Company	-	COLEMBERT.
Vacant. 1 Company	-	LONGUEVILLE.
227 — 1 Company	-	BAINGHEM LE COMTE.
13th Bn. Gloster Regt. (Pioneers)	-	BOURNONVILLE.

Billets will be obtained from Area Commandant 'C' Area.

    (d) The 50th Mobile Vet.Section, Salvage Coy & 236th Employment Company will be billeted at NIELLES LEZ BLEQUIN.

    (e) 228th (Divl.) Machine Gun Coy. will be billeted at VAL de LUMBRES.
Billets will be obtained from Area Commandant, LUMBRES.

4. SUPPLIES

Preserved Rations will be issued for troops travelling by train on 8th, 9th & 10th instant.
Arrangements will be made by units whose transport moves on 7th, 8th & 9th for rations for consumption on these days to be cooked on the previous day.
Train Companies will accompany transport of units. Baggage wagons will march with the First Line Transport.
Rations for transport of Brigade Groups for consumption 8th, 9th & 10th respectively will be carried on the Supply Wagons.
Rations for Brigade Groups for consumption 9th, 10th & 11th respectively will be dumped near MAISON BLANCHE and conveyed by Supply Wagons to Brigade Areas where they will be issued to units on arrival.

5. LORRIES.

The following Lorries will be provided for move of units to the LUMBRES Area.
All Formations and Units mentioned below will wire 39th Div."Q" the rendezvous and time at which they wish lorries to report.
All lorries will make one journey only.

8th inst.	118th Brigade	–	16 lorries.
	228th Machine Gun Coy.	–	2 "
	Divl. Rest Station	–	1 lorry.
9th inst.	117th Brigade	–	16 lorries.
	Divl. Rest Station	–	1 lorry.
10th inst.	116th Brigade	–	16 lorries.
	13th Gloster Regt.	–	3 "
	227th Field Coy., R.E.	–	2 "
	234th Field Coy., R.E.	–	2 "
	39th Div. Salvage Coy.	–	1 lorry.
	39th Div. Gas School	–	1 "
	Divl. Rest Station	–	1 "

6. STRENGTHS.

The following are the strengths of units attached to Brigade Groups.
Brigades are responsible for the issue of all instructions necessary to move these units to the LUMBRES Area.

116th Brigade Group.	By Train.	By Road.	
13th Gloucesters.	506 men	64 men	89 animals.
227th Field Coy. R.E.	75 "	93 "	73 "
234th Field Coy., R.E.	93 "	89 "	74 "
134th Field Ambl.	150 "	36 "	44 "
117th Brigade Group.			
133rd Field Ambulance.	180 "	36 "	45 "
118th Brigade Group.			
228th Machine Gun Coy.	146 "	41 "	51 "
39th Div. Salvage Coy.	61 "	2 "	2 "

P.T.O.

(4)

7. **BATHS.**

Baths are situated in the LUMBRES Area as follows :-

116th Brigade Area in - SENINGHEM.
117th   "   "   "   - SELLES.
118th   "   "   "   - HENNEVEUX.

Applications for baths will be made to Baths Officer, 39th Division who will be situated at Divl. Headquarters.
Brigades will take over these Baths on arrival and place a Caretaker at the Bath until the arrival of the Bath personnel.
It is hoped to be able to supply clean clothing about the 13th instant.

8. **AREA STORES.**

All Area Stores including R.E. material, tents and tent bottoms will be handed over to Area Commandants or their representatives in the STEENVOORDE Area and receipts obtained. No Area Stores are to be taken out of the Area.

9. **TRAFFIC CONTROL.**

The A.P.M. will make the necessary arrangements for the control of traffic during the move of Brigade. Transports.
He will arrange direct with the 58th Division to take over Traffic Control Posts in the LUMBRES Area.

10. **DIVISIONAL UNITS.**

The following units will move by train on the 10th instant, all transport to proceed by road on the 9th instant under an Officer to be detailed by O.C. 39th Divl. Signal Coy., R.E.

39th Divl. Headquarters.
39th Divl. Signal Coy., R.E.
39th Divl. Salvage Coy.
39th Divl. Gas School.
236th Employment Company.

11. **LEAVE TRAINS.**

Whilst in the LUMBRES Area leave takers proceeding via CALAIS will entrain at ST. OMER at 3.15 a.m., and those via BOULOGNE at LUMBRES at 18.00 or DESVRES at 18.45.

12. **ACKNOWLEDGE.**

Lieut.-Colonel.
A.A. & Q.M.G., 39th Division.

6th December, 1917.

Issued at 8.0 p.m.
Copies to:-

G.O.C.	39th Div.R.A.	S.S.O.	Area Commandants:-
G.	39th Div.R.E.	Supply Colm.	RENESCURE,
A.Q.	116th Inf.Bde.	Camp Comdt.	LUMBRES,
A.D.M.S.	117th Inf.Bde.	Xth Corps "Q"	LOTTINGHEM,
D.A.D.V.S.	118th Inf.Bde.	VIII Corps "Q"	HENNEVEUX,
D.A.Q.O.S.	13th Glosters.	S.M.T.O. VIII Corps	WATOU,
A.P.M.	Divl.Train.	Div. Gas Officer.	WINNIZEELE,
War Diary.	Salvage Officer.	228th M.G.Coy.	EECKE.
Signals.	Baths Officer.	Divl. Wing.	Town Major, STEENVOORDE.

SECRET. 39/1658/AQ6.

ADMINISTRATIVE INSTRUCTIONS No. ISSUED WITH REFERENCE
to DIVISIONAL OPERATION ORDER No.199 dated 5.12.17.

Ref. Map 1/10,000, Sheet 28 N.W.

1. Battalions proceeding by train to rejoin their Brigades in the STEENVOORDE Area will do so in accordance with the attached Table.

2. Lorries will be provided as follows:-

Date.	UNIT.	No. of Lorries	RENDEZVOUS.	Time.
6th inst.	1/6th Cheshire R.	3	21 Place Berthen, POPERINGHE.	8.0 a.m.
"	4/5th Black Watch	3	Road Junction, G.11.c.6.3.	8.0 a.m.
"	1/1st Cambs.R.	3	ST. JEAN Church.	8.0 a.m.
"	1/1st Herts R.	3	Cross Roads, POTIJZE, I.4.a.30.05.	8.0 a.m.
7th "	16th Sherwood Forst.	3	Road Junction, LA BRIQUE, C.28.d.7.4.	8.0 a.m.
" "	17th " "	3	Road Junction, C.27.c.1.8.	8.0 a.m.
" "	17th K.R.R.Corps.	3	1 Rue des Pots, POPERINGHE	8.0 a.m.
" "	16th Rifle Bde.	3	I.1.c.1.6.	8.0 a.m.
8th "	11th Rl.Sussex	3	I.2.d.7.7.	8.0 a.m.
" "	12th Rl.Sussex	3	21 Place Berthen, POPERINGHE.	8.0 a.m.
" "	13th Rl.Sussex	3	Convent, YPRES, I.7.d.5.5.	8.0 a.m.
" "	14th Hants.R.	3	Road Junction, I.28.b.1.4.	8.0 a.m.

3. Units will take over billets which they previously occupied in the STEENVOORDE Area.

4. Brigades will detail an Officer to superintend the entraining in the forward area

5. Administrative Instructions & Train Arrangements with reference to the move from the STEENVOORDE Area to the LUMBRES Area will be issued later.

6. ACKNOWLEDGE by wire.

H. F. Dawes, Capt.

for Lieut.-Colonel,
A.A.& Q.M.G., 39th Division.

5th December, 1917.

Copies issued at to -
G.O.C.   Signals.   S.S.O.
G.   39th Div.R.A.   Supply Column.
A.Q.   39th Div.R.E.   1/6th Cheshire Regt.
A.D.M.S.   116th Inf.Bde.   4/5th Black Watch
D.A.D.V.S.   117th Inf.Bde.   1/1st Cambs.Regt.
D.A.D.O.S.   118th Inf.Bde.   1/1st Herts Regt.
A.P.M.   13th Glouc.R.   Town Major, POPERINGHE.
War Diary.   Divl. Train.   VIII Corps 'Q'.
                Salvage Coy.   S.M.T.O. VIII Corps.

TRAIN TABLE.

Date.	Unit.	Entrain.	Depart.	Detrain.	Arrive.
6-12-17.	1/1st Bn. Cambs Regt. 1/1st Bn. Herts Regt. 39th.Divnl.Salvage Coy.	ST. JEAN.	9.10 a.m.	GODEWAERSVELDE.	10.15 a.m.
7-12-17.	16th Sherwood Foresters. 17th Sherwood Foresters. 16th Rifle Brigade.	ST. JEAN. YPRES ASYLUM.	9.10 a.m. 9.30 a.m.	ABEELE. do	10.0 a.m. 10.0 a.m.
8-12-17.	11th Bn.R.Sussex Regt. 13th 14th Bn.Hampshire Regt.	ST. JEAN YPRES ASYLUM.	9.10 a.m. 9.10 a.m. 9.30 a.m.	GODEWAERSVELDE. do do	10.15 a.m. 10.15 a.m. 10.15 a.m.

All troops will be ready to entrain twenty minutes before the time of departure of the train.

58th (LONDON) DIVISION.   S E C R E T.

LOCATION OF UNITS at 8 a.m. 5th December, 1917.
(Reference HAZEBROUCK 5A, CALAIS 13, and Sheet 28 1/40,000.)

Unit.	Headquarters.	Transport Lines.	Moving after 8 a.m. to :-
58th Divl. H.Q.	NIELLES-LES-BLEQUIN.	NIELLES-LES-BLEQUIN.	
58th Div. Arty.H.Q.	ST. MOMELIN.	ST. MOMELIN.	CANAL BANK.
290th Bde. R.F.A.)		ST. MOMELIN.	ZERMEELE Area.
291st -do-)	ST. MOMELIN.		
58th Divl. A.C.)			
173rd Inf. Brigade.	Chateau d'ALINCTHUN.		
2/1st London Rgt.	HENNEVEUX.		HENNEVEUX.
2/2nd -do-	BOURNONVILLE Chateau.		BOURNONVILLE.
2/3rd -do-	Chateau LE VAST.		LE VAST.
2/4th -do-	Chateau BELLEBRUNE.		BELLEBRUNE.
208th M.G. Coy.	BRUNEMBERT.		BRUNEMBERT.
173rd T.M. Battery	HABRINGHEN.		
174th Inf. Brigade.	VELINGHEN.		LOTTINGHEN.
2/5th London Rgt.	LOTTINGHEN.		QUESQUES.
2/6th -do-	QUESQUES.		SELLES.
2/7th -do-	SELLES.		SURQUES & ESCOEUILLES.
2/8th -do-	SURQUES & ESCOEUILLES.		WATTERDAL.
198th M.G. Coy.	WATTERDAL.		
174th T.M. Bty.	T.M. School, VALHEUREUX.	-	
175th Inf.Brigade.	SANETTE.	ST. MOMELIN.	) Siege Camp
2/9th London Rgt.	COUREMBY.	"	) Area B.&C.
2/10th -do-	BAYENGHEM.	"	)
2/11th -do-	SENINGHEM	"	)
2/12th -do-	SENINGHEM & AFFRINGUES.	"	)
215th M.G. Coy.	AFFRINGUES.		
175th T.M. Battery	T.M. School, VALHEUREUX.		
214th M.G. Coy.	VAL DE LUMBRES.	VAL DE LUMBRES.	CANAL BANK.
C.R.E.	CANAL BANK.	ST. MOMELIN	C.13.c.0.7.
503rd Fd. Coy.	SANETTE.	COLEMBERT.	
504th -do-	COLEMBERT.	BAINGHEN-LE-COMTE.	LUMBRES.
511th -do-	BAINGHEN-LE-COMTE.		
A.D.M.S.	NIELLES-LES-BLEQUIN.		
2/1st Fd. Amb.	BRUNEMBERT.	BRUNEMBERT.	
2/2nd -do-	VIEIL MOULIER.	VIEIL MOULIER.	
2/3rd -do-	LART.	LART.	175th Bde. area.
58th Divl. Train.	NIELLES-LES-BLEQUIN.		
509 Coy. A.S.C.	ST. MOMELIN.		
510 -do-	ALINCTHUN		
511 -do-	QUESQUES.		SANETTE.
512 -do-	ST. MOMELIN.		ST. JAN TER BIEZEN
A.P.M., D.A.D.O.S.)			
French & Belgian)	NIELLES-LES-BLEQUIN.		
Missions.)			
Sen. Chaplains)			
C.E. & Non C.E.)			

[signature]
Major,
for Lieut.-Colonel,
General Staff, 58th (London) Division.

5/12/17.

D.O.199/3.

SECRET.

ADDENDUM NO. 2 TO 39th DIVISION ORDER NO. 199.

1. C.R.E. 39th Division will detail the following:-

(a). One Section Field Company, R.E. and necessary transport to proceed to XVIII Corps Reinforcement Camp at MONDECOVE on 10th December, 1917, ready to commence work on the 11th December, 1917.

(b). One Section Field Company, R.E. and necessary transport to proceed to Fifth Army Musketry Camp at NORTBECOURT on 10th December, 1917, ready to commence work on the 11th December, 1917.

2. All details regarding the move of personnel and transport will be arranged by A.A. and Q.M.G. 39th Division.

3.(a) Reference para. 2 of Addendum to 39th Division Order No. 199 (D.O. 199/1 d/5-12-17) -
Transport of 39th Divisional R.E. Headquarters and Field Companies, R.E., and 13th Bn. Gloucester Regt. proceeding to "C" Area, LUMBRES, will stage the night 10/11th December, 1917, at SAMETTE, proceeding on the morning of the 11th December, 1917 to join their units.

(b) Any further details for this move will be notified by A.A. and Q.M.G. 39th Division.

4. C.R.E. to acknowledge.

Lieut.-Colonel,
General Staff,
39th Division.

7th December, 1917.

To all recipients of
    39th Division Order No. 199.

AFTER ORDER
39th DIVISION ORDER No. 199.

D.O. 199/2.

With reference to 39th Division Order No. 199 :-

1. (a). 118th Infantry Brigade Group (less 228th Machine Gun Coy.) on arrival at NIELLES-LEZ-BLEQUIN (LUMBRES Area) will proceed by route march to "B" Area, where they will billet for the night 8/9th December, 1917, (billets from Area Commandant, LOTTINGHEN) and will proceed by route march on the morning of 9th December (billets to be cleared by 10 am.) to "C" Area where they will remain. Billets in "C" area from Area Commandant, HENNEVEUX.

(b). 228th Machine Gun Coy. on arrival at NIELLES-LEZ-BLEQUIN will proceed by route march to VAL DE LUMBRES where they will remain. Billets from Area Commandant, LUMBRES.

2. 117th Infantry Brigade Group on arrival at NIELLES-LEZ-BLEQUIN will proceed to "B" Area and remain there. Billets from Area Commandant, LOTTINGHEN.

3. (a). 116th Infantry Brigade Group (less 39th Divisional R.E.H.Q., 2 Field Companies, R.E., and 13th Bn. Gloucester Regt.) on arrival at NIELLES-LEZ-BLEQUIN will proceed to "A" Area and remain there. Billets from Area Commandant, LUMBRES.

(b). 39th Divisional R.E. Headquarters and 2 Field Companies on arrival at NIELLES-LEZ-BLEQUIN will proceed to "C" Area and remain there. Billets from Area Commandant, HENNEVEUX.

(c). 13th Bn. Gloucester Regt (Pioneers) on arrival at NIELLES-LEZ-BLEQUIN will proceed to "C" Area and remain there. Billets from Area Commandant, HENNEVEUX.

4. 39th Division Headquarters will close at STEENVOORDE at 10.0 am. on 10th December, 1917, and open at NIELLES-LEZ-BLEQUIN at the same hour.

5. For further details of advance parties, moves, and accommodation in the LUMBRES Areas "A", "B", and "C" see Administrative Instructions issued in connection with this Order by the A.A. and Q.M.G. 39th Division.

6. ACKNOWLEDGE.

[signature]
Lieut.-Colonel,
General Staff,
39th Division.

6th December, 1917.

To all recipients of
39th Division Order No. 199.

SECRET.

D.O.199/1.

ADDENDUM TO 39th DIVISION ORDER No. 199.

Reference para. 5 of above mentioned Order:-

1. (a). The Headquarters and two Field Companies, 39th Divisional R.E., and the 13th Bn. Gloucester Regt. will proceed on the morning of the 8th December, 1917, as follows:-

   (i). Personnel by train to GODEWAERSVELDE and thence by route march to billets at EECKE.

   (ii). Transport by route march through POPERINGHE - ABEELE to EECKE in accordance with attached Table "C".

   (b). Billets will be allotted by the Town Major, EECKE, upon application.

   (c). Advanced parties will report to the Town Major, EECKE, by 2 pm. on 7th December, 1917.

2. For the move from EECKE to LUMBRES the units mentioned in above para. 1 (a), will be grouped and will move with the 116th Infantry Brigade Group (see para. 3 (a),(b),(c), of 39th Division Order No. 199).

3. (a). One Field Company, 39th Divisional R.E., (less one Section) will proceed on the morning of the 8th December, 1917, from YPRES to BOESCHEPE as follows -

   Personnel by train to GODEWAERSVELDE and thence by route march to BOESCHEPE and will, on arrival, report to the Commandant, X Corps School.
   Transport will move by route march in accordance with attached Table " C".
   The Sections of above party should not be less than 20 strong and will be rationed by X Corps School from day after arrival inclusive.

4. One Section Field Company, 39th Divisional R.E., will proceed direct to CLAIRMARAIS (billets at COIN PERDU) by train and will report, on arrival, to X Corps Heavy Artillery.
   This party will be rationed by the X Corps Heavy Artillery from the day after arrival inclusive.

5. No transport is to enter POPERINGHE before 11 am.

6. A.A. and Q.M.G. 39th Division will arrange for above train accommodation and will notify units concerned.

7. Attention is directed to para. 6 of 39th Division Order No. 199.

8. ACKNOWLEDGE.

Lieut.-Colonel,
General Staff,
39th Division.

5th December, 1917.

To all recipients of
39th Division Order No. 199.

P.T.O.

TABLE "C". TABLE TO ACCOMPANY ADDENDUM TO 39th DIVISION ORDER No. 199. (D.O.199/1.).

Serial No.	Date.	Unit.	From.	To.	Route.	Remarks.
1.	8/12/17.	Transport 225th Fd.Co.R.E.	VLAMERTINGHE	BOESCHEPE	POPERINGHE - ABEELE	Head to reach POPERINGHE at 11 am.
2.	8/12/17.	Transport 227th Fd.Co.R.E.	VLAMERTINGHE	ECKE	POPERINGHE - ABEELE	Head to reach POPERINGHE at 11.20 am.
3.	8/12/17.	Transport 234th Fd.Co.R.E.	VLAMERTINGHE	ECKE	POPERINGHE - ABEELE	Head to reach POPERINGHE at 11.45 am.
4.	8/12/17.	Transport Hdqrs. 39th Divl.R.E.	VLAMERTINGHE	ECKE	POPERINGHE - ABEELE	Head to reach POPERINGHE at 12.Noon.
5.	8/12/17	Transport 13th Br.Glouc. Regt.	YPRES	ECKE	POPERINGHE - ABEELE	Head to reach POPERINGHE at 12.30 pm.

SECRET.   Copy. No. 4.

39th DIVISION ORDER No. 199.

5/12/17.

Ref. Map 1/100,000
HAZEBROUCK 5A.

1. The battalions of the 39th Division, with transport, will rejoin their Brigades in the STEENVOORDE Area in accordance with attached Table "A".
(less Artillery)

2. The 39th Division will proceed to the LUMBRES Area in accordance with attached Table "B" and will, on arrival, come under orders of the X Corps.

3. (a) For the move units will be grouped as in Appendix "A"

(b) Personnel will move by train in accordance with attached Table "B" -
    i. Entraining at GODEWAERSVELDE.
    ii. Detraining at NIELLES
Time of departure of trains will be communicated later by the A.A. and Q.M.G. 39th Division.

(c). Transport will move by route march in accordance with Table "B".

4. Infantry Brigades will wire entraining strength to A.A. and Q.M.G. 39th Division at once.

5. Instructions for 39th Division Field Companies, R.E. and 13th Bn. Gloucester Regt will be issued later.

6. The following distances will be maintained on the march -

Between Companies	100 yards.
Between unit and its transport	100 ,,
Between Battalions	500 ,,
When transport is Brigaded between each Battalion Transport	100 ,,

A distance of 100 yards between each group of 6 vehicles will be maintained when moving from STEENVOORDE Area to LUMBRES Area.

7. ACKNOWLEDGE.

[signature]
Lieut.-Colonel,
General Staff,
39th Division.

Copies issued at 10.30 am. to -

G.O.C.	39th Divl. R.A.	Ammn. Sub-Park
G.	39th Divl. R.E.	228th M.G. Coy.
A.Q.	116th Inf.Bde.	Div.Wing.IX Corps
A.D.M.S.	117th Inf.Bde.	Reinforcement Camp.
D.A.D.V.S.	118th Inf.Bde.	Div.Gas Officer.
D.A.D.O.S.	13th Glouc.R.	VIII Corps.
A.P.M.	Divl. Train.	IX Corps.
War Diary.	S.S.O.	X Corps.
Signals.	Supply Column.	Town Major POPERINGHE.

P.T.O.

To accompany 39th Div. Order 199.

APPENDIX "A".

116th Infantry Brigade Group.

    116th Inf. Bde. Headquarters.
    4 Battalions.
    116th M.G. Coy.
    116th L.T.M. Bty.
    No. 2 Co. Divl. Train.
    134th Field Ambulance

117th Infantry Brigade Group.

    117th Inf. Bde. Headquarters.
    4 Battalions.
    117th M.G. Coy.
    117th L.T.M. Bty.
    No. 3 Co. Divl. Train.
    133rd Field Ambulance.

118th Infantry Brigade Group.

    118th Infantry Bde. Headquarters.
    4 Battalions.
    118th M.G. Coy.
    118th L.T.M. Bty.
    228th M.G. Coy.
    No. 4 Co. Divl. Train.
    132nd Field Ambulance.

TABLE "B". TABLE TO ACCOMPANY 39th DIVISION ORDER No. 199.

Serial No.	Date.	Unit.	From.	To.	Route.	Remarks.
1.	7-12-17.	Transport of 118th Brigade Group.	STEENVOORDE	RENESCURE	CASSEL.	Head to reach CASSEL 2 pm. Billets from Area Commandant RENESCURE.
2.	8-12-17.	118th Brigade Group. 39th Division.	STEENVOORDE Area.	LUMBRES Area.	Train from GODEWAERSVELDE.	Detrain NIELLES. Details later.
3.	8-12-17.	Transport of 118th Brigade Group.	RENESCURE	LUMBRES.	ARQUES WIZERNES	To start about 10 am., i.e., as soon as French troops have vacated RENESCURE Area.
4.	8-12-17.	Transport of 117th Brigade Group.	STEENVOORDE	RENESCURE	CASSEL	Head to reach CASSEL 2 pm. Billets from Area Commandant RENESCURE.
5.	9-12-17.	117th Brigade Group. 39th Division.	STEENVOORDE Area.	LUMBRES Area.	Train from GODEWAERSVELDE	Detrain NIELLES. Details later.
6.	9-12-17.	Transport of 117th Brigade Group.	RENESCURE	LUMBRES	ARQUES WIZERNES	To start about 10 am. i.e., as soon as French troops have vacated RENESCURE Area.
7.	9-12-17.	Transport of 116th Brigade Group.	STEENVOORDE	RENESCURE	CASSEL	Head to reach CASSEL at 1 pm. Billets from Area Commandant RENESCURE.
8.	10-12-17.	116th Brigade Group and 39th Division H.Q.	STEENVOORDE Area.	LUMBRES Area.	Train from GODEWAERSVELDE	Detrain NIELLES. Details later.
9.	10-12-17.	Transport of 116th Brigade Group.	RENESCURE	LUMBRES	ARQUES WIZERNES.	Clear of billets at 10 am.

TABLE "A".   TABLE TO ACCOMPANY 39th DIVISION ORDER No. 199.

Serial No.	Date.	Unit.	From.	To.	Route.	Remarks.
1.	6-12-17.	1/6th Cheshires 118th Brigade.	POPERINGHE	STEENVOORDE Area.	March.	To be clear of POPERINGHE by 10 am.
2.	6-12-17.	4/5th Black Watch 118th Brigade.	BRANDHOEK	STEENVOORDE Area.	March.	Transport by road. Route – POPERINGHE.
3.	6-12-17.	1/1st Cambs. 118th Brigade.	I.3.b.8.2.	STEENVOORDE Area.	Train.	Transport by road – Route – POPERINGHE. Not to enter POPERINGHE before 10 am.
4.	6-12-17.	1/1st Herts. 118th Brigade.	I.3.b.2.5.	STEENVOORDE Area.	Train.	Transport not to enter POPERINGHE before 10.30 am.
5.	7-12-17.	16th Sherwood For. 117th Brigade.	WILLJE Area.	STEENVOORDE Area.	Train.	Transport by road. Route – POPERINGHE.
6.	7-12-17.	17th Sherwood For. 117th Brigade.	C.27.b.50.25	STEENVOORDE Area.	Train.	Transport by road. Route – POPERINGHE.
7.	7-12-17.	17th K.R.R. 117th Brigade.	POPERINGHE	STEENVOORDE Area.	March.	Transport by road. Route – POPERINGHE. To be clear of POPERINGHE by 10 am.
8.	7-12-17.	16th Rifle Bde. 117th Brigade.	H.6.c.6.4.	STEENVOORDE Area.	Train	Transport by road. Route – POPERINGHE.
9.	8-12-17.	11th R.Sussex R. 116th Brigade.	I.2.d.7.5.	STEENVOORDE Area.	Train	Transport by road. Route – POPERINGHE.
10.	8-12-17.	12th R.Sussex R. 116th Brigade.	POPERINGHE	STEENVOORDE Area.	March.	To be clear of POPERINGHE by 10 am.
11.	8-12-17.	13th R.Sussex R. 116th Brigade.	VERKS WIEHJE	STEENVOORDE Area.	Train.	Transport by road, route POPERINGHE. Not to enter POPERINGHE before 10 am.
12.	8-12-17.	14th Hants. 116th Brigade.	WILLJE YPRES	STEENVOORDE Area.	Train.	Transport by road. Route – POPERINGHE. Not to enter POPERINGHE BEFOR 10.30 am.

P.T.O

D.R.L.S.

VIII CORPS ADMINISTRATIVE INSTRUCTIONS NO: 2

1.   39th Division (less Artillery) move to LUMBRES area on 8th, 9th and 10th by empty supply trains from GODEWAERSVELDE to NEILLES.

  50th Division (less Artillery) move from EPERLECQUES area on 10th, 11th and 12th to relieve 33rd Division (less artillery). Two personnel and one omnibus train are placed at disposal of 50th Division for this move on 10th, 11th and 12th December.

  33rd Division move from the forward area to STEENVOORDE area. Trains are authorised for the carriage of the personnel of two brigades from YPR'S to GODEWAERSVELDE, on 11th and 13th.

2.   33rd, 39th and 50th Divisions will send a Staff Officer to see Traffic, HAZEBROUCK, as soon as possible to arrange details of these railway moves, which have been authorised by Second Army G. 20/127 (G) of 3rd December.

3.   Changes in railheads will be wired to the Divisions concerned as soon as arranged.

4.   Supply Columns are placed at the disposal of Divisions between the following dates inclusive for the carriage of blankets and stores, where not required for supplies, and for train loading

  33rd from 10th to 14th (inclusive)
  39th from 7th onwards.
  50th until 12th.

5.   Trench stores which include Hot Food Containers, Gum Boots thigh, Flapper Fans, O.P. Equipment (telescopes, sextants and watches) etc., will be handed over by 33rd Division to 50th Division.

  Area stores which include tents, chaffcutters, Soyer Stoves, lamps, washing tubs, latrine buckets, laundry machinery will be transferred in situ.

  Any stores issued specially for operations such as water carts and harness, packsaddilery, extra waterbottles etc., will be transferred by 33rd to 50th Division.

  The following are divisional stores and will be retained by Divisions :-

  100 Yukon packs.
  500 bags waterproof for socks.
  Any special carriers made up by formations and not issued by the Army.

  Lieutenant-Colonel.
4th December 1917.   A.Q.M.G. VIII Corps.

  33rd Division (2 copies)   A.D.O.S.
  39th Division (-"-)   D.A.D.P.S.
  50th Division. (-"-)   Traffic HAZEBROUCK.
  G.S., VIII Corps.   Area Comdt. BRANDHOEK.
  Second Army "Q"   Area Comdt. STEENVOORDE.
  S.M.T.O.

SECRET.

Copy No. 8
4th. December, 1917.

VIII CORPS ORDER NO. 84.

(1) 50th. Division (less Artillery) will relieve the 33rd. Division (less Artillery) in the right sector of the Corps front between the 10th. and 13th. December, in accordance with the attached table.

(2) The 50th. Division will relieve all working parties being found for VIII Corps by 33rd Division at the time of relief.

(3) All details of defence arrangements, work in progress and proposed will be handed over to incoming Division.

(4) The 33rd. Division will be in Corps reserve whilst in the STEENVOORDE Area.

(5) All troops of 50th. Division on arrival in 33rd. Divisional Area, and until 12 noon on December 13th., will be under orders of G.O.C. 33rd. Division.

(6) G.O.C. 50th. Division will assume command of the front at noon on the 13th. December.

(7) ACKNOWLEDGE.

B.G., G.S.,
VIII Corps.

Issued to Signals at 3 am

PTO.

DISTRIBUTION.

Copy No. 1 & 2 to	8th. Division.	20	A.&.Signals.
3 & 4	14th. Division.	21	A.D.O.S.
5 & 6	23rd. Division.	22	'I'
7 & 8	39th. Division.	23	C.M.G.O.
9 & 10	50th. Division.	24	A.P.M.
11	VIII Corps H.A.	25	21st Squadron RFC.
12	Second Army.	26	2nd. Wing R.F.C.
13	II Corps	27	A.D.C. for G.O.C.
14	II Anzac Corps	28	War Diary.
15	'A'	29	War Diary.
16	'Q'	30	File.
17	G.O.C.R.A.	31	11th. Balloon Coy RFC.
18	C.L.		
19	D.D.M.S.	32	X Corps.
		33	Area Comdt. Zermezeele.

MARCH TABLE TO ACCOMPANY VIII CORPS ORDER NO. 62.

SERIAL NO.	DATE.	FORMATION. 32nd Div.	FORMATION. 50th Div.	FROM.	TO.	ROUTE.	REMARKS.
1.	9 Dec		Tpt. A Bde.	EPERLECQUES	ZEGERZEELE	LEDERZEELE-STATION - WAEMERS CAPPEL.	Not to pass LEDERZEELE Station bfr. 11 a.m. Billets from Area Cmdt. ZEGERZEELE.
2.	10 Dec		A Bde.	WATTEN	BRANDHOEK	Train	Details later.
3.	10 Dec	A Bde.		BRANDHOEK Area.	STEENVOORDE Area.	POPERINGHE.	March.
4.	10 Dec		Tpt. A Bde.	ZEGERZEELE	BRANDHOEK	WINNEZEELE-WATOU-POPERINGHE.	To be E. of WORMHOUDT-CASSEL Rd. by 9 a.m.
5.	10 Dec		Tpt. B Bde.	EPERLECQUES	ZEGERZEELE	LEDERZEELE Stn.-WAEMERS CAPPEL.	To be clear of LEDERZEELE Stn. by 10 a.m.
6.	11 Dec		A Bde.	BRANDHOEK	POTIJZE	Train	Details later.
7.	11 Dec	2 Bns. A Bde.		POTIJZE	INTERMEDIATE Supp rt.	March.	As ordered by 33rd Div.
8.	11 Dec	2 Bns. A Bde.		INTERMEDIATE Supp rt.	POTIJZE	March.	
9.	11 Dec	B Bde.		POTIJZE	STEENVOORDE.	Train	Transport by Road. Route POPERINGHE.
10.	11 Dec		B Bde.	WATTEN	BRANDHOEK	Train	Details later.
11.	11 Dec		Tpt. B Bde.	ZEGERZEELE	BRANDHOEK	WINNEZEELE-WATOU-POPERINGHE.	To be E of WORMHOUDT-CASSEL Rd. by 9 a.m.
12.	11 Dec		Tpt. C Bde.	EPERLECQUES	ZEGERZEELE	LEDERZEELE STATION-WAEMERS CAPPEL.	Not to pass LEDERZEELE Stn. bfr 11 a.m.

(2)

NO.	DATE.	FORMATION.		FROM.	TO.	ROUTE.	REMARKS.
		23rd. Div.	50th. Div.				
13	12 Dec	2 Bns C Bde.			ST. INVOOIDE.	Train.	March route under orders of 23rd. Division.
14	12 Dec		B. Bde.	POTIJZE.	POTIJZE.	VLAMERTINGHE.	Details later.
15	12 Dec		C. Bde.	BRANDHOEK.	BRANDHOEK.	Train.	
16	12 Dec		(pt. C Bde.	WATTEN.	BRANDHOEK.	VINIZEELE - WATOU - POPERINGHE.	To be E. of VOLKHOUDT - CASEL Road by 9 a.m.
17	12/13 Dec		A. Bde.	POTIJZE & INFANTRY DIV TH SUPPORT.	LINE.		To relieve C Brigade of 23rd. Division.
18	12/13 Dec	C Bde. (Less 2 Bns)		LINE.	ST. JEAN AREA		As relieved by A Bde 50 Division.
19	13 Dec	C Bde. (Less 2 Bns)		ST. JEAN AREA	ST. ENVOODI AREA.	Train.	Transport by road. Route POPERINGHE.
20	13 Dec		Div.H.Q.	EPERLECQUES.	RAMPARTS, YPRES		To relieve 23rd. Divn. H.Q.
21	13 Dec	Div.H.Q.		RAMPARTS, YPRES.	ST. INVOOIDE.		As relieved by 50th. Div H.Q.

TO ACCOMPANY VIII CORPS ORDER NO. 64

Following distances will be maintained on the march:-

    Between Companies ....100 yards.

       "   Unit & its transport.................100 yards.

       "   Battalions..........................500 yards.

When transport is brigaded,
       between each battalion transport......100 yards.

A distance of 100 yards will be maintained between every 6 vehicles., during march of transport between ZERMEZEELE and BRANDHOEK.

[signature]
B.G., G.S.
VIII Corps.

S E C R E T.

39/1724/A.Q.3.

ALMINISTRATIVE INSTRUCTIONS
in
Connection with 39th Divisional Order No.203.

1. Train Tables will be issued separately with arrangements for lorries.

2. Accommodation. Vide attached Location of Units, 32nd Division, Appendix "A". Accommodation will be taken over by corresponding Units of this Division, except
   (a) in the case of Infantry Transport vide para.3 (d) below.
   (b) The 13th Bn. Gloucester Regt. will be accommodated at SIEGE CAMP.
   (c) The 228th Machine Gun Company will be accommodated at IRISH FARM on arrival until the 219th Machine Gun Company moves out of the CANAL BANK. Its transport will double up with that of the 219th Machine Gun Company.

3. Transport.
   (a) Transport will march in accordance with the attached March Table - Appendix "B" under Command of the Officer Commanding the Train Company.
   (b) Brigade Groups for the march of the transport are formed as under.

   ### 116th Infantry Brigade Group.

   Divisional Headquarters.
   Headquarters 39th Divisional R.E.
   13th Bn. Gloucester Regt.
   Headquarters Divisional Train.
   116th Infantry Brigade.
   Divisional Signal Company.
   No. 2 Company 39th Divisional Train.

   ### 117th Infantry Brigade Group.

   117th Infantry Brigade.
   228th Machine Gun Company.
   134th Field Ambulance. (less transport of tent sub-divisions.)
   No. 3 Company 39th Divisional Train.

   ### 118th Infantry Brigade Group.

   118th Infantry Brigade.
   234th Field Company, R.E.
   132nd Field Ambulance (less tent Sub-divisions).
   50th Mobile Veterinary Section.
   No. 4 Company 39th Divisional Train.

   (c) The necessary orders will be issued by Brigade Commanders to all Units of their Groups.
   (d) Transport Lines will be taken over as follows:-

   116th Infantry Brigade take over those of 97th Inf. Bde.
   117th   "   "   "   "   "   "   96th "   "
   118th   "   "   "   "   "   "   14th "   "

P.T.O.

-2-

(e) Advance parties of 117th Infantry Brigade Transport will leave LOTTINGHEM by the 6.15 p.m. train on the 26th so as to take over the lines of the 96th Infantry Brigade Transport on the evening of the 27th inst.
Advance parties of the 116th Infantry Brigade Transport will leave LUMBRES by the 7.15 p.m. train on the 27th so as to take over the Lines of the 97th Infantry Brigade Transport on the evening of the 28th inst.
Advance parties of the 118th Infantry Brigade Transport will leave DESVRES by the 6 p.m. train on the 28th so as to take over the Lines of the 14th Infantry Brigade Transport on the evening of the 29th inst.
Parties in each case will billet the night in HAZEBROUCK and proceed to POPERINGHE by train leaving HAZEBROUCK 8.50 a.m. next morning.

4. Advance Parties to take over camps will be sent to arrive 24 hours in advance of troops.
The advance party of the 117th Infantry Brigade Group will proceed by the 6.15 p.m. train from LOTTINGHEM on the 27th inst. staying the night 27/28th at HAZEBROUCK.
Those of the 116th and 118th Infantry Brigade Groups on the trains shown on the Entraining Tables.

5. Supply Arrangements.
   (a) For move.
      (i) Supply Railhead will change to REIGERSBURG on the 30th inst.
      (ii) Feeding programme for the move is attached, Appendix "C".
   (b) On taking over the Line.
      (i) Refilling Points
         1 Coy. - A.21.b.3.3.
         2 Coys - H.3.d.6.8.
         Coal Dump - H.6.a.6.8.
      (ii) Battalions moving into the front line will take two days' rations and solidified alcohol on the man.

6. Ammunition.
   (a) The Divisional S.A.A. & Grenade Dump is at HILL TOP C.21.c.5.4.
   (b) The following dumps will be taken over by the 117th Infantry Brigade at 12 noon on the 30th inst.

      HUBNER FARM - D.1.d.2.6.
      STROPPE FARM D.1.d.2.2.

      These Dumps serve the ALBERTA and MOUSETRAP tracks respectively.

      The following advanced dumps in process of formation will also be taken over by the 117th Infantry Brigade.

      D.1.b.9.3.
      D.2.d.9.6.

      The 117th Infantry Brigade will report to this Office as regards the contents, the cover provided for ammunition, and the personnel at these 4 dumps.
   (c) The Divisional Dump Officer and personnel will proceed by train on the 29th inst. and take over the Divisional Dump on the 30th inst.

7. Water.
   (a) Water for the Line is taken up in petrol tins under Brigade arrangements.
   (b) The O.C., 39th Divisional Train will issue 300 tins to the 117th Infantry Brigade which will be taken up on their lorries on the 29th inst.
   (c) The 117th Infantry Brigade will take over the following reserves of water from the 38nd Division.
      (i)   200 filled petrol tins at CORNER COT.
      (ii) 100   ditto   at D.1.b.9.3.
      (iii) 100   ditto   at D.2.d.9.6.
   The Brigade in the Line will be responsible for maintaining these reserves at the above establishment and for turning over water twice during each tour in the trenches.

8. Trench Feet.
   (a) Trench foot rooms have been established at the following Battalion Camps.
      HOSPITAL FARM.
      SIEGE CAMP.
      DAMBRE CAMP.
      IRISH FARM.
      HILL TOP.
   One will be established on the CANAL BANK as soon as possible. Until this is done the Battalion there will share the room at IRISH FARM.
   Each of the above Huts is fitted out with
      1 Soyer Stove.
      30 Basins.
      30 Nail Brushes.

   (b) Units will draw the soap and powder for the preventive treatment laid down in Fourth Army Standing Orders para. 597 from Field Ambulances who are supplied by the Divisional Train.

9. R.E. Dumps.
   Corps Main Dump   PESELHOEK   A.20.d.
   "   Forward "   ZOUAVE VILLA C.20.c.
   Main Divisional Dump   CANAL BANK   C.25.c.9.3.

   Advanced Divisional Dumps :-   (YORK FARM.
                                  (CORNER COT.
                                  (KRONPRINZ.
   Divisional Concrete Dump. MERRYTHOUGHT SIDING
                                  WIELTJE.

10. Trench Tramways.
    A trench tramway runs from CORNER COT to the vicinity of KRONPRINZ Farm.
    Applications for trucks will be addressed to Officer i/c of Railhead at CORNER COT who is found by the 225th Field Coy. Pushing parties will be provided by the Unit indenting for trucks.

11. Divisional Baths & Laundry.
    (a) Dirty clothes are washed at the G.H.Q. Laundry ABBEVILLE.
    (b) The Divisional Laundry Store is at SIEGE CAMP. Clean clothes are distributed from there as required.
    (c) Baths are established at
           SIEGE CAMP   Capacity 200 per hour.
           REIGERSBURG CAMP   "   200 "   "
           IRISH FARM   "   80 "   "
    (d) A Sock laundry and Drying room is established at REIGERSBURG.
        Dry socks required for the Line will be drawn from there by Units.
    (e) The Divisional Baths Officer and personnel will take over the above on the 30th inst.

P.T.O.

-4-

Canteens.
- (a) Main Canteen and Depot SIEGE CAMP.
  Branch Canteen & Order Office CANAL BANK.
  Branch Canteen   IRISH FARM.
- (b) Canteens in this area will close on the 28th inst.
- (c) Canteen personnel will proceed by train on the 29th and take over canteens in para (a) above, on the 30th.inst.

A Soup Kitchen will be established at CORNER COT. and will supply soup or tea free to wounded, working parties, reliefs, runners, despatch riders, etc.

12. **Medical Arrangements.**
    - (a) Regimental Aid Posts.
      Right Sector WALLEMOLEN D.4.a.1.8 (at present at Pill-box 83 D.4.a.8.4. but will be moved when Battalion Headquarters is moved to WINCHESTER FARM.)
      Left Sector OXFORD HOUSE, V.26.b.8.1.

    - (b) Bearer Relay Posts.
                 ((1) KRONPRINZ   D.3.c.5.4.
      Right   ((2) ALBATROSS   D.2.d.2.5.
      Sector.   ((3) SPRINGFIELD FARM C.12.b.8.4.

      Left   ((1) WINCHESTER FARM D.2.a.5.4.
      Sector.   ((2) HUBNER FARM.   D.1.c.Central.

    - (c) Advanced Dressing Station and Walking Wounded Collecting Station, ST. JULIEN, C.18.a.2.8.

    - (d) Corps Main Dressing Station DUHALLOW (CANAL BANK).

    - (e) Ambulance Stand at advanced Dressing Station ST. JULIEN.

13. **Leave Takers.**
    For arrangements for leave takers see II Corps Circular Memorandum No.36 attached, Appendix "D".

14. **Cemeteries.**
    KRONPRINZ D.3.c.8.6.
               C.21.d.2.5.
               C.17.b.9.7.

15. **Tivolies.**
    Will move to POPERINGHE by lorry on the 31st inst.

16. **Salvage Company.**
    Orders re move will be issued later.

17. **Employed Officers and Men.**
    - (a) Appendix "E" attached shows the employed Officers and men to be found by this Division in relief of the 32nd Division.
    - (b) These Officers and men will proceed, with two days' rations, under Command of Capt. J.H.COOLING, 11th Bn.Royal Sussex Regt., by train on the 29th from WIZERNES and will be accommodated at SIEGE CAMP on the night 29/30th.
      The reliefs will be carried out on the 30th inst. The 32nd.Division are sending guides to SIEGE CAMP at 9.a.m. on the 30th in those cases where guides are necessary.
    - (c) Arrangements for the conveyance of these parties to WIZERNES Station on the 29th will be issued later.

18. ACKNOWLEDGE.

26th December,1917.

Lieut-Colonel,
A.A.&.Q.M.G.,39th Division.

COPIES ISSUED TO:-

G.O.C.	117th Inf.Bde.	O.C.,Divl.Canteons.
G.S.	118th Inf.Bde.	O.C.,224th Empl.Coy.
A.Q.	13/Glouc.Regt.	O.i/c Baths & Laundry.
A.D.M.S.	Divl.Train.	O.i/c Bomb Stores.
D.A.D.V.S.	S.S.O.	O.i/c Tivolies.
D.A.D.O.S.	Supply Column.	Senior Chaplain.(C.of E)
A.P.M.	Ammn.Sub.Park.	Area Commdt.LUMBRES.
War Diary.	228th M.G.Coy.	32nd Div.
Signal Coy.	Camp Commandant	IInd Corps.
39th Div.R.A.	Divl.Gas Officer.	
39th Div.R.E.	Divl.Salvage Officer.	
116th Inf.Bde.		

APPENDIX "A".

LOCATION OF UNITS - 32ND DIVISION - 22nd.Decr.,1917.

Ref. 1/40,000 Map. Sht. 27 & 28.

UNIT.	LOCATION.	Transport and Wagon Lines.
Divisional Headquarters.	C.25.d.0.0.	
Divisional Signal Coy.	-do-	
C.R.A.	-do-	
161st Brigade, R.F.A.	C.11.c.90.70.	C.19.d.5.3.
168th Brigade, R.F.A.	C.17.c.42.35.	B.26.b.8.0.
A/161st Battery, R.F.A.	D.7.c.15.75.	B.22.d.3.3.
B/ " " "	D.1.b.05.15 & D.7.a.65.15.	B.22.d.7.2.
C/ " " "	C.18.b.05.55.	B.22.d.1.5.
D/ " " "	C.12.b.6.3.	C.19.d.5.3.
A/168th Battery, R.F.A.	D.7.a.65.30.	B.26.b.8.0.
B/ " " "	C.12.b.6.4.	B.22.d.3.9.
C/ " " "	C.12.b.35.75.	C.25.a.3.2.
D/ " " "	C.12.d.80.58.	B.26.b.8.0.
Divisional Ammn.Column.	B.26.a.4.1.	
No.1 Section.	-do-	B.26.a.1.5.
No.2 Section.	-do-	B.26.a.3.3.
No.3 Section.	-do-	H.4.a.6.3.
Trench Mortar Batteries.	H.2.a.1.7.	
C.R.E.	C.25.d.0.0.	
206th Field Coy., R.E.	CALIFORNIA TRENCH	C.25.c.7.4.
218th Field Coy., R.E.	" "	H.6.d.7.5.
219th Field Coy., R.E.	" "	(Ford. C.19.d.55.20 (Rear. HOSPITAL FARM CMP.
14th Infantry Brigade.	C.25.d.2.9.	HOSPITAL FARM CMP.
5/6th Royal Scots.	IRISH FARM.	SIEGE CAMP.
1st Dorset Regt.	SIEGE CAMP	"
2nd Manchester Regt.(Support)	CANAL BANK.	HOSPITAL FARM CMP.
15th High.L.Infy.	IRISH FARM.	SIEGE CAMP.
14th Machine Gun Coy.	CANAL BANK.	" "
14th Trench Mortar Bty.	HILL TOP FARM.	" "
14th Pioneer Coy.	CANAL BANK EAST.	
96th Infantry Brigade.	HOSPITAL FARM.	B.19.d.2.2.
16th North'd Fusrs.	SIEGE CAMP.	A.30.c.4.5.
15th Lancs.Fusrs. (Reserve).	HOSPITAL FARM.	B.27.c.7.6.
16th Lancs.Fusrs.	SIEGE CAMP.	H.3.b.2.7.
2nd R.Innis.Fusrs.	HILL TOP FARM.	A.30.c.2.5.
96th Machine Gun Coy.	SIEGE CAMP.	B.27.c.7.6.
96th Trench Mortar Bty.	" "	B.27.c.3.6.
96th Pioneer Coy.	CALIFORNIA TRENCH.	
97th Infantry Brigade.	ALBERTA.C.11.c.90.70.)	)
11th Border Regt.	Line Right. Pt.53. V.28.c.6.4.)	)
2nd.K.O.Y.L.I. (Line)	HILL TOP FARM.	)
16th High.L.Infy.	Line Left. HUBNER FARM.	)B.28.d.3.2.
17th High.L.Infy.	WURST FARM.	)
97th Machine Gun Coy.	Line.	)
97th Trench Mortar Bty.	Line.	)
97th Pioneer Coy.	CALIFORNIA TRENCH.	
219th Machine Gun Coy.	CANAL BANK.	BORDER CAMP.

Infant Brigade (margin note beside 14th Brigade)
Reserve Brigade (margin note beside 96th Brigade)
Brigade in Line (margin note beside 97th Brigade)

P.T.O.

UNIT.	LOCATION.	Transport and Wagon Lines.
Divisional Train & S.S.O..	H.3.d.5.5.	
No. 1 Company.	A.21.b.3.3.	A.21.b.3.3.
No. 2 Company.	H.3.d.7.7.	H.3.d.7.7.
No. 3 Company.	-do-	-do-
	-do-	-do-
Supply Refilling Point.		
14th Infantry Brigade.	H.3.d.6.8.	
96th Infantry Brigade.	H.3.d.2.8.	
97th Infantry Brigade.	H.3.d.6.8.	
Divisional Troops.	A.21.b.3.3.	
Divisional Supply Column.	A.21.c.	
A.D.M.S.	BORDER CAMP.	F.29.d.5.9.
90th Field Ambulance.	F.29.d.5.9.	"A" Sect. A.23.c.2.9.
91st " "	A.23.c.2.9.	A.23.c.2.9.
92nd " "	I.1.b.2.6.	A.23.c.2.9.
D.A.D.O.S.	BORDER CAMP.	
D.A.D.V.S.	" "	
Mobile Vet. Section.	A.28.c.2.4.	A.28.c.2.4.
Divnl. Salvage Coy.	C.27.b.6.3.	
Divnl. Employment Coy.	BORDER CAMP.	
Supply Railhead.	REIGERSBURG.	
Personnel Railhead.	REIGERSBURG.	

APPENDIX "B".

MARCH TABLE FOR TRANSPORT.

DATE.	TROOPS.	FROM.	TO.	ROUTE.	Report for billets to
26th	Transport of 133.Fld.Amb. and transport of tent Sub-divisions 132 & 134 Fld.Ambs.	Present Billets.	ST.MOMELIN.	ST.MARTIN au-LAERT.	Area Commdt. ST.MOMELIN.
27th	ditto	ST.MOMELIN.	ST.JANSTER BIEZEN.	WAEMARS CAPPEL -WINNEZEELE- WATOU	Area Commdt. ST. JANSTER BIEZEN.
28th	ditto	ST.JANSTER BIEZEN.	Destination vide Appendix "A".	---	---
28th	Transport of 117th Inf.Bdo.Group.	LUMBRES Area.	ST.MOMELIN.	ST.MARTIN au LAERT.	Area Commdt. ST.MOMELIN.
29th	Transport of 117th Inf.Bdo. Group.	LUMBRES Area.	ST.MOMELIN.	ditto	ditto
29th	Transport of 117th Inf.Bdo. Group.	ST.MOMELIN.	ST.JANSTER BIEZEN.	WAEMARS CAPPEL -WINNEZEELE- WATOU.	Area Commdt: ST. JANSTER BIEZEN.
29th	Transport of 118th Inf.Bdo. Group.	Present Positions.	(Transport lines (now occupied by (11f Inf.Bdo in ("A" Sub-Area of (LUMBRES Area and (SAMETTE (Staging Camp.	---	---
30th	Transport of 118th Inf.Bdo. Group	ST.MOMELIN.	ST.JANSTER BIEZEN.	(WAEMARS CAPPEL (-WINNEZEELE- (WATOU	Area Commdt. ST.JANSTER BIEZEN.

P.T.O.

DATE.	TROOPS.	FROM.	TO.	ROUTE.	Report for billets to
30th	Transport of 117th Inf.Bde. Group.	ST.JANSTER BIEZEN	Destinations vide Appendix "A".	—	—
30th	Transport of 118th Inf.Bde. Group.	Present Transport Lines 118th Inf.Bde. Group.	ST.MOMELIN.	ST.MARTIN au LAERT.	Area Commdt.ST.MOMELIN
31st	Transport of 117th Inf.Bde. Group.	ST.JANSTER BIEZEN.	Destinations vide Appendix "A".	—	—
31st	Transport of 118th Inf.Bde. Group.	ST.MOMELIN.	ST.JANSTER-BIEZEN.	WATMARS CAPPEL -WINNEZEELE- -WATOU.	Area Commdt.ST.JANSTER -BIEZEN.
1st Jan.'18.	do do do	ST.JANSTER BIEZEN.	Destinations vide Appendix "A".	—	—

APPENDIX "C".

LUMBRES RAILHEAD.	27th DECEMBER.	28th DECEMBER.	29th DECEMBER.	30th DECEMBER. NEW RAILHEAD.	31st DECEMBER.	1st JANUARY.
117th Inf. Bde. Group.	Rations for transport on supply wagons. Rations for rail parties delivered by M.T. to present Camps for 29th.	Transport Moves. Rations dumped at ST.MOMELIN for 30th. Rations for 30th for rail parties delivered by M.T. at destination (Battalion camps) to Advance parties. Transport rations carried on Supply Wagons.	Rations for 31st. dumped at ST.JANS-TER-BIEZEN (two days rations, viz. 31st & 1st. for rail parties of battalions.) These two days rations for rail parties delivered four Battalions delivered by M.T. in forward area. These Units thus on 30th. having in their possession rations for 31st.& 1st. Transport rations for 31st. on Supply Wagons.	Supplies for 1st Jan. less four Btns. rail parties dumped at destination and picked up complete by Supply wagons.	Normal	Normal.
118th Inf. Bde. Group.	Normal	Rations for 30th.for first line transport on supply wagons. Rations for 30th for rail parties delivered to Units.	Transport moves. Rations for 31st.dumped at ST.MOMELIN. Rail parties rations delivered by M.T. at destination to advance parties. Road parties rations on Supply wagons.	Rations for 1st. Jan dumped at ST.JANS-TER-BIEZEN and loaded complete on Supply wagons.	Rations for 2nd.Jan dumped at Refilling Point in new area and loaded on to Supply wagons.	Normal.
118th Inf. Bde. Group.	Normal.	Rations for 30th.for 1st Line transport taken on Supply wagons to "A" Area and delivered. Rations for Rail parties delivered in "B" Area by Supply Wagons.	Rations for 31st.for rail parties delivered in "A" area. Rations for 1st Line transport kept on Supply wagons.	Transport leaves LUMBRES area. Supplies for 1st Jan.dumped at ST. MOMELIN. Rail parties rations for 1st delivered to advance parties at Bttn. Camps in new area by M.T. on the 31st. Rations for road parties on Supply wagons.	Rations for 2nd.Jan.dumped at ST.JANS-TER -BIEZEN. Loaded Refilling Point complete on Supply wagons.	Rations for 3rd.Jan. dumped at Refilling Point in new area and loaded on Supply wagons.

APPENDIX "D"
II CORPS CIRCULAR MEMORANDUM NO. 36.

RAILHEAD ACCOMMODATION.

9th December, 1917.

1. To provide for the comfort of officers and other ranks at Railheads in the Corps Area, the following institutions have been organised.

   (a) POPERINGHE.

      II Corps Railhead Rest Camp "LE FILATURE" on road loading from Station to ELVERDINGHE (Map Ref. S.28., G.2.d.8.4) with Canteen and accommodation for 20 Officers and 600 Other Ranks.

      II Corps Railhead Refreshment and Waiting Room at POPERINGHE STATION.

   (b) PROVEN.

      II Corps Railhead Refreshment and Waiting Room.

   (c) Refreshment and Waiting Rooms are also being constructed at ELVERDINGHE and VLAMERTINGHE, by neighbouring Corps. Refreshment Rooms at Railheads are available for use by all troops, irrespective of the formation to which they belong.

2. The Corps Railhead Rest Camp at LE FILATURE will be in charge of an officer appointed by Corps Headquarters assisted by a permanent staff found by the Corps.

In addition to the above the following personnel will be detailed by units concerned to administer their own troops arriving and departing by rail.

Each Division :-
      1 A/Q.M. Sergeant.
      1 Storekeeper.
      3 Privates (Guides)
      1 Private (Cook)

The above personnel will be under the command of the officer in charge of the Corps Railhead Rest Station, and will only be changed when a Division or Unit concerned leaves the Corps.

3. A Railhead Disbursing Officer will be located at the Corps Railhead Rest Station.

4. The duties of the Officer in charge of the Corps Railhead Rest Station will be as follows :-

/ (a) To administer the Rest Station.

4.   (a) To administer the Rest Station.
     (b) To keep in close touch with the R.T.O. POPERINGHE, as regards the arrival and departure of trains.
     (c) To provide guides to meet all trains.
     (d) To receive and administer all troops whom the R.T.O. POPERINGHE may send him, either of his own or neighbouring Corps, until such time as they can be despatched by train or returned to their Units.
     (e) To demand any necessary lorry transport from II Corps "A" to convey men to their Units when the distance exceeds 4 miles. This applies to cases not provided for by formations and units for their own men and does not relieve formations and units from the responsibility of arranging horse and lorry transport to collect their men from Railheads which are more than 4 miles distant.
     (f) To supervise the Corps Railhead Refreshment Room.

5.   *   **   **   **   **   **   *

6.   The Corps Railhead Rest Station will receive at any time any Officers or other ranks who may be sent there by Corps or Divisions either arriving or departing by rail.

   (i) Accommodation for the night will be available.
   (ii) Meals will be provided.

7.   Divisions will provide horse transport or, when horse transport is not available, will demand lorry transport from the S.M.T.O., II Corps for officers or other ranks proceeding on leave when the distance from Camp, Transport or Wagon Lines to Railhead exceeds 4 miles. Such demand being made by 3 p.m. on the day previous to the lorries being required, the time and rendezvous for lorries and numbers to be carried being stated.

   Units of Corps Troops will send demands giving the necessary details to O.C., Corps Troops by 12 noon previous to the day the lorries are required. O.C., Corps Troops will then demand on S.M.T.O., II Corps by 3 p.m. for the necessary transport.

   All demands for lorries made on the S.M.T.O., II Corps will be repeated to II Corps "A".

                             (Signed) R.M. FOOT, Brigadier-
                                                  -General,
                                   D.A. & Q.M.G., II Corps.

APPENDIX "E".

EMPLOYED OFFICERS AND MEN.

(a) To be found by 116th Infantry Brigade

Area Commandant CANAL BANK 1 Officer, 2 N.C.O's and 20 men.

(b) To be found by 117th Infantry Brigade.

    (i) Camp Adjutant IRISH FARM, 1 Officer, 1 N.C.O., 1 Man.

    (ii) Corps Baths, TUNNELLING CAMP, 1 N.C.O., and 3 men.

    (iii) Area Commandant REIGERSBURG, 1 Officer and 1 man.

    (iv) Guard POPERINGHE Town Hall, 1 N.C.O. and 6 men.

    (v) Duty with Forward Area Commandant HILL TOP, 1 N.C.O., and 5 men.

    (vi) Soup Kitchen CORNER COT, 6 men (to include 2 Cooks) N.C.O., being provided by Employment Company.

(c) To be found by 118th Infantry Brigade

    (i) Corps Baths ST. JANSTER BIEZEN, 1 N.C.O., and 3 men.

    (ii) Camp Adjutant DAMBRE CAMP, 1 Officer, 1 man.

    (iii) Corps Prisoners of War Cage B.19.c.7.5., 1 N.C.O., and 6 men.

    (iv) Divisional S.A.A. & Grenade Dump HILL TOP, 6 bombers.

    (v) IInd Corps Railhead Rest Camp LE FILATURE (near POPERINGHE Station) 1 Acting Q.M.S., 1 Cook, 1 Storeman, 3 guides.

NOTE:- It is intended to replace as many of the above by Employment Company men, as soon as it is known how that Unit will be situated in the new area.

S E C R E T. 39/1724/A.G.5.

AMENDMENT TO 39th DIVISIONAL ADMINISTRATIVE INSTRUCTIONS - APPENDIX 'C' dated 26.12.17.

Rations for 117th and 116th Infantry Brigades rail parties for consumption day after train journey will be dumped at WIZERNES Station and carried by Units on the train.

Rations for 118th Infantry Brigade rail party for consumption day after train journey will be dumped at detraining station.

27th December, 1917.

Lieut.-Colonel.
A.A.& Q.M.G., 59th Division.

War Diary

SECRET.   39/1724/A.Q.4.

ENTRAINING ARRANGEMENTS.

1. The move will be carried out by Tactical trains in accordance with attached Table "A".

2. <u>Entraining Station.</u>   WIZERNES.

   <u>Detraining Station.</u> (a) Personnel Trains 29th and 31st Dec,
   ST. JEAN. (IRISH FARM), 30th Dec, VLAMERTINGHE.
   (b) Omnibus Trains all at
   VLAMERTINGHE.

3. <u>Personnel Trains.</u> - Consist of the following :-

   2 Brake Vans (not to be used for troops or baggage)
   44 3rd Class Coaches. (40 men each - at 8 men to each
                         compartment gives total of 1760).
   2 First Class Coaches
   2 Covered Goods Wagons.

   Personnel will arrive at WIZERNES Station 1 hour before time of departure of train.

4. <u>Omnibus Trains.</u> - Consist of the following :-

   1 Passenger Coach.
   30 Covered Wagons (each carry 6 H.D. or 8 L.D. horses
                     or 40 men).
   17 Flats. (4 axles each).
   2 Brake Vans (for Railway Personnel only).

5. <u>Transport.</u>
   (a) The detail of transport to be carried in the Omnibus Trains is given in Table "B" attached.
   (b) Units will provide breast ropes for horse trucks.
   (c) All transport will arrive at WIZERNES Station 3 hours before time of departure of train.
   (d) Brigades will detail a party of 2 Officers and 50 men to report R.T.O., 3½ hours before departure of Omnibus Train to load vehicles.

6. <u>Baggage.</u>
   (a) All baggage will be conveyed by Omnibus Trains except where otherwise stated in Lorry Programme, attached.
   (b) Parties to load baggage on the train will be conveyed in the lorries to the station, proceed with the baggage in the train and unload it at detraining station and reload it onto lorries there.
   (c) Lorries conveying baggage to the train must arrive at WIZERNES Station 1½ hours before departure of train.

7. <u>Entraining Officer.</u>
   Brigades will detail an Officer to act as Entraining Officer at WIZERNES. He will report to R.T.O. WIZERNES 1½ hours before departure of first train on the day his Brigade moves and will proceed by last train of his group.
   <u>Detraining Officer.</u>
   Brigades will detail an Officer to act as Detraining Officer for Omnibus trains at VLAMERTINGHE.

P.T.O.

8. Marching Out States showing number of Officers, Other Ranks, Animals H.D. & L.D., Vehicles and bicycles, will be handed to Entraining Officer by Units on arrival at Station.

9. No lighted braziers are allowed in the trains.

10. No men are allowed to travel on the tops of carriages or to sit on the steps or buffers.

11. Lewis Guns will be taken on the trains.

12. ACKNOWLEDGE.

[signature]

27th December, 1917.
Lieut-Colonel,
A.A. & Q.M.G., 39th Division.

Copies issued to all recipients of Administrative Instructions, 39/1724/A.Q.3 dated 26.12.17.

===== ** =====

Table A

ENTRAINING TABLE.

DATE.	Type of train.	Time of departure.	UNIT.	STRENGTH.
29th.	Personnel	7 a.m.	Units of 117 Bde. 228 M.G. Coy. A. P. M.	Not to exceed 1400 130 70
29th.	Omnibus.	10 a.m.	Adv.Parties 116 Bde. 117 T.M.Bty. 134 Fld.Amb. Transport loading party. Baggage " "	30 50 110 50) To be detailed by 50) 117 Bde.
29th.	Personnel	11 a.m.	Units of 117 Bde. 133 Fld.Amb.	Not to exceed 1400. 150.
30th.	Personnel	7 a.m.	Adv.Parties 118 Bde. Units of 116 Bde.	30 Not to exceed 1400
30th.	Omnibus.	10 a.m.	116 T.M.Bty. Divl.Headquarters. D.A.D.V.S. H.Q., Divl. R.E. Divl.Signal Coy. 236 Divl.Emplt.Coy. Transport loading party. Baggage " "	50 30 10 10 120 20 50) To be detailed by 50) 116 Bde.
30th.	Personnel	11 a.m.	Units of 116 Bde. 13th.Gloucesters. Divl.Band.	Not to exceed 1100.) 500
31st.	Personnel	7 a.m.	Units of 118 Bde. 274 Field Coy.R.E.	Not to exceed 1500. 80
31st.	Omnibus.	10 a.m.	118 T.M.Bty. Transport loading party. Baggage " "	50 50) To be detailed by 50) 118 Bde.
31st.	Personnel	11 a.m.	Units of 118 Bde. Divl.Salvage Coy.	Not to exceed 1500 60

Entraining Station, all trains, WIZERNES.

Detraining Station, all omnibus trains, VLAMERTINGHE.

" " Personnel trains 29th & ST. JEAN
            31st Dec. (IRISH FARM.)

" " Personnel trains 30th Dec. ELVERDINGHE.

about
The journey to ST. JEAN and ELVERDINGHE should take/3½ hours
and to VLAMERTINGHE 3 hours.

======== ** ========

DETAIL OF OMNIBUS TRAIN 29th DEC. TABLE "B"

Vehicles.			Axles.	Horses.	
				H.D.	L.D.
Cookers	3 per Bttn.	= 12	24	24	
Water Carts.	1 " "	= 4	4		8
Medical "	1 " "	= 4	4		4
Mess "	1 per Bn.1 per M.G.Coy.	= 6	6		6
G.S.Limbd.Wagons.	2 per Bttn.	= 8	16		16
	1 per M.G.Coy.	= 2	4		4
	1 per Bde.H.Q.	= 1	2		2
	1 per Fld.Amb.	= 2	4		4
Chargers	4				4
			64	24	48

	= 10	Covered Wagons.
Baggage per Bde.H.Q.	1 = 1	" "
per Battn.	1 = 4	" "
M.G.Coy. & T.M.Bty.	= 1	" "
Divl.M.G.Coy.	1 = 1	" "
Fld.Amls.	= 1	" "
T.M.B. Hand-carts.	= 2	" "
Personnel.	= 8	" "
Spare.	= 2	" "
	30	

DETAIL OF OMNIBUS TRAIN 30th DEC.

Vehicles.			Axles.	Horses.		REMARKS.
				H.D.	L.D.	
Cookers *	3 per Bttn.	= 15	30	30		* 2 Cookers
Water Carts.	1 " "	= 5	5		10	& 1 Limbd.
Medical "	1 " "	= 5	5		5	Wagon may
Mess "	1 per Bttn.1 per M.G.Coy	= 6	6		6	be taken
G.S.Limbd.Wagons.	per 118 Bde.	= 2	4		4	instead
Chargers.	per 118 Bde.	= 3			3	of 3
			50	30	28	Cookers
						if
						required.

	= 8	Covered Wagons.
Baggage per Bde.H.Q.	= 1	" "
per Bttn.	1 = 5	" "
M.G.Coy. & T.M.B.	= 1	" "
T.M.B. Hand-carts.	= 2	" "
Personnel	= 10	" "
Spare	= 3	" "
	30	

===============

Detail of Omnibus Train on 31st Dec. will be similar
to that on 29th. though there will be rather more
spare accommodation.

LORRY PROGRAMME.

DATE.	Number of Lorries.	PURPOSE.	REMARKS.
29th.	25	Move baggage of 117 Inf.Bde. to WIZERNES Station.	
"	2	Move baggage of 228 M.G.Coy. to WIZERNES Station.	
"	1	Move baggage of 133 Field Amb. to WIZERNES Station.	
"	1	Move baggage of 134 Field Amb. to WIZERNES Station.	
"	8	Move 116 Inf.Bde from "B" to "A" Sub-area.	Found from Sub-Park. Two trips if required.
"	3	Move Gloucesters from BOURNONVILLE to HARLETTES.	Found from Sub-Park Two trips.
"	13	Move 118 Inf.Bde.from "C" to "B" Sub-area.	Two trips.
"	1	To convey employed men of 116 Inf.Bde.(vide appendix "E") to WIZERNES Station for Omnibus Train.	
"	1	To convey employed men of 118 Inf.Bde.(vide appendix "E") to WIZERNES Station for Omnibus Train.	
			Total for 29th...55.
30th.	25	Move baggage of 116 Inf.Bde. to WIZERNES Station.	
"	15	Move Divnl.Headquarters to POPERINGHE & BORDER CAMP.	
"	5	Move baggage of 13th Gloucs. to WIZERNES Station.	
"	13	Move baggage of 118 Inf.Bde. from "B" to "C" Sub-area of LUMBRES Area.	Two trips.
"	1	Move baggage of 132 Field. Amb. to WIZERNES Station.	
			Total for 30th..49.
31st.	25	Move baggage of 118 Inf.Bde. to WIZERNES Station.	
"	5	Move Divnl.Concert Party from LOTTINGHEM to POPERINGHE.	
"	8	Move clothing of Divnl.Baths to Forward Area.	
			Total for 31st..38.

NOTE:— Brigades and Divisional Troops will wire this Office time and place at which lorries will be required to rendezvous.

H-Q Brandes

Army Form C. 2118.

WAR DIARY
or
INTELLIGENCE SUMMARY.
(Erase heading not required.)

Page 1

Place	Date	Hour	Summary of Events and Information	Remarks and references to Appendices
CAMEL BANK YPRES	Jan 1918 1st		118 Inf Bde moved from LUMBRES area to SUPPORT area.	
	2nd		Transport – 118 Inf Bde gone from ST JAMSTER BIEZEN to Sulfur and to complete a move of 39 Divn.	
	3rd		In defence situation a number of 466 I.R. 239 Divn was transferred to Hostile bombardments and counter-attacks among Signal Coy at 39 Div HQ.	
	4th		One prisoner captured during a raid at 107 Inf Bgde - 58 Divn	
	11th		118 Inf Bde relieved 117 Inf Bde in the line.	
	12th		39 D.O. No. 2 JS received. Includes list of 39 Divn Arty programme.	
	13th		One prisoner captured, belongs to 237 R.I.R. 199 F. Divn	
	14th		On prisoner captured and identified as 237 R.I.R. 199 F. Divn	
	15th		One found wounded J.C. — identified as 466 I.R. 239 Divn	
	16th		II Corps Intsum received re moves of 39 Divn, 35th & 29 Divns.	
	17th		39 D.O. No. 08 received re relief of 39 F Divn by 35 Divn.	
	18th		39 D.O. No. 8 or received re relief of 39 Div Arty by 35 Div Arty.	
	20th		II Corps Intsum 189 received re move of Supply Columns.	

'F' 'Q' Branches.

WAR DIARY
or
INTELLIGENCE SUMMARY.
(Erase heading not required.)

Army Form C. 2118.

Page 2

Place	Date 1918	Hour	Summary of Events and Information	Remarks and references to Appendices
CANAL BANK YPRES.	Jan 20th (Contin- ued)		III. Corps Order received re Relief of French Divisions in Line South of ST QUENTIN.	
"	21st		" " " re Move of 39 Divn to MERICOURT SUR SOMME area.	
"	"		39 Divn on relief proceeded to PROVEN area.	
"	"	10 PM	Command of WESTROOSEBEKE Sector handed over to 9th & 29 Divn & 9 & 25 DM.	
"	22nd	10AM	39 Divn HQ closed at CANAL BANK and reopened at COUTHOVE CHATEAU.	
"	"		39 A.D.M.S. 212 received re movements of Divn.	
COUTHOVE CHATEAU	23rd		39 Divn in Corps Reserve	
"	24th	12 Noon	39 Div HQ entrained for MERICOURT L'ABBÉ: refn- entre-cleany at COUTHOVE CHATEAU at 12.30 pm and reopening at HOTEL du R.H.IV AMIENS at its same hour. 117 Inf Bde entrained for MERICOURT L'ABBÉ.	
MERICOURT SUR SOMME	25th	1.10 AM	39 Div HQ opened. 39 Div. HQ detrained at MERICOURT L'ABBÉ and marched to MERICOURT SUR SOMME.	
"	"		116 Inf Bde entrained at PROVEN: 117 Inf Bde arrived at MERICOURT L'ABBÉ and marched to SUZANNE area.	
"	26th		118 Inf Bde detrained at MERICOURT L'ABBÉ and marched to BRAY area.	
"	"		116 Inf Bde entrained at PROVEN.	

Army Form C. 2118.

Page 3

"A" + "Q" Branches.

WAR DIARY
or
INTELLIGENCE SUMMARY.
(Erase heading not required.)

Place	Date	Hour	Summary of Events and Information	Remarks and references to Appendices
MERICOURT SUR SOMME	1918 Jan 27th		39 D.O. No 213 received re Div to hold itself in readiness to move at 24 B hr notice	
"	28th		116 Infty Bde arrived at SAILLY LAURETTE area.	
"	29th		39 Do. No 214 received re move of 39 DivRA which is in ETTINEHEM area. Completion of statement of 39 Div RA	
"	30th		117 Inf Bde went into the line in relief of left Bde 21st Divn.	
"	31st		118 Inf Bde went into the line in relief of left Bde of 1st Divn.	

31/1/1918.

J.C. Owen Major
Major General
Commanding 39 Divn.

Army Form C. 2118.

A&Q branches

WAR DIARY
or
INTELLIGENCE SUMMARY

(Erase heading not required.)

AQ a70390
Page 1

Place	Date 1918	Hour	Summary of Events and Information	Remarks and references to Appendices
MERICOURT SUR SOMME	10th Feb		116 Inf Bde relieved the Right Bde of the 9th Divn.	
"	21st Feb	10 am	39 Div. HQ opened at MÉRICOURT SUR SOMME and relieved at NURLU G.O.C. 39 Div HQ took over command from G.O.C. 21st and G.O.C. 9th Div.	
"	"	10 am	The 16th Div. is on the right and the 2nd Div. (V. Corps) on the left.	
NURLU	4th Feb		Completion of relief of 9th Div. Arty by 39 Div Arty in accordance with 39 D.O. No. 214.	
"	5th		TITH Info rec'd re enemy to our front at 150th & AFA Bde & 39 Divn	
"	6th		39 DO No. 215 received re arrival of 150th AFA Bde	
"	9th 11am		Hostile raid upon our trenches; two men reported missing. A woman & her child who had escaped from French camp at FRAMERVILLE mentioned.	
"	12th		One Company of 52 Inf Regt 157 Divn captured. 39 D.O. No. 216 received re detachment of 9 & 28 Seaforth Highlanders proceeding from 39 Divn.	
"			39 DO No 217 received re attachment of 197 machine gun coy to 39 Divn.	

A.Q Branches WAR DIARY or **INTELLIGENCE SUMMARY.**
(Erase heading not required.)

Army Form C. 2118.

Page 2

Place	Date 1918	Hour	Summary of Events and Information	Remarks and references to Appendices
NURLU	Feb 15th		The Commander-in-Chief British Armies in France Sir Douglas HAIG visited 39 Div. H.Q.	
"	16th		Inspection of 186 Bde R.F.A. by Lt-General CONGREVE V.C., G.O.C. VII Corps.	
"	17th		H.Q. VII Corps heavily bombed by E.A. between 7pm & 1am (18th)	
"	19th		VII Corps order received re moves of Artillery units.	
"	20th		39 D.O. No. 218 received re Battalion Cyclist Coy R.E. rejoining from this	
"	22nd		39 A.O. No. 219 received re attachment of Btt Rn General Regt (21st Divn) to 39 Divn for work.	
"	28th		A. fo 113 & R. 116 Cheshire Regt (T.F.) 118 Inf Bde raided the enemy line opposite GOUZEAUCOURT — 2 prisoners of 120th & 85th Inf Regt 18th Div. captured: 1 M.G. 3 dugouts blown up and 20 of the enemy killed. 39 D.O. received re Clothing on the left sector of the Corps battle front. Relief of 11th Infty Bde by 62nd Inf Bde (21st Divn) and withdrawal 83 Divn Reserve at HEUDECOURT, SOREL AND DESART WOOD	

28/2/1918.

J. C. Owen Major for
G.S.C. 39 Divn

A/Q Branch

WAR DIARY
or
INTELLIGENCE SUMMARY
(Erase heading not required.)

Army Form C. 2118.

WO 95/397
Page 1

Place	Date 1918	Hour	Summary of Events and Information	Remarks and references to Appendices
MORLU	March 1st to 5th 6th		Nothing to report	
"	6th		Hostile raid on front S.E. of GAUCHE WOOD. Two of our men missing, one German prisoner belonging to 227 R.I.R. 107 Divr remained in our hands. He reports 52nd R.I.R. 107 Divn arrived in GAUCHE WOOD. Major General E. FEETHAM C.B. C.M.G. proceeded on leave to the United Kingdom. Brigadier General GANS, C.of S. assumed command of 39 Divr.	
"	7th			
"	8th		39 Div. D.O. No 223 issued re relief of 39 Div A/5 by 1 R. Div A/5 39 Div A/5 by a certain Q. Hut. S.I.C.	
"	9th	11am	The Commander in Chief B.A.E.F. arrived at HQ. VII Corps and had a talk with GOC 39 Divr and visited him at "Villa line" en route to METZ	
"	10th		39 Div Order No. 224 issued re relief of 39 Divn by 1 R. Divn drawn up & distributed at 1 p.m.	
"	11th		H.Q. 117 Inf. Bde moved from HEUDICOURT to NURLU. 26 Inf Bde (39 Divn) relieved 118 Inf Bde in the line 118 Inf Bde moved to MOISLAINS.	

A. & Q. Branches.
WAR DIARY
or
INTELLIGENCE SUMMARY.

Army Form C. 2118.

Page 2

Place	Date 1918	Hour	Summary of Events and Information	Remarks and references to Appendices
MURLU	March 12th		Command of GOUZEAUCOURT Sector handed from G.O.C. 39 Divn to G.O.C. 9 Divn	
		3pm	39 DHQ closed at MURLU and reopened at HAUT ALLAINES. 39 Divn came under 9th Corps and ready to move at 12 hours notice.	
			116 Inf Bde relieved by S.A. Inf Bde & proceeded to GURLU WOOD.	
			117 " " " " " " in SOREL—HEUDICOURT area.	
			39 Divn Machine Gun Battalion formed under Lt Col A FLEETWOOD-WILSON	
HAUT-ALLAINES	13th		116 Inf Bde despatched one Battn for work to HEM under A.D.G.T 5th Army	
			117 " " " employed work in forward area under 9th & 21st Divns.	
			118 " " " started training in the MOISLAINS area	
"	14 Apl to 16th		Nothing to report.	
"	17th		39 D.O. No. 225 received re relief of 117 Inf Bde by 118 Inf Bde	
"	18th		Brigadier Gen L.A.S CAPE CMG (CRA 39 Divn) temporarily in command of the Divn in lieu of Genl— G.O. Ronssoy.	
			Brigm M.L. HORNBY CMG DSO, assumed command of the Divn. Colonel AH. CARTER CMG (Comdg DAC) assumed command of the Div. Arty	

A/Q Branch

WAR DIARY
or
INTELLIGENCE SUMMARY.
(Erase heading not required.)

Army Form C. 2118.

Page 3

Place	Date 1918 March	Hour	Summary of Events and Information	Remarks and references to Appendices
HAUT-ALLAINES	23rd		Brig-General 4 MS CAPE CMG arrived in the British Military Cemetery PERONNE	I
" "	21st	AM 4.50A	Enemy opened intense bombardment along the whole Corps front with very heavy minnies.	
" "	23rd	8 AM	Maj-Gen EFFETHAM CB CMG returns from leave and took over command of the 39 Divn from Brig-Gen M.L. HORNBY CMG DSO who resumed command of 116 Infantry Bde	
CLERY-SUR-SOMME		6.30AM	39 Div. HQ closed at HAUT ALLAINES and re-opened at CLERY-SUR-SOMME. With drawal to the line BIACHES-LA MAISONETTE was successfully carried out — during the afternoon the enemy following up closely. All telephone was cleared with very few exceptions.	
FRISE		4 PM	39 Divl HQ closed at CLERY-SUR-SOMME and re-opened at FRISE. Transport lines established at HERBECOURT where stragglers were collected, fed, and rested and after a little rest sent back to their units. Teams becoming disorganised owing to 3 days continuous fighting, night and day.	

Army Form C. 2118.

HQ Branches

WAR DIARY
or
INTELLIGENCE SUMMARY.
(Erase heading not required.)

Page 4

Instructions regarding War Diaries and Intelligence Summaries are contained in F. S. Regs., Part II. and the Staff Manual respectively. Title pages will be prepared in manuscript.

Place	Date 1918 March	Hour	Summary of Events and Information	Remarks and references to Appendices
FRISE.	24th		Operations continued.	
CHUIGNES	25th	11am	39 Div HQ closed at FRISE and re-opened at CHUIGNES.	
		6.35pm	39 Div. handed from VII Corps and came under the orders of XIX Corps. Orders received directing withdrawal to HERBECOURT-FRISE line.	
	26th	7.10am	Orders received re line of withdrawal to PROYART-FRAMERVILLE line.	
PROYART	27th	9am	39 Div HQ closed at CHUIGNES and re-opened at PROYART.	
HAMEL.		3pm	39 Div HQ closed at PROYART and re-opened at HAMEL. Brigadier General THOMSON 39 Div assumed command of 39 Div. Arty.	
	27th	3pm	39 Div HQ closed at HAMEL and re-opened at HAMELET.	
HAMELET		3.30pm	39 Div HQ closed at HAMELET and re-opened at FOUILLOY.	
FOUILLOY.	28th	10.30am	39 Div HQ closed at FOUILLOY and re-opened at DOMART-SUR-LA-LUCE.	
		6pm	XIX Corps HQ opened at ST FUSCIEN. Orders received for 39 Div to hold a line from 1000 yds E of CAYEUX to MARCELCAVE.	
DOMART-SUR-LA-LUCE	29th	11am	Major General E FEETHAM CB CMG killed by shell in IGNAUCOURT.	
BOVES.		3.30pm	39 Div HQ closed at DOMART-SUR-LA-LUCE and re-opened at BOVES.	

HQ Branches

WAR DIARY
or
INTELLIGENCE SUMMARY.
(Erase heading not required.)

Army Form C. 2118.

Page 5

Place	Date	Hour	Summary of Events and Information	Remarks and references to Appendices
BOVES.	Mar. 1918 30th	1pm	Considerable fighting in forward zone of the Division. Warning order received for relief of 39th & 66th Divns.	
		6pm	Major General BLACKLOCK CMG DSO took over command of the Divn from Brigadier General THOMPSON CRA	
		MIDNIGHT	Relief of 39th and 66th Divn by 18th Divn in progress by 39 I.B. & 2 I.B.	

31/3/1918.

Lt. Colonel General
G.O.C. 39 Divn

FUNERAL OF THE LATE BRIGADIER-GENERAL G.A.S. CAPE, C.M.G.
ROYAL ARTILLERY, C.R.A., 39th. DIVISION - On WEDNESDAY
20th. MARCH, 1918.
==

1. The body will be conveyed by Motor Ambulance from 133rd. Field Ambulance at MOISLAINS to I.16.a.3.3. where it will be met at 10.30 am. and transferred to a gun-carriage to be detailed by the C.R.A., 39th Division.

2. The Band and Drums of the 1/6th.Bn.Cheshire Regt., and a firing party (strength 1 Officer, 1 Sergt., and 20 other ranks) to be detailed by the C.R.A. will rendezvous at I.16.a.3.3. at 10.15 am. and report on arrival to the D.A.A.G.

3. The following will act as pall bearers :-

   Brigadier-General M.L. HORNBY, C.M.G., D.S.O.
   Brigadier-General E.C.H.P. BELLINGHAM, C.M.G., D.S.O.
   Colonel A.H. CARTER, C.M.G.
   Lt.-Col., F.W. GOSSET, C.M.G., D.S.O.
   Lt.-Col., E.W.S. BROOKE, C.M.G., D.S.O.
   Lt.-Col., LORD A.E. BROWNE

4. Pall bearers, Staff Officers 39th Division and Officers of the R.A., will rendezvous at I.16.a.3.3. at 10.15 a.m.

5. The cortege will leave the rendezvous at 10.35 am. and proceed to the British Military Cemetery PERONNE (I.21.d.5.9.)

6. All Officers and troops NOT mentioned above attending the funeral will proceed direct to the cemetery and will be formed up by the Staff Captain 39th.Divnl.R.A., according to attached plan, by 10.30 a.m.

7. The A.P.M., will arrange for the control of traffic on the MT. ST. QUENTIN - LE QUINCONCE Road between 10. and 11.30 a.m.

8. DRESS. Service Dress, DRILL Order, Caps will be worn.

9. At the conclusion of the service troops will return to camp.

                                           F.C. Owen
                                           Major,
19th.March,1918.   A/A.A. & Q.M.G., 39th.Division.

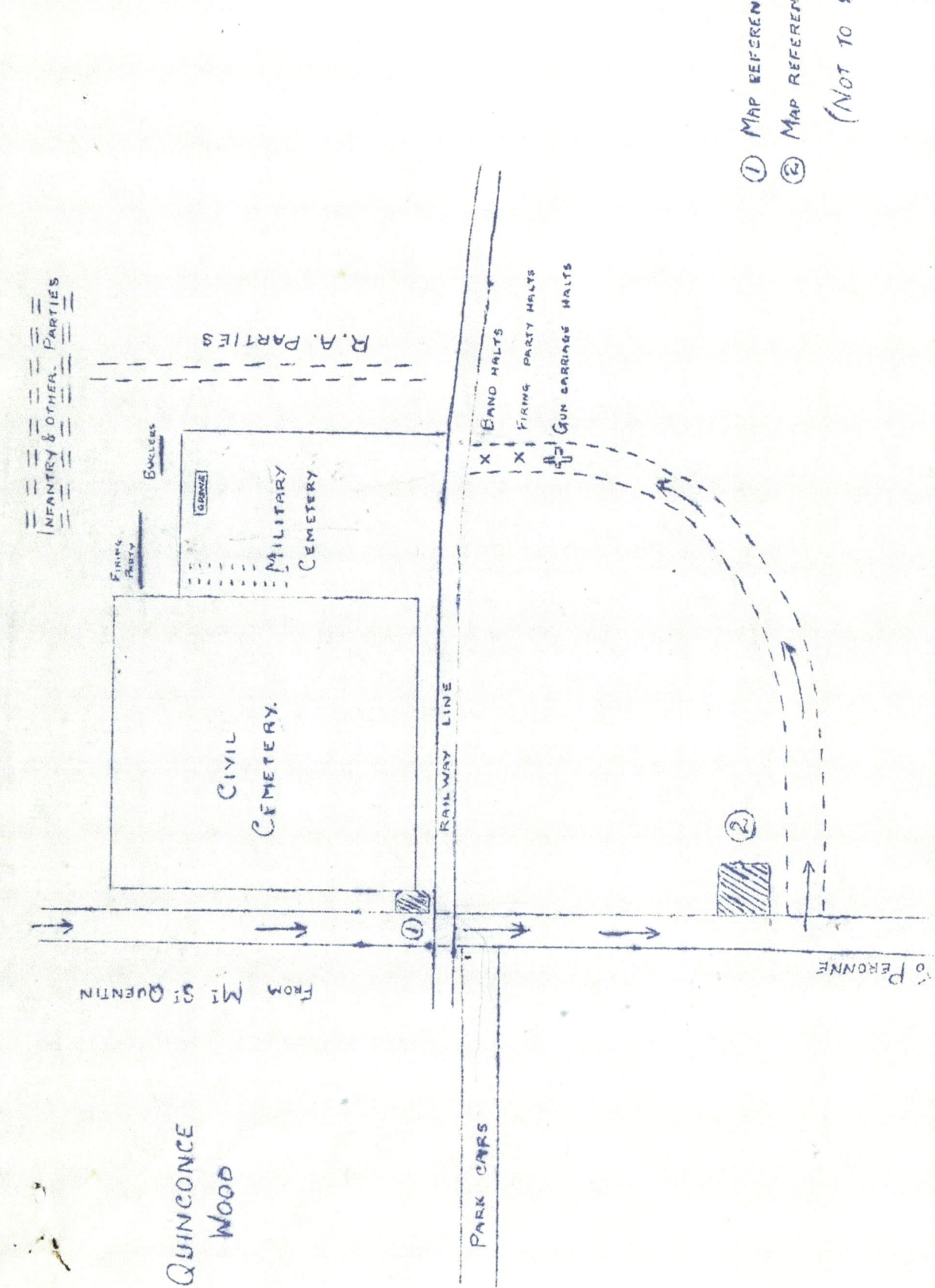

39th Divisional Administrative

A. & Q.

39th DIVISION

APRIL 1918.

SECRET

"A" & "Q"
39 Divr.

WAR DIARY
or
INTELLIGENCE SUMMARY.
(Erase heading not required.)

Army Form C. 2118.

Page 1

Place	Date 1918	Hour	Summary of Events and Information	Remarks and references to Appendices
GUIGNEMI-COURT	April 1st		Remainder of 39 Divr. embarked at LONGEAU. 116, 117 and 118 Inf Bdes 225, 227 & 234 Field Coy R.E. and 39 M.G. Bn concentrated at GUIGNEMICOURT and BOVELLES. 39 Divr. Arty. remained in line in VILLERS BRETONNEUX Area.	
		3 PM	Major General E. FEETHAM CB. CMG. burned in the French Cemetery at GUIGNEMICOURT.	
			39 D.O. No 220 received re move to OISEMONT Area by march route. Moving overnight of 2/3 April in ALLERY-AIRAINES Area.	
BELLOY ST LEONARD	2nd	AM to PM	39 Div HQ closed at GUIGNEMICOURT and reopened at NEUILLY ST LEONARD. 39 Divl Arty moved by march route to AILLERY-AIRAINES area.	
			39 D.O. No 231 received re march to OISEMONT area.	
			VIII Corps order received re probable move of 39 Divr to YPRES salient.	
OISEMONT	3rd	10	39 Div HQ closed at NEUILLY ST LEONARD and reopened at OISEMONT. 39 Div Arty moved by march route to OISEMONT area from ALLERY-AIRAIMES area.	
			VIII Corps received re Transfer of 39 Divr. from Fourth Army on night 5/6 April.	

HQ branches

WAR DIARY
or
INTELLIGENCE SUMMARY

Army Form C. 2118.
Page 2

Place	Date 1918	Hour	Summary of Events and Information	Remarks and references to Appendices
OISEMONT	April 4th		Troops refitted and rested.	
"	5th		Brig-General HUGBACK assumed command of 118th Inf Bde.	
"	6th		XVIII Corps order and 39 D.O. No 283 received re move of 39 Div by road & rail from OISEMONT to GAMACHES Area preparatory to entrainment for Second Army area.	
GAMACHES	7th	10. AM	39 Div HQ closed at OISEMONT and re-opened at GAMACHES. 39 Div (less RA) proceeded by road & rail from OISEMONT to GAMACHES area. XVIII Corps order received re entrainment of 39 Div. 39/9/24 received re future employment of 39 Div, as a Training Divn to the American Expeditionary Force.	
"	8th		39 Divn Gen Staff began to distribute at WOINCOURT, EU and FEUQUIÈRES. Following orders 117, 116 and 118 Brigade groups for HOULLE, ST MARTIN-AU-LAERT & ARQUES respectively delivery at ST OMER and ARQUES.	
"	13th	Noon	39 Div. HQ closed at GAMACHES and re-opened at ST OMER. 227 & 234 Field Coys RE and 221ᵛᵗʰ Corps remained in GAMACHES area to carry out salvage & clearing, also as railway detachments.	

WAR DIARY or INTELLIGENCE SUMMARY

A.Q. Branch

Army Form C. 2118.

Page 3

Place	Date 1918	Hour	Summary of Events and Information	Remarks and references to Appendices
GAMACHES	9th		Move by train of 116, 117, 118 Bde Groups from GAMACHES area. 39 Div HQ closed at ST OMER and re-opened at COCOVE CHATEAU.	
COCOVE CHATEAU	10th		39 Div Order No 2 & 3 received. Remainder of Bde groups for training area. EPERLECQUES RECQUES and WATTEN (see 39 Div O.O. for details) by 77th American Division. 39 D.O.O. 235 received in formation of 39 Control Regts under Bn Cmdr HUBBACK CMG. HQ Control Regts was formed. No output as report to HQ XXII Corps. Arrived at 77th Div Adv HQrs.	
"	11th	2AM	Final Pos of 39 Composite Bde entrained ST OMER. Remainder (arriving 3 hours)	
EPERLECQUES	12th	11AM	39 Div HQ closed at COCOVE CHATEAU on relief and opened at EPERLECQUES. Remainder of Bde groups moved to RECQUES & EPERLECQUES area. 39 Div Order No 236 re arrangement re formation of No 5 Composite Bn under Lt Col HT SEYMOUR DSO comdg 17th KRRC from details of 116, 117, 118 & P.B.s and 13th Gloucester Regt. BM forwarded by Lt Col W. ORDAVSQUES dom UPM to LES CINQUES RUES on relief from 1st Australian Divn. Br Gnls G.A. Armytage CMG DSO, L. WYATT DSO, Captain McCann MC & G.S.O. 3 and Cmr J Cooley SO II O arrived Dvn HQ 3 Div at 2 pm for Conference as to Handing over to 39 Divn. M.M.R. MNR	

T2134. Wt. W708—776. 500000. 4/15. Sir J. C. & S.

Army Form C. 2118.

APO Dunkirk

WAR DIARY
or
INTELLIGENCE SUMMARY.
(Erase heading not required.)

Page 4.

Place	Date	Hour	Summary of Events and Information	Remarks and references to Appendices
EPERLEQUES	April 1918 16th		39 Infantry Bn in action on WYTSCHAETE Ridge under orders 21st Div.	
"	18th		MAJOR A.E.Q.F. Perkins MC assumed duties of 9502 vice Lt Col W.W. Burland DSO to IX Corps	
"	20th		Bn Genl Armytage Captains Cave & Cockburg returned to 39 Div from Infantry Depot WL-335 Div	
"	21st		71 American Div. HQ moved from COCHOVE CHATEAU to EPERLECQUES CHATEAU	
"	26th		39 Composite Bn heavily attacked in Kepple Park. No 2 Bn suffered heavy casualties.	
"	29th		Move of American Engineers from RUMINGHEM and NUVE MURLET to VON KER MOKOVE and MERCGHEM.	
"	30th		Bere Relieved of No 5 Corporation Bn: disbanding of it on being placed to provide reinforcements to other units.	

30/4/1918

JC Owen Major
GOC 39 Div.

Original ~~Confidential~~

WAR DIARY or INTELLIGENCE SUMMARY
(Erase heading not required.)

A&Q Headquarters 39 Div.

Army Form C. 2118
Page 1.

Place	Date 1918	Hour	Summary of Events and Information	Remarks and references to Appendices
EPERLEC-QUES	May 6th		Return of 39th Composite Bde from forward area.	
"	9th		11 Herts Regt (T.F.) and 11 Cambs Regt (T.F.) entrained at AUDRUICQ on transfer to 37th Division and 12th Division respectively.	
"	14th		4/5th Black Ward (Royal Highlanders) T.F. entrained at RAMBERT on transfer to 15th Division.	
"	15th		Orders received for Major ?. C. Owen DAAG to 5th Div on appointment as DAAG 1X Corps vice Major D. Tidbury M.C. is appointed DAAG 39 Div. Capt. M. Carr M.C. 4 So. 3. appointed RSM Major 102 Int Bde. 39 Div vice Major Rupert Fiennes approved 450 3 Capt???? defence Corps M.C. vice Capt???	See. Map.

Nob. 22 3D

Original.

Copy. 2.

WAR DIARY A&Q Headquarters 39 Div.
or
INTELLIGENCE SUMMARY Page 2.

Army Form C. 2118

(Erase heading not required.)

Place	Date	Hour	Summary of Events and Information	Remarks and references to Appendices
EPER- LECQUES	16 May		Division being made up to 4 Battns. Training Staffs per Brigade.	
	20"		9th Black Watch Training Staff 60 officers 50 other ranks arrive.	
	21"		7th Suffolk Training Staff arrive.	
	23rd		Advanced party 30th American Div arrive — 30 Div A.E.F. to be attached to 39 Div for training. 78th	
	25th		Allotted new area S. of HARDINGHEN for the American Div to billet in. Division now allotted	
	28th		Advance party of 30th American Division now allotted Reception Area, southern portion.	
	29th		Nothing new.	

29th June 1918.

Krisson Major
for GOC 39 Div.
for GOC 39 Div.

WAR DIARY or INTELLIGENCE SUMMARY

Army Form C. 2118

A&Q Headquarters 39 Div

Page 1

Place	Date	Hour	Summary of Events and Information	Remarks and references to Appendices
EPERLECQUES N. of ST OMER	1st June		Reduction of establishments to cadre strength complete.	
	8th "		Prepare WIERRE area for 78 American Div who is now arriving in contingents at CALAIS.	
	14th-15th		Corps recon South - we are now administered by XVII Corps	
			VIIth Corps who we are at present under, moves A&Q 77th Div to WOLPHUS and NIELLES lez ARDRES	
WOLPHUS	6th-7th		A&Q 39 Div move	
	15th		Training continues. 34 Div going to 1st Army and the Div takes over training of 78 Division	
	16th		Black Watch 80 off tomorrow to Boulogne & proceed to England. 16th & 16½ Division.	
	21st		11th Cheshires join 39 Div. Get orders to be prepared to leave to WINNEZEELE LINE by the 30th Div A.E.T. in the event of a heavy attack on the 2nd Army front.	

Army Form C. 2118

Page 2

WAR DIARY
or
INTELLIGENCE SUMMARY

A&Q Headquarters 39 Div.

(Erase heading not required.)

Place	Date	Hour	Summary of Events and Information	Remarks and references to Appendices
WOLPHUS	22 June		78 Div A.F.F. tak over from 34 Div for training.	
	23 "		Placed in Jun 116 Bde (afas Div HQrs) Wielte to Belgium Area.	
	24 "			
	25 "			
	26 "		80th Div AEF taken over from 2nd Div for training	
	27 "		Placed under 117 Bde (actg as Div HQrs) SAMER Area	
	28 "			
	29 "			
	30 "			

[signature] 2/8
[signature] 1 Aug 39

Army Form C. 2118

WAR DIARY
or
INTELLIGENCE SUMMARY

Short Cadre A+Q Headquarters 39 Div.

Page 1.

(Erase heading not required.)

Place	Date	Hour	Summary of Events and Information	Remarks and references to Appendices
WOLPHUS	1st July		Still Cadre Division. Train Americans.	
	2"		30 Div A.E.F move to 2nd British Corps.	
	3"		80 Div A.E.F moved to move to Third Army tactical	
			Train - transport by boat horse — 30 train BOULOGNE	
	11—12th		212	
	13th			
	18th		78th Am Div leaves for 1st Army — Reconnaissance	Division
	24th		M.G Units of 80th Div A.E.F leave for Third Army	
	28th		Following Cadre Battn Staff have been up and over to Third Army	
			2/6 Lincoln 2/6 Sherwood	
			8 KRRC 9.0 Aug 2/5 KRRC	
			6 Munster Dr. 3.0 Aug 9 RB	
			6 Connaught	
			11 Cheshire	
			6 Bedford	

Army Form C. 2118

WAR DIARY
or
INTELLIGENCE SUMMARY

A.P.O. 29 Div. August 1918.

W.D 30

Place	Date	Hour	Summary of Events and Information	Remarks and references to Appendices
WALPHUS (CALAIS AREA)	1st Aug		The Div. has to cadre Battns. looking after reinforcements will be different Corps.	Cot
	2nd Aug		11 A & S. Highrs, 7 Canadians 8/10 Gordons, 15 R. Scots	Cot
	3rd "		16 Bn. 4 cadre Battns. taken from Front Line by 78 Am. Div.	Cot
			Cadre Battns. formed in accordance with A.G.'s instructions	
			11 Cheshires – 8 K.R.R.C. – 6 Borders – 6 Munsters – 6 Connaught Rangers	
			16 Bedfords – 2/5 Shrops – 9 K.R.R.C. – 8 Fifth Bn. 9 Rifle Bde	
	10th "		order to move to POURVILLE with Bde. Hqrs. at CALAIS, Etaples	Cot
			ROUEN and HAVRE.	Cot
	11th "		Following cadre Battns. broke up 16 R. Scots 16 R. Scots	Cot
			11 A & S Highrs 8/10 Gordons 13 Essex R.	Cot
	12th "		Following Battns. ordered to proceed to L of C under 66 Div	Cot
			18, 23, 26 Northumbld. Fus, 10 Lincoln, 7 Suffolk	Cot
			13 Gloster, 16 N. & Derby, 17 KRRC, 14 H.L.I, 16 Rifle Bde	Cot
	15th "		The above cadre Battn. entrained at NORTKERQUE to L of C. under 66 Div.	Cot
			117th & 115th Bdes entrained for HAVRE and ROUEN. Div. Hqrs. for VERANGVILLE.	Cot
	16th "		Div. Hqrs. closed at WALPHUS at 10 am. Reopening at same hour at VERANGVILLE	Cot
	17th "		8/10 Gordon Highlanders entrained for L of C. to 66th Div	Cot
	18th "		39th Div. Train ordered to LUMBRES to Admin. 30th American Div. Artillery.	Cot
	20th "		B. Major O.H. Dodbury M.C. Middx Rs. DAAG 39 Div. appointed DAHG 2nd Div. Received from leave and	Cot
	21st "		ordered to report direct to 2nd Div	Cot
			Major T/ Lt Col R.E. Holmes A'Court DSO AA & QMG 39 Div. proceeded 21/8/18 for temporary duty as AQMG XVII Corps	Cot

WAR DIARY
or
INTELLIGENCE SUMMARY

(Erase heading not required.)

Army Form C. 2118

Instructions regarding War Diaries and Intelligence Summaries are contained in F. S. Regs., Part II. and the Staff Manual respectively. Title Pages will be prepared in manuscript.

Place	Date	Hour	Summary of Events and Information	Remarks and references to Appendices
VARENGEVILLE DIEPPE.	22nd Aug		Owing to lack of private accommodation at LE HAVRE approval was obtained for the 116th Infy Bde. Officers Training Depot to be retained at FECAMP, and Bde. was ordered to move on 23rd.	Copy
	23rd		116th Infy Bde completed move to FECAMP.	Copy
	24th		Programme for Recreational Training arranged for Musketry, Cricket, Football, Riding, Swimming &c.	Copy
	30th		Remarks of move spent by Staff visiting the four Officers Training Depots. Major Gen. G.A. Blacklock C.M.G. D.S.O. G.O.C. 39th Div ordered to assume command of 63rd Div & left same day.	Copy
	31st		Brigadier Gen. H.B. Hulbert C.M.G. G.O.C. 116th Infy Bde. assumed command 39th Div.	Copy

M. Cook
Brigadier Gen.
Comdg 39th Division

1875 Wt. W593/826 1,000,000 4/15 J.B.C. & A. A.D.S.S./Forms/C. 2118.

Confidential

WAR DIARY
or
INTELLIGENCE SUMMARY

(Erase heading not required.)

Army Form C. 2118

Army Headquarters 39th Divn Hdqrs

September 1917

Place	Date	Hour	Summary of Events and Information	Remarks and references to Appendices
VERANGEVILLE	1st to 30th		The Divisional Engr. personnel at VERANGEVILLE, and the organizing of Nos 1, 2, 3 & 4 Officers Training Schools was supervised from these Hqrs. The Staff Officers of the Division visited these Training Depots from time to time during the month.	Cont
	10		Major Gen N McLeod joined Division and assumed command & proceeded on temporary duty to G.H.Q. same day	Cont
	18th		Major J.C. Cooke MC %AA & QMG attended conference at G.H.Q.	Cont
	19th		Lt. Col. J.W. Scott CMG DSO. proceeded to 20th Div. for temporary duty as G.S.O.1.	Cont
	26th		4th Batn. Lincolnshire Regt. left 116th Brigade, joining 116th Bde at Etaples.	Cont
	22nd		G.S. Essay, 3rd Batn. Argyle and Sutherland Highlands joined Division thus upon appointment of A.D.C. to Maj. Gen. McLeod.	Cont
	28th		Lt. Col. R.E. Holmes a Court confirmed in appointment at 17th Corps.	Cont
	26th		Maj. Gen N McLeod DSO arrived at Division & proceeded to Decamps and Rouen	Cont
	28th		Capt. J.J. Jollero G.S.O.3 ordered to report to Division of Staff duties, War Office but order cancelled following day	Cont

McL
Maj Gen
Cmg. 39th Division

WAR DIARY Army Form C. 2118
or
INTELLIGENCE SUMMARY

(Erase heading not required.)

Secret Confidential
HQ Branch 39 Divn

Vol. 3

Place	Date	Hour	Summary of Events and Information	Remarks and references to Appendices
VERANGEVILLE DIEPPE SHEET	1 & 31st Oct.		Staff Officers of the Division visited and supervised the work at Young Officers Training Schools at Fecamp, Etaples, Rouen, & Calais.	Ent
	4th		Brig. Gen. E.A. Armytage CMG. DSO (117th Bde) to 40th Div. & command 97th Infy Bde.	Ent
	8th		Major O.E. Knight MC DADMS to 4th Army for temporary duty.	Ent
	10th		Lt Col. J.W. Gosset CMG DSO psc R.A. to 62nd Div. for duty as G.S.O. 1.	Ent
	17th		Brig. Gen. Hon Ruthven CMG DSO proceeded to command 120 Infy Bde.	Ent
	17th		Brig. Gen. E.W. Compton CB. CMG to command 117th Infy Bde.	Ent
	20th		Brig. Gen. C.B. Lawrence CMG. DSO (118th Infy Bde) to command 63rd Infy Bde.	Ent
	22nd		Major J.C. Crofton M.C. DAQMG. to Cmdt. LILLE for temp. duty	Ent
	27th		Brig. Gen. M.L. Hornby CMG. DSO to command 116th Infy Bde	Ent
	29th		Major J.C. Cooke DAQMG from Cmdt Lille to Hqrs L of C.	Ent

Major W. Mapoppes Co.
for Maj. Gen.
Comdg. 39th Division.

WAR DIARY or INTELLIGENCE SUMMARY
Army Form C. 2118

(Erase heading not required.) AQ Branch 39 Divn

Secret / Confidential

Place	Date	Hour	Summary of Events and Information	Remarks and references to Appendices
VERANGEVILLE / DIEPPE	Nov 1st		Orders received for demobilization of following Battns. (OB 2257)	
			116th Infy Bde :— 1/4th East Yorks — 1/4th Yorks — 1/5th Yorks — 4th S. Staffs — 5th Staffs	Cort
			117" — — 1/6th Durham Light Infy, 1/5th D.L.I. and 1/8th D.L.I.	Cort
			118" — — 1/4th Northumberland Fusiliers — 1/5th N.F. — 1/6th N.F. and 4th Lincolns	Cort
			No 4 OTC — — 4th East Lancs and 7th Notts & Derby Regt	Cort
	4th		Brig Genl L.J. Wyatt DSO left 116th Infy Bde to assume command 196th Infy Bde.	Cort
	6th		" M.L. Hearn CMG DSO left 118th Infy Bde to join 8th Div	Cort
			" C.W. Compton left 117th Infy Bde to join 4th Div	Cort
	7th		Maj. J.C. Cooke MC. DAQMG 39th Divn left LofC to take up duties DAQMG 1 Cavalry Area.	Cort
	9th		116th & 117th units demobelized	Cort
	10		118 Bde units demobilized	Cort
	11		Commandr Officers of Demob. units at A.D.O.s Port Etaples.	Cort
			Order received from L of C Demobilizing 236 Empcy Coy.	Cort
	16"		Demobilization of 4th E. Lancs & 7th Notts & Derby Regt cancelled. Order received for reinstatement	Cort
			I Div. No 4 OTC as follows 4th E. Lancs and 7th Notts Derby to form 116th Infy Bde.	
			Balce of Boulogne Convalescents to be mounted 117th Infy Bde.	
			197th I.W. Bde with Training Staff to replace 118 Infy Bde.	
			Orders received for reduction of 236 Empcy. Cy under orders of M.E.F.C. for duty at Dunkerk.	Cort
1st to 30th			Staff Officers of Division continued visits to Brigades and Corps.	Cort

Coloy (Major) ADAQS

for Major-General

Comdg. 39th Division

Secret & Confidential

No. A.A.D. 39 R

Army Form C. 2118

WAR DIARY
or
INTELLIGENCE SUMMARY
(Erase heading not required.)

Vol 34

Place	Date	Hour	Summary of Events and Information	Remarks and references to Appendices
VERANGEVILLE	1st Dec.		Orders issued for 18th, 23rd & 25th Northumberland Fus., 13th Glosters, 14th Highland Light Infy, 7th Seaforth and 4th East Yorks to be held in readiness to proceed Devonlyk Camp, Dunkirk. Orders received for 225 Field Coy RE to proceed to Convsct. Camps Dunkirk for duty.	Copy
DIEPPE	3rd		225 Coy R.E. proceeded to Dunkirk.	Copy
	4th		Appointment made of H.Q. L.9.C. for Major A.E. Kruger DSO, MC, DADOS 39th Div. the personnel from 8th Corps to Divl. for duty.	Copy
	8th		Orders received for Batn. Rest in readiness to proceed & Devon. Camps Dunkirk to proceed at once to move Convalescent Camp.	Copy
	9th		Orders received from L.9.C. for 14th HLI & 116th Infy Bde to move & Horse Compets 17pm onwd for Convalescent Camp.	Copy
	12th		Orders issued by L.9.C. for all m/t material at HAUDRICOURT and MARTIN EGLISE Camps & the Material to No 3 Convalescent Depot at TREPORT.	Copy
	13		Move 7.116th Infy Bde Competd. Major (A/T.F. Read DSO) DA at Recent Rep. (DDSC H9 L9C) appointed AD.OMG 39th Div. for & proceed for duty with L9.C.	Copy
	20th		7th Bn. Suffolk Regt & 17th KRRCorps passes & 116th Infy Bde. afts deployment of No 2 & 3 Young Soldiers Bns.	Copy
	23rd		Orders issued for L.9.C. for Maj. Gen. McLachlan DSO taken over Command of 30th Div. — 13 Gen. J. Kennett took CMG DSo Cmdg. 191 Infy Bde assumed Cmnd of 39th Div.	Copy
	27th			Copy

Col. Taylor Major
i/c DAMC
for Brig. Gen.
Cmdg. 39 Div. Division.

WAR DIARY
or
INTELLIGENCE SUMMARY

Army Form C. 2118

HQ 993 39D

Ref. Map 1/250,000 Rut. Calais & Le Havre

Place	Date	Hour	Summary of Events and Information	Remarks and references to Appendices
VARENGEVILLE	Jan 1		Break up of 39" Divisional R.E. Headquarters commenced.	Ent
	2		General Office Routine	Ent
	3		— do —	
	4		— do —	
	5		— do —	Ent
	6		— do —	
	7		— do —	
	8		— do —	
	9		— do —	
	10		— do —	
	11		— do —	
	12		— do —	
	13		Brig. Gen. J.H. Hall C.M.G. D.S.O. and 197 Infantry Brigade consisting of Brigade Hdqrs. and three Cadre Battalions – 10th Lincoln Rgt.; 16th Sherwood Foresters, and 16th Rifle Brigade, ordered by L.of C. to move to Le Havre and to take over command of Clothing & Kit General (late R.A.S.C.) Base Depot. The Brigade to also be known as 197 Infantry Brigade (Authority L of C letter W.R.13325 of 13/1/19).	Ent

Army Form C. 2118

WAR DIARY
or
INTELLIGENCE SUMMARY
(Erase heading not required.)

Ref. Map 1/250,000 sheet _____ Calais to Le Havre

Instructions regarding War Diaries and Intelligence Summaries are contained in F. S. Regs., Part II. and the Staff Manual respectively. Title Pages will be prepared in manuscript.

Place	Date	Hour	Summary of Events and Information	Remarks and references to Appendices
YARENGEVILLE	Jan 14		General Office Routine	Capt
	15		do	
	16		197 Infantry Brigade established at No.6 Camp Le Havre (General Base Reinforcement Depot) Capt
	17		General Office Routine	
	18		do	
	19		do	
	20		do	
	21		do	Capt
	22		do	
	23		do	
	24		do	
	25		do	
	26		do	
	27		do	
	28		do	

1875 Wt. W593/826 1,000,000 4/15 J.B.C. & A. A.D.S.S./Forms/C. 2118.

Army Form C. 2118

WAR DIARY
or
INTELLIGENCE SUMMARY
(Erase heading not required.)

Place	Date	Hour	Summary of Events and Information	Remarks and references to Appendices
VRRENGEVILLE	Jan 29		↑ of E. WWW. W.R. 13325/6 of 29th received ordering Brig. Gen. J.L. Hall C.M.G. D.S.O. to proceed to Le Havre today to take over command of General Base Depot and assume temporary duty as O.C. Reinforcements vice Colonel Young proceeding on leave.	Ap 1
	30		Visit of Civilian Advisory Board to Divisional Headquarters. To give advice to Officers and other ranks on Education and employment after demobilisation.	Ap 2 Ap 3
	31		General Office Routine	
			— do —	

C.J.U. M?
C of S. 7/BDPC
for Brigadier General
Commanding 39th Division

WAR DIARY
INTELLIGENCE SUMMARY
(Erase heading not required.)

Army Form C. 2118

Ref. Map:- 1/200,000 sheet
Boulain to Le Havre.

Place	Date	Hour	Summary of Events and Information	Remarks and references to Appendices
VARENGEVILLE.	Feb 1		General Office Routine	Apps
	2		" " "	
	3		do	
	4		do	App.
	5		do	
	6		do	
	7		do	
	8		do	
	9		do	
	10		do	
	11		do	
	12		do	
	13		do	
	14		do	
	15		do	
	16		AAG letter O.B. 2231 dated 14/2/19 received ordering the breaking up of 39° Divisional Signal Company's personnel to be disposed of by the Adjutant-General, transport by the Quartermaster-General.	App.
	17		General Office Routine.	
	18		" do "	App.
	19		" do "	App
	20		" do "	App

Army Form C. 2118

WAR DIARY
INTELLIGENCE SUMMARY
(Erase heading not required.)

Place	Date	Hour	Summary of Events and Information	Remarks and references to Appendices
VARENGEVILLE	Feb 21		General Office Routine	Cet
	22		— do —	Cet
	23		— do —	Cet
	24		— do —	Cet
	25		A.G.'s letter No. A.G. 6459(0) dated 21/2/19 received returning personnel of 39th Divisional Signal Company to proceed to Signal Base Depot ABBEVILLE for disposal on drafts to other units.	Cet
	26		General Office Routine	Cet
	27		— do —	Cet
	28		— do —	Cet

C. Taylor Major
A.D.M.S.
p. Brigadier General
Commanding 39 Division

WAR DIARY
or
INTELLIGENCE SUMMARY
(Erase heading not required.)

Army Form C. 2118

AQ OOB 39²
Vol 37

Place	Date	Hour	Summary of Events and Information	Remarks and references to Appendices
VARENGEVILLE	March 1		L.G.C. wire 996 Q.L. received ordering move of 39th Divisional Headquarters from VARENGEVILLE to ROUEN	Copy
	2		General Office Routine	Copy
	3		do	
	4		Advance party of 39th Div. Std. Sgd. for ROUEN	Copy
ROUEN	5		Main body of 39th Div. P.B.O. moved to ROUEN. Headquarters established in (late) No.12 General Hospital	Copy
	6		Instruction No 6266 (Q.B.2.) of 27/2/19 received — giving instructions as to disposal of equipment and horses of 39th Divisional Signal Co. R.E.	Copy
	7		General Office Routine	Copy
	8		do	
	9		do	
	10		do	
	11		do	
	12		do	Copy
	13		do	

Army Form C. 2118

Ref. No. 1/250,000 Pad.
Earon to L. House.

WAR DIARY
INTELLIGENCE SUMMARY
(Erase heading not required.)

Instructions regarding War Diaries and Intelligence Summaries are contained in F. S. Regs., Part II. and the Staff Manual respectively. Title Pages will be prepared in manuscript.

Place	Date	Hour	Summary of Events and Information	Remarks and references to Appendices
ROUEN	March	14	General Office Routine	Ort
		15	— do —	
		16	— do —	Ort
		17	— do —	
		18	— do —	
		19	— do —	Ort
		20	— do —	
		21	Major R.E. KNIGHT D.S.O. M.C. R.A.O.T.C.'s 39 Division proceeded to England for Demobilization	Ort
		22	Major J.H. PEELE D.A.D.V.S. 39 Division proceeded to England for Demobilization	
		23	General Office Routine	Ort
		24	— do —	
		25	— do —	Ort
		26	Brig-Genl N. Hall C.M.G. D.S.O took of his quarters with 39 Ros P.S.R.	
		27	Rev. H.D. Hanford S.C.F. Capt Lewis Kaplan 39 Division proceeded to England for Demobilization	Ort
		28	Lt Col Keith MA y & MG relieved to report No 1 G.B. for duty; Lt Col Keith was attached A.D.M.S. C.B. on temporary duty at H.Q. Troops Rouen	
		29	General Office Routine	Ort
		30	— do —	
		31	— do —	Ort

A J Younger
Major R.A.M.C.
for Brigadier General
Commanding 39 Division

1875 Wt. W593/826 1,000,000 4/15 J.B.C. & A. A.D.S.S./Forms/C. 2118.

ORIGINAL.

SECRET.

WAR DIARY

OF

39th DIVISION

("A" & "Q" BRANCH)

1st to 30th APRIL, 1919.

Army Form C. 2118

WAR DIARY
~~INTELLIGENCE SUMMARY~~
(Erase heading not required.)

Instructions regarding War Diaries and Intelligence Summaries are contained in F. S. Regs., Part II. and the Staff Manual respectively. Title Pages will be prepared in manuscript.

Ref map 1/250,000 Sheet
Calais Le Havre

Place	Date	Hour	Summary of Events and Information	Remarks and references to Appendices
ROUEN	April 1		General Office Routine	Ant
	2		do —	
	3		do —	
	4		do —	
	5		do —	
	6		do —	
	7		do —	
	8		do —	Cu.
	9		do —	
	10		do —	
	11		do —	
	12		do —	
	13		do —	
	14		do —	
	15		do —	
	16		do —	
	17		do —	
	18		do —	
	19		do —	
	20		do —	
	21		do —	
	22		do —	Cu
	23		do —	

Army Form C. 2118

WAR DIARY
or
INTELLIGENCE SUMMARY
(Erase heading not required.)

Instructions regarding War Diaries and Intelligence Summaries are contained in F. S. Regs., Part II. and the Staff Manual respectively. Title Pages will be prepared in manuscript.

Place	Date	Hour	Summary of Events and Information	Remarks and references to Appendices
ROUEN	April 24		General Office Routine	Cop
	25		— do —	Cop
	26		— do —	
	27		— do —	Cop
	28		116th Infantry Brigade H.Q. and Cadre Battalions relieved by 18th Middlesex Regiment, and completely withdrawn from Ben-Helisabeth Base. Staff.	
	29		General Office Routine	Cop
	30		— do —	

A.H. Wylde Major
for Brigadier General
Commanding 39 Division

1875   Wt. W 593/826   1,000,000   4/15   J.B.C. & A.   A.D.S.S./Forms/C. 2118.

ORIGINAL.

S E C R E T.

W A R D I A R Y

O F

39th D I V I S I O N.

("A" & "Q" BRANCH)

1st to 31st MAY, 1919.

WAR DIARY
INTELLIGENCE SUMMARY
(Erase heading not required.)

Army Form C. 2118

Reg. Prop. 1/30000 Sheet
Calais to Le Havre

Place	Date	Hour	Summary of Events and Information	Remarks and references to Appendices
ROUEN	May 1		General Office Rouen.	Cpt
	2		Consecration of Colours - The following battalions' Colours were consecrated and presented to the Battalion by Maj. Gen. H.C.C. Uniacke C.B. C.M.G.:- 1st Bn. Northumberland Fusiliers, 23rd Bn. Northumberland Fusiliers, 25th Bn. Northumberland Fusiliers, 14th Bn. Highland Light Infantry, 16th Bn. Sherwood Foresters, 10th Bn. Lincolnshire Regiment, 13th Bn. Gloucester Regiment, 7th Bn. Suffolk Regiment. (programme of presentation attached)	Cpt
	3		Major Campbell reported from D.A.P.S. to take up appointment of D.A.P.S., but telephone message received to say he was to proceed to 61st Division.	Cpt
	4		Orders received for Lt. Col. Sander, Gordon Highlanders to proceed and assume command 1/8th Argyll & Sutherland Highlanders. General Office Rouen.	Cpt
	5-6			Cpt
	7		Proceed for move of General Office Rouen.	Cpt
	8,9,10,11		General Office Rouen.	Cpt
	12		G.O.C. proceeded on 14 days leave to England	Cpt
	13		106 "C" Inf. Bde took over command of Division during absence or leave of Brigadier General Gale, C.M.G. D.S.O	Cpt

WAR DIARY
or
INTELLIGENCE SUMMARY

(Erase heading not required.)

Army Form C. 2118

Place	Date	Hour	Summary of Events and Information	Remarks and references to Appendices
ROUEN	May 14		General Office Rouen	
	15		do	Apt
	16		do	
	17		do	
	18		do	Apt
			2.15 received D.A.740 of 17th received cancelling orders for Bn. Edone and Divisional Headquarters Cadres to proceed to England. These Cadres no longer required in England. 1164.17 Brigade Headquarters only to proceed as before.	Apt
	19		General Office Rouen	Apt
	20		do	
	21		do	
	22		do	Apt
	23		do	
	24		do	
	25		do	
	26		do	
	27		do	
	28		Col. returned from leave	Apt
	29		General Office Rouen	Apt
	30		do	Apt
	31		do	

Commanding 39th Division

Presentation of Colours

by

Major-General **H. C. C. UNIACKE**, C. B., C. M. G.

COMMANDING LINES OF COMMUNICATION AREA

~~On Monday, 28th April,~~ *Friday 2nd May* 1919.

To the following Cadre Battalions of

39th DIVISION.

Brigadier-General **J. H. HALL**, C.M.G., D.S.O., Commanding.

A/A. A & Q.M.G.   Major G. TAYLOR, M. C. the Rifle Brigade.

116th INFANTRY BRIGADE.

Lieut-Col. **F.R.F. SWORDER**, Commanding Parade.

A/Staff Captain, Captain A. E. H. SAYERS, West Riding Regiment.

18th Bn. Northumberland Fusiliers (1st Tyneside Pioneers).
23rd Bn. Northumberland Fusiliers (4th Tyneside Scottish).
25th Bn. Northumberland Fusiliers (2nd Tyneside Irish).
14th Bn. Highland Light Infantry.

117th INFANTRY BRIGADE.

Lieut-Col. **A.K.M.C.W. SAVORY**, D.S.O., Commanding.

A/Staff Captain, 2/Lieut. R. EVANS, Sherwood Foresters.

16th Bn. Sherwood Foresters.
10th Bn. Lincolnshire Regiment.

197th INFANTRY BRIGADE.

Lieut-Col. **LE PREVOST**, D.S.O., Commanding.

A/Staff Captain, Captain THIRSFIELD, K.S.L.I.

13th (Forest of Dean) Bn. The Gloucester Regiment.
7th Bn. Suffolk Regiment.

18th Bn.
Northumberland Fusiliers
(1st Tyneside Pioneers).

Lieut.-Col. J. A. METHUEN, D.S.O.
2nd-Lieut. R. W. WALKER.
2nd-Lieut. N. CAMERON
                (Officer receiving Colours).

R.S.M.   SWEET.
R.Q.M.S.   WILLEY.
C.S.M.   BALMAIN.
C.S.M.   STOTT.
C.Q.M.S.   CHISHOLM.
C.Q.M.S   SHERRINGTON, M.M.
Sergt.   PEART, M.M.
»   WALTON.
Corpl.   GOODFELLOW.
L/Cpl.   EACOTT.
L/Cpl.   HUNTER.
»   WOOD.
Pte.   MCLEAN.
Pte.   RITSON.
Pte.   RUTHERFORD.
Pte.   SIMS.

23rd Bn.
Northumberland Fusiliers
(4th Tyneside Scottish).

Major   W. J. HUNT.
Captain   W. GERRARD.
Captain   R. M. HUNTRODS
                (Officer receiving Colours).

R.S.M.   GOODLET.
C.S.M.   MALLINSON.
C.Q.M.S.   MIDDLETON.
Sergt.   DENT.
»   BASTABLE.
Corpl   PRATT.
»   NICHOLSON.
»   MITCHELL.
L/Cpl.   PARKER, M.M.
»   WELBON.
Pte.   WORSDALE.
»   CHESTERS.
»   HALL.
»   HOUSE.
»   SPENCE.
»   ROBERTSON.
»   MCKENZIE.
»   HALLIDAY.
»   BOWMAN.
»   WHITE.
»   LEES.
»   HILLMAN.

25th Bn.
Northumberland Fusiliers
(2nd Tyneside Irish).

Lieut-Col. A. H. CATCHPOLE.
Captain   G. COLEBY, M.C. M.M.
Captain   A. BLAKE
                (Officer receiving Colours).
Captain   F. TREANOR.

R.S.M.   IREDALE.
C.S.M.   HALL.
C.S.M   ROGERS, M.M.
C.S.M.   SCOTT.
R.Q.M.S.   TUXILL.
C.Q.M.S.   GOODHEAD.
»   PEARSON, D.C.M.
»   SANDS.
Sergt.   BELL, M.M.
»   LEACH.
»   THOMAS.
»   WILLIAMS.
L/Sgt.   ROBSON.
Corpl.   CHADWICK.
»   DEMPSTER.
L/Cpl.   MARSHALL.

10th Bn.
Lincolnshire Regiment.

Lieut.   C. L. PETTITT.
Lieut.   J. SCOTT
                (Officer receiving Colours).
Lieut.   H. L. THOMSON.

C.S.M.   FOOTTIT.
Sergt.   BEAUMONT.
»   THOMAS.
Corpl.   CLAY.
»   EVANS.

16th Bn.
Sherwood Foresters.

Lieut. DAVIES.
Lieut. T. F. CARTER.
2nd-Lt. W. T. J. RUMSEY
    (Officer receiving Colours).

R.S.M. ARKINSTALL.
C.Q.M.S. PERKINS.
" SHAW.
Corpl. BARKER.
Pte. BROADHEAD.
" ANSCOMBE.
" JOHNSTON.
" WISBEY.
" LOVATT.

7th Bn.
Suffolk Regiment.

Major P. C. BALL, D.S.O.
Captain G. L. GRANDON, M.C.
Lieut. W. L. BROOKES
    (Officer receiving Colours).

R.S.M. FOOKES, M.M.
C.S.M. NORRIS, M.M.
C.Q.M.S. JOHNSON, M.S.M.
Sergt. SPINDLER, M.M., C. de G.
" KING, M.M.
" CLITHEROE.
" EMMERSON.
" ALLEN.
" HAZLEWOOD, D.C.M, M.M.
" BAKER, M.M.
" SKEMMING.
Corpl. PEARS.
" KENT.
Pte. WILLS.
" SPALL.
" PIZZEY.
" PIZZEY.
" RICHARDSON.
" WARDLAW.
" PARKER.

13th (Forest of Dean) Bn.
The Gloucester Regiment.

Captain B. J. LAMPLUGH.
Lieut. P. E. GARDINER
    (Officer receiving Colours).
Lieut. A. J. RADLEY.

R.S.M. MAKEPEACE.
C.S.M. CROSIER, M S M.
" DAWE.
C.Q.M.S. BROWN.
Sergt. RICHARDS.
" CRONQUIST.
" GUEST.
" VAUGHAN.
" SPRING.
" HAYNES, M M.
Corpl. POWELL.
Pte. BRAIN.
" BEER.
" STEVENS.
" BOWDEN.
" NORTH.
" WILLIAMS.
" WILLIAMS.
" LUMLEY.

14th
Highland Light Infantry.

Captain P. H. MARSHALL.
Captain R. D. W. NICOLSON.
Lieut. D. L. STEWART
    (Officer receiving Colours).
Captain J. DICKS, M.C.

R.S.M. LOGAN.
C.S.M. SHIELDS.
" CRAWFORD.
C.Q.M.S. BOATH.
" McCRINDLE.
" CHITTY.
" FERGUSON.
Sergt. GATHERAL.
" COWAN, D.C.M.
" DONALD, M.M.
Corpl. SILVER.
Pte. TEMPLE.
" WHITE.
" RANKIN.
" CAMPBELL.
" WILKINSON.
" DEAN.
" HASTINGS.

AQ AQQ 39R
Vol 40
June 1919
Secret
Caucasus

Original

War Diary

of

3rd Division

(Administrative Branch)

June 1919.

WAR DIARY

INTELLIGENCE SUMMARY

(Erase heading not required.)

Army Form C. 2118

Ref Map 1/250,000 sheet
Calais to L Fère

Place	Date	Hour	Summary of Events and Information	Remarks and references to Appendices
ROUEN	June 1		General Office Routine	Capt
	2		do —	Capt
	3		Orders received for the disbandment of the following Battalions and Brigade Headquarters of this Division:— H.Q. 119th Infantry Brigade, 18th Northumberland Fus, 25th Northumberland Fus, 10 Lincolns, 7th Suffolks, 13th Gloucs Regt, 4th E Lancs, 9th Sherwoods, 12th Sherwoods, 17th K.R.R.C, 14th K.O.Y.L.I. and 16th R.B.	Capt
	4		General Office Routine	Capt
	5		do —	Capt
	6		Orders received for the 23rd Northumberland Fus to be disbanded with the remainder of Divisional Units. 119th Infantry Brigade reported that arrangements for the disbandment of the Brigade were complied with, and the following units disbanded:— Brigade Headquarters, 10th Lincolns, 4th E Lancs, 9th and 16th Sherwoods Fusiliers.	Capt
	7		General Office Routine	Capt
	8		do —	Capt
	9		116th Infantry Brigade H.Q. reported that instructions for the disbandment of Battalions were complied with and the following Units disbanded:— 18th, 23rd, and 25th Northumberland Fusiliers, 14th K.O.Y.L.I.	Capt
	10		General Office Routine	Capt

WAR DIARY
INTELLIGENCE SUMMARY
(Erase heading not required.)

Army Form C. 2118

Ref No:- 1/250,000 sheet
Calais to Le Havre

Place	Date	Hour	Summary of Events and Information	Remarks and references to Appendices
Rouen	June 11		Orders received for Brig. Genl. J. Hamilton Hall, C.M.G., A.S.O., 2.i.c. 39th Division to proceed to take over command of 179th Infantry Brigade.	Cal
	12		General Office Routine	Ct
	13		179th Infantry Brigade refused that instructions for disbandment of Battalions were complied with, and following Battalions disbanded:- 13" Gloucesters, 7" Suffolks, 16" R.B. and 7" KRRC.	Cat
	14		Brig. Genl. J. Hamilton Hall, C.M.G., A.S.O. proceeded to take over command of 179th Infantry Brigade Ext.	Cal
	15		General Office Routine	Cat
	16-22		General Office Routine	Cat
	23		Summary informed Officers that they were willing to sign the Peace Treaty.	Cat
	24-27		General Office Routine	Cat
	28		Peace Treaty signed	Cat
	29		General Office Routine	Cat
	30		General Office Routine	Cat

C V Taylor Major
A/AA & QMG
Sy Brouken

~~Duplicate~~
Original

HQ A9Q 39D
1/8/41

Secret.
"
Final

War Diary

of

39th Division.

(Administrative Branch)

1st to 10th July.

Army Form C. 2118

R.J. Mop. 1/250,000 Sheet
Calais to Havre.

WAR DIARY
or
INTELLIGENCE SUMMARY
(Erase heading not required.)

Place	Date	Hour	Summary of Events and Information	Remarks and references to Appendices
ROUEN	July 1		General Office Routine.	
	2		do	
	3		do	
	4		do	
	5		Verbal instructions received from 2.G.C. that remainder of Division ought to broken up.	
	6		General Office Routine.	
	7		Major G.V. Taylor D.S.O. M.C. DDMS 29" Division left for Boulogne for demob. General Office Routine.	
	8		Orders received for Division to be disbanded.	
	9		29'ND AD. closed down. Remaining Officers sent 2 N.C.O's proceeded to England making of Records.	
	10			

G.W. Southend 2/L.
for A.D. 2 M.C.
29" Division

www.ingramcontent.com/pod-product-compliance
Lightning Source LLC
Chambersburg PA
CBHW081432300426
44108CB00016BA/2355